Amazon Fire™ Phone

A Wiley Brand

by Dan Gookin

D0573152

A Wiley Brand

Amazon Fire™ Phone For Dummies®

Published by
John Wiley & Sons, Inc.
111 River Street
Hoboken, NJ 07030-5774
www.wiley.com

Copyright © 2015 by John Wiley & Sons, Inc., Hoboken, New Jersey

Published by John Wiley & Sons, Inc., Hoboken, New Jersey

Published simultaneously in Canada

For general information on our other products and services, please contact our Customer Care Department within the U.S. at 877-762-2974, outside the U.S. at 317-572-3993, or fax 317-572-4002.

For technical support, please visit www.wiley.com/techsupport.

Wiley also publishes its books in a variety of electronic formats and by print-on-demand. Not all content that is available in standard print versions of this book may appear or be packaged in all book formats. If you have purchased a version of this book that did not include media that is referenced by or accompanies a standard print version, you may request this media by visiting http://booksupport.wiley.com. For more information about Wiley products, visit us www.wiley.com.

Library of Congress Control Number: 2014945050

ISBN 978-1-118-81034-7 (pbk); ISBN 978-1-118-81048-4 (ebk); ISBN 978-1-119-00419-6 (ebk)

Manufactured in the United States of America

10 9 8 7 6 5 4 3 2 1

Table of Contents

Introduction

I'm naturally nervous whenever electronics are named after something that burns. Apple's *FireWire* technology was terrifying, but somehow the Fire phone doesn't seem as scary. No, I imagine it's something a firefighter would use to save lives and property. That's a happy thing.

What makes having a Fire phone even better is reading a good book that helps unweave the multitudinous mysteries that surround the device. Amazon packed a lot of magic into that tiny box. Most everyone to whom you show a Fire phone is amazed. It also helps to be comfortable with what the phone does and know how to use it. That's why I wrote this book.

This book's goal is to make a complex subject like the Fire phone easy to understand. Here I carefully explain all its magical features in a friendly, informative way. The tone is light and entertaining, but that doesn't distract from the solid information. With this book in your possession, you'll find yourself more comfortable with the phone and happy to know that you're getting the most of its technology.

About This Book

Despite what you've been taught, do not read this book from cover to cover. This book is a reference. It's designed to be used as you need it. Look up a topic in the table of contents or the index. Find something about your phone that vexes you or something you're curious about. Look up the answer, and get on with your life.

Every chapter in this book is written as its own, self-contained unit, covering a specific topic about using the Fire phone. The chapters are further divided into sections representing a task you perform with the phone or explaining how to get something done. Sample sections in this book include

- Exploring the onscreen keyboard
- Making a conference call
- Creating a new contact from scratch
- Uploading a picture to Facebook
- Navigating to your destination

> ✔ Printing to a Bluetooth printer
>
> ✔ Dialing an international number
>
> ✔ Saving battery life

Every section explains a topic as though it's the first one you read in this book. Nothing is assumed, and everything is cross-referenced. Technical terms and topics, when they come up, are neatly shoved to the side, where they're easily avoided. The idea here isn't to learn anything. This book's philosophy is to help you look it up, figure it out, and get back to your life.

How to Use This Book

This book follows a few conventions for using your phone, so pay attention!

The main way to interact with the Fire phone is by using its *touchscreen,* which is the glassy part of the phone as it's facing you. In an ironic twist that shakes the tech industry to its roots, the physical buttons on the Fire phone are called *buttons.* These items are discussed and explained in Part I of this book.

Various techniques are used to touch the screen, which are described in Chapter 3.

Chapter 4 covers typing text by using something called the *onscreen keyboard.* And when you tire of typing, you can dictate your text. It's all explained in Chapter 4.

This book directs you to do things on your phone by following numbered steps. Every step involves a specific activity, such as touching something on the screen; for example:

1. Choose Downloads.

This step directs you to touch the text or item on the screen labeled Downloads. You might also be told to do this:

1. Tap Downloads.

 Various phone settings are turned off or on, as indicated by a box next to the setting. Touch this box on the screen to add or remove the check mark. When the check mark appears, as shown in the margin, the option is on; otherwise, it's off.

OFF   ON   Some settings feature a master control, which looks like the on–off switch shown in the margin. Slide the button to the right to activate the switch, turning on a phone feature. Slide the button to the left to disable the feature. Often, the master control is labeled Off and On, which helps.

Foolish Assumptions

Even though this book is written with the gentle handholding required by anyone who is just starting out or is easily intimidated, I have made a few assumptions.

I'm assuming that you're still reading the introduction. That's great. It's much better than getting a snack right now or discovering who's going to die next on *Game of Thrones*.

My biggest assumption: You have an Amazon Fire phone. There's only one, so if you have a Fire phone, you're good. And if you haven't yet bought the phone but are perusing this book to see what's up, why, you're also good.

You don't need to own a computer to use your Fire phone. If you have a computer, great. The Fire phone works well with both PCs and Macs. When directions are specific to a PC or Mac, the book says so.

Finally, this book assumes that you have an Amazon account. If you don't, I'd be puzzled how you purchased a Fire phone, because only Amazon sells them. Still, if you don't have an Amazon account, get one. Also, send me an email and tell me how you got a Fire phone without an Amazon account.

How This Book Is Organized

This book has been sliced into six parts, each of which describes a certain aspect of the Fire phone or how it's used.

Part I: Have a Little Fire

Part I serves as an introduction to your Fire phone. Chapters cover setup and orientation and familiarize you with this interesting and unusual device. This part is a good place to start — plus, you discover things in this part that aren't obvious from just guessing how the phone works.

Part II: The Phone Part of Smartphone

Nothing is more basic for a phone to do than make calls, which is the topic of the chapters in Part II. As you may have suspected, the Fire phone can make calls, receive calls, and serve as an answering service for calls you miss. It also manages the names of all the people you know and even those you don't want to know but have to know anyway.

Part III: Stay Connected

The modern cell phone is about more than just telephone communications. Part III explores other ways you can use your phone to stay in touch with people, browse the Internet, check your email, do your social networking, exchange text messages, engage in video chats, and more.

Part IV: It Does Miraculous Things

Part IV explores the nonphone things your phone can do. For example, your phone can find locations on a map, give you verbal driving directions, take pictures, shoot videos, play music, play games, and do all sorts of wonderful things that no one would ever think a phone can do. The chapters in this part of the book get you up to speed on those activities.

Part V: Nitty Gritties

The chapters in Part V discuss a spate of interesting topics, from connecting the phone to a computer, using Wi-Fi and Bluetooth networking, and taking the phone overseas and making international calls to customizing and personalizing your phone and performing the necessary chores of maintenance and troubleshooting.

Part VI: The Part of Tens

Finally, this book ends with the traditional _For Dummies_ The Part of Tens, where every chapter lists ten items or topics. For the Fire phone, the chapters include tips, tricks, shortcuts, and things to remember.

Icons Used in This Book

This icon flags useful, helpful tips or shortcuts.

This icon marks a friendly reminder to do something.

This icon marks a friendly reminder _not_ to do something.

This icon alerts you to overly nerdy information and technical discussions of the topic at hand. Reading the information is optional, though it may win you a pie slice in *Trivial Pursuit.*

Where to Go from Here

Thank you for reading the introduction. Few people do, and it would save a lot of time and bother if they did. Consider yourself fortunate, although you probably knew that.

Your task now: Start reading the rest of the book — but not the whole thing, and especially not in order. Observe the table of contents and find something that interests you. Or look up your puzzle in the index. When these suggestions don't cut it, just start reading Chapter 1.

My email address is dgookin@wambooli.com. Yes, that's my real address. I reply to every email I receive, especially when you keep your question short and specific to this book. Although I enjoy saying Hi, I cannot answer technical support questions, resolve billing issues, or help you troubleshoot your phone. Thanks for understanding.

My website is www.wambooli.com. This book has its own page on that site, which you can check for updates, new information, and all sorts of fun stuff. Visit often:

    www.wambooli.com/help/fire-phone

Bonus information for this title can be found online. You can visit the publisher's website to find an online Cheat Sheet at

    www.dummies.com/cheatsheet/amazonfirephone

Supplemental online material has been created for this book. That supplemental stuff can be found at

    www.dummies.com/extras/amazonfirephone

Updates to this book will be found at

    www.dummies.com/extras/amazonfirephone

Enjoy this book and your Android phone!

Part I
Have a Little Fire

getting started
with
**Amazon Fire
Phone**

In this part . . .

- ✔ Get started with your Fire phone
- ✔ Work through the setup of your phone
- ✔ Discover important phone parts
- ✔ Learn how to operate your phone

The Out-of-the-Box Experience

*E*verything has a first time. Baby takes her first step. You take your first trip in an airplane. A congressman keeps a promise. Yet when it comes to technology, taking that first step can often be an odd or awkward experience.

With electronics, the first step starts with taking the thing out of the box, which can often be an ordeal. That's why I wrote this chapter. My purpose is help you do some initial orientation, take care of first-order duties, and become more comfortable with what could be a brand-new experience: using the Fire phone.

Hello, Phone!

Studies show that high-tech equipment works faster when it's removed from the box. Your Fire phone came in a delightful box, filled with goodies. Many of these items are highly useful, so don't get them lost in your mad frenzy to rip out the phone and start using it.

Inside the Fire phone box, you'll find the following goodies:

- ✔ The phone itself, which is cocooned in a clingy plastic sheet wrapper
- ✔ The USB charging cable, which is also used for data transfer
- ✔ A charger head, which is a wall adapter for the USB charging cable

✔ Some fancy, stylin' earbuds

These are the high-quality earbuds that don't tangle. They also feature a microphone for hands-free operation.

✔ A teensy card labeled *Getting to know your fire phone*. If it says *Conoce tu teléfono Fire* instead, you're reading the Spanish-language version.

You can remove the clingy plastic sheet at this time. Dispense with it.

Once freed from its clingy plastic sheet cocoon, the phone is ready to use. No further assembly is required, although if you purchased the Fire phone at a Phone Store, they may have to install a SIM card. Good! That's something that they do for you:

✔ The Fire phone lacks removable storage, so you don't need to buy a Micro SD memory card for use with the phone.

✔ A list of optional accessories available for the Fire phone is in the later section "Adding accessories."

Charge the Battery

Don't count on the Fire phone shipping with a fully charged battery. That would be nice, but most of the time it's not true. Therefore, one of your first phone duties is to charge the battery. Follow these steps:

1. **Plug the USB charging cable into the charger head.**

   The cable plugs in only one way.

2. **Plug the charger head and cable into a wall socket.**

   You may have to extend the two prongs on the charger head.

3. **Plug the Fire phone into the USB cable.**

   The cable connects on the bottom edge of the phone. It goes in only one way. Don't force it!

The phone charges stealthily, so don't bother looking for a blinking light or icon indicating that it's rapidly sucking the juice. It is.

The phone may turn on when you plug it in for a charge. That's okay, but read Chapter 2 to find out what to do the first time the Fire phone turns on:

✔ I recommend fully charging the phone before you use it. Even so:

✔ You can use the Fire phone while it's charging. The USB cable does impede mobility, but you can still use the phone.

✔ You can charge the phone in your car, if you have something called a Micro USB charging adapter. One end plugs into the phone, and the other into the receptacle once known as a cigarette lighter.

✔ The phone also charges itself whenever it's plugged into a computer by way of a USB cable. The computer must be on for charging to work.

✔ The Fire phone charges more quickly when it's plugged into the wall.

✔ You don't need to worry about fully discharging your phone before recharging it. If the phone needs a charge, even when the battery is just a little low, feel free to do so.

✔ The Fire phone's battery is nonremovable. That's okay! It's a robust battery that should serve you well, either until the desire to get the Fire II phone overwhelms you or you exhaust your cellular provider's contract.

Fire Phone Orientation

You may be high-tech savvy. You may be trying out your first smartphone. Either way, it helps to know what you're looking at when you hold a Fire phone in your hand. Each of those features, holes, and buttons is important. And they all have a specific name.

Finding things on the phone

Don't call it a *doodad* or *thingamabob*. Yes, I succumb to that fault as well, but it's not accurate. Instead, soak in Figure 1-1, which illustrates important items found on your Fire phone.

The terms referenced in Figure 1-1 are the same as the terms used elsewhere in this book and in Amazon's documentation as well. Here are the details:

Power button: Don't be mistaken and refer to this button as the On–Off button. It's not. It has more than one function, the details of which are found in Chapter 2.

Dynamic Perspective Sensor: Four of these eyeballs dwell in each of the phone's four corners. These sensors help enable the captivating 3D magic on the phone's touchscreen.

Volume button: The Volume button is really two buttons in one. Press the top end to set the volume higher; press the bottom end to set the volume lower. This volume button — both ends — can also be used as the shutter button when using the Fire phone to take pictures. See Chapter 14.

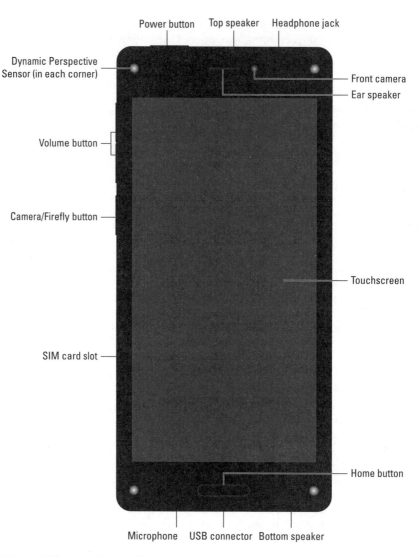

Power button   Top speaker   Headphone jack

Dynamic Perspective
Sensor (in each corner)

Front camera

Ear speaker

Volume button

Camera/Firefly button

Touchscreen

SIM card slot

Home button

Microphone   USB connector   Bottom speaker

Figure 1-1: Fire phone's facial features.

Camera/Firefly button: Press this button to activate the phone's Camera mode and start taking pictures. If you press and hold the button, you activate the Fire phone's Firefly feature. See Chapter 14 for information on using the phone as a camera; Firefly is covered in Chapter 17.

SIM card slot: This spot is where the phone's SIM card is inserted. I point this out to sate your curiosity; odds are that you'll never need to insert or remove the SIM card.

Microphone: The phone's microphone is found on the bottom edge. It works great in that location, so don't believe that you need to hold the phone at a weird angle so that people can hear you.

USB connector: On the bottom center edge is where the USB cable attaches to the phone. The cable is used to charge the phone and to exchange information with a computer. Charging the phone is covered in this chapter; see Chapter 19 for information on sharing files with a computer.

Speaker(s): The Fire phone features three speakers. The ear speaker is at the top center on the device's front. That's the speaker you stick up to your head while you're on a phone call. Two other speakers are found on the top and bottom edges of the phone. Those are the stereo speakers that are used when you're playing a game, watching a movie, or otherwise goofing off.

Headphone jack: The hole on top of the phone is where you plug in a standard set of headphones. I recommend using the no-tangle earbud speakers that come with the Fire phone.

Front camera: The phone's front-facing camera is found just to the right of the ear speaker. It's used for taking self-portraits as well as for video chat.

Touchscreen display: The main part of the phone is its *touchscreen* display. It's a see-touch thing: You look at the display and also touch it with your fingers to control the phone. That's where it gets the name *touch*screen.

Home button: At the bottom center of the phone, below the touchscreen, is the Home button. This button's function is covered in Chapter 3.

Not shown in Figure 1-1 is the exciting backside of the Fire phone. You'll find two interesting items there — and only two, so an illustration isn't necessary:

Rear camera: The larger of the two round holes in the upper left of the phone's back is the rear camera. It's the phone's main camera.

LED flash: The smaller round hole is the camera's LED flash, used for flash photography, to illuminate low-light videos, or as a flashlight.

Anything else you find on your phone: Yeah, that's a mystery. I've asked, but Amazon is tight-lipped about those items. My guess is that if it's not illustrated in Figure 1-1, you probably don't need to worry about it.

Using the earphones

The Amazon Fire phone comes with a fine set of earphones, perhaps the best ever to be included with any phone. And if your Fire didn't come with those phones, perhaps it's late in the quarter and Amazon's bean-counters are looking to save a few bucks. Shame on them.

The earphones are officially known as the Premium Headset. It features a flat cable that promises never to tangle.

The cable has three ends. Two of the ends are the earbuds, which you stick into your ears. The other end has a pointy thing that you don't want to stick into your ear. Instead, stick that end into the top of your phone.

Between the ends is a control, something I call the *noodle*. It has + (plus) and – (minus) buttons, used to adjust the earphone volume up or down, respectively.

A button in the center of the earphone is used to play or pause music. You can also press the button to answer or disconnect a call.

A teeny microphone hole on the noodle allows you to use the earphones for hands-free phone operation. Just plug them into the Fire phone and you're ready to go:

- You can use any earphones with your Fire phone, although the premium headset that ships with the phone is one of the best I've used.

- The earbuds are labeled L and R for left and right. The label is on the back of the earbud, although the right earbud features a concave end and the left earbud is convex.

- The earbuds ends are *magnetic,* so you can stick them together when you're not using the earphones.

- If you use another set of earphones with the Fire phone, ensure that they feature a microphone. You need that option so that you can listen to the phone and talk on it while using the earphones.

- See Chapter 15 for more information on using your phone as a portable music player.

- Be sure to fully insert the earphone connector into the phone. The person you're talking with can't hear you well when the earphones are plugged in only part of the way.

- You can also use a Bluetooth headset with your phone, to listen to a call or some music. See Chapter 18 for more information on Bluetooth.

Adding accessories

As this book goes to press, few accessories are available for the Fire phone. The most common are carrying cases, which you can find on Amazon, although some may also be hanging around the Phone Store.

Eventually, a nighttime docking stand may appear for the phone. That item is truly handy, especially when you use your phone as an alarm clock.

A car charger is also a good accessory to obtain. You don't need a specific brand; any car charger with a Micro-USB connector does the job.

 If it's your desire to watch your Fire phone's image on an HDTV or a monitor, you need to obtain a Miracast adapter. The adapter attaches to the TV and accesses a Wi-Fi network. As long as your phone uses the same network, you can connect to the Miracast adapter and see the phone's screen on the TV.

Your Phone's Home

It's perfectly normal to carry around your Fire phone in your pants pocket. Belt-clip holsters are also appropriate, as is tossing the phone into a purse or even a backpack. The point is to keep your phone with you where it's handy. Even so:

 Don't forget when the phone is in your pocket, especially in your coat or jacket. You might accidentally sit on the phone, or it can fly out when you take off your coat. The worst fate for any cell phone is to take a trip through the wash. I'm sure your phone has nightmares about it.

When you're not toting the phone about, I recommend that you find a single place for it: on top of your desk or workstation, in the kitchen, on the nightstand — you get the idea. Phones are as prone to being misplaced as are your car keys and glasses. Consistency is the key to finding your phone.

Then again, your phone rings, so you can always have someone else call your cell phone to help you locate it:

- ✒ I store my Fire phone on my desk, next to my computer. Conveniently, I have the charger plugged into the computer so that the phone remains plugged in, connected, and charging when I'm not using it.

- ✒ Phones on coffee tables get buried under magazines and are often squished when rude people put their feet on the furniture.

- ✒ Avoid putting your Fire phone in direct sunlight. Despite its name, heat is bad news for your phone — any electronic gizmo, for that matter.

- ✒ See Chapter 23 for information on properly cleaning the phone.

Hello and Goodbye

*I*n the book *Lamps For Dummies*, the chapter about turning a lamp on and off is only one page long. Can you imagine? I accused the author of padding, but he insisted that a full page was necessary to describe all the nuances of the On–Off switch, especially for 3-way lamps.

Here in *Amazon Fire Phone For Dummies*, this On–Off chapter is several pages long. That's because the phone doesn't have an On–Off button — it has a Power button. That button has many functions, and indeed you have many options for turning your Fire phone off or on, all carefully described in this chapter's ten pages.

How to Start a Fire

Forget the book of matches, and don't bother looking for two sticks and some kindling. When it comes to starting a Fire phone, you really need to know only one thing: how to use the Power button.

Turning on your phone for the first time

The very first time you turn on a Fire phone is a special occasion. The phone recognizes that it hasn't yet been set up, so it asks you a bunch of configuration questions. This happens only once. After the phone is configured, turning it on works differently, as described in the next section.

Details regarding the setup may change in the future. For now, the first-time setup process generally works like this:

1. **Turn on the phone by pressing the Power button.**

   Press and hold the button until you see the Amazon logo on the screen. You can then release the key.

   It's okay to turn on the phone while it's plugged in and charging.

2. **Answer the questions as they appear on the screen.**

   You're asked to select options for the following items:

   • Select your language.

   • Activate the phone on the cellular network, which may have already been done for you.

   • Register your phone by signing in with your Amazon account and password.

   • Choose a Wi-Fi network (can be done later).

   • Enable location services.

   • Activate the automatic backup.

   • Sign in to your Facebook and Twitter accounts (can also be done later).

   • Peruse any offers or trials for services (which you can skip).

   • Review a quick interactive guide on how to use the phone (also skippable).

   To fill in text fields, use the onscreen keyboard. Specific directions for using the keyboard are found in Chapter 4.

3. **After each choice, tap the Next button.**

   Tapping the Next button on the screen lets you proceed between steps. Some you must answer, some you can skip. Skipping a question is fine; you won't screw up anything by skipping an option. For example, you can wait to set up accounts until later.

4. **Touch the Finish button.**

   The Finish button appears on the final screen, meaning that you've completed the setup and configuration.

From this point on, starting the phone works as described in the next few sections.

After the initial setup, you're taken to the Home screen. Chapter 3 provides information on how to work the Home screen as well as general operations information for the Fire phone. Turn there quickly, before the urge to play with your phone becomes unbearable:

✓ Skipping steps in the setup procedure is fine because the phone offers many ways to do things, and you can change settings at any time.

✓ *Your Amazon account* refers to the name and password you use to access Amazon on the Internet. You must have an Amazon account to get the most from the Fire phone.

✓ Refer to Chapter 18 for details on connecting to a Wi-Fi network.

✓ *Location services* refers to how the phone knows its position on Planet Earth. I recommend activating all location services to get the most from your Android phone.

✓ Chapter 11 contains information about accessing social networking sites. Refer there if you skipped signing in to a social networking account during setup.

Turning on the phone

To turn on your Fire phone, press and hold the Power button. It's found on the phone's top edge. After a few moments, you see the Amazon logo. The phone is starting.

Eventually, you see the lock screen. It shows the date and time and any pending messages or appointments, similar to what's shown in Figure 2-1. You can tilt and move the phone to view the lock screen scene in 3D. That's fun, but it's not the point of the lock screen.

To unlock the phone, swipe the touchscreen, as illustrated in Figure 2-1: Touch the screen near the bottom, and then drag your finger up to the top.

After the phone unlocks, you can begin using it:

✓ If you tilt the phone to the left or right, the status bar atop the screen becomes visible. It lists signal strength, battery life, and other information.

✓ You can change the lock screen scene (the background) or supply your own image. Refer to Chapter 21 for information.

✓ Turning on the phone is something you'll not often do. Instead, you unlock it. See the next section.

Figure 2-1: Unlocking the phone.

Unlocking the phone

Rather than turn the phone on or off, most of the time you lock and unlock it. To unlock the phone, press the Power button. A quick press is all that's needed. The phone's touchscreen comes to life, and you see the lock screen.

The standard screen lock is called None, and it's shown in Figure 2-1. For more security, you can choose the PIN lock or Password lock, both of which are illustrated in Figure 2-2.

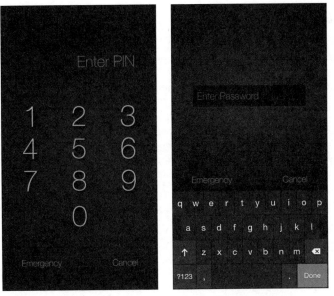

PIN lock   Password lock

Figure 2-2: The PIN and Password lock screens.

The PIN lock requires that you type a secret number to unlock the phone. Swipe up the screen to unlock and you'll see the PIN keypad, shown in Figure 2-2. Type the PIN and the phone is unlocked.

The password lock is more secure than the PIN. It requires that you type a multicharacter password to unlock the phone. Tap the Enter Password field to view the onscreen keyboard, shown in Figure 2-2. Type the password and tap the OK button to unlock the phone:

✔ You can also unlock the phone by pressing the Home button.

✔ Pressing the Camera button unlocks the phone and immediately starts the Camera app, so you can use the phone to take pictures.

✔ Specific directions for setting and removing screen locks are found in Chapter 21.

✔ It isn't necessary to unlock the phone for an incoming call. For information on receiving phone calls, see Chapter 5.

✔ For additional information on working with the onscreen keyboard, see Chapter 4.

✔ See the later section "Locking the phone" for information on manually locking the phone.

Account Setup

To make your phone useful, you need to add your various online personas and existences. You do this by incorporating those online accounts, allowing the Fire phone to access information such as names, phone numbers, and email addresses, as well as your schedule, appointments, and other information kept on the Internet.

The Fire phone is already aware of your Amazon account. You may have added more accounts during the initial setup process. If not, or to add an account at any time, follow these steps:

1. **Go to the Home screen.**

   The *Home screen* is the main screen on your phone. Display it by pressing the Home button.

2. **Display the App Grid.**

   Press the Home button again to view all apps in the App Grid, as shown in Figure 2-3.

Settings app

Home screen   App Grid

Figure 2-3: Getting to the App Grid.

3. **Tap the Settings icon to start the Settings app.**

   You may have to swipe the touchscreen from bottom to top to find the Settings icon. See Chapter 3 for specific screen swiping instructions.

   The Settings app is where you access internal options, change settings, or adjust features on your Fire phone.

4. **Tap My Accounts.**

   The My Accounts area expands to list options.

5. **Choose Manage Email Accounts.**

   A list of any existing accounts appears.

6. **Choose the Add Account item.**

7. **Type the account's email address.**

   Use the onscreen keyboard to type the address. You'll find an at-key (@) as well as the .com (dot-com) key to assist your typing.

   For example, to add your Google account to the Fire phone, type your Gmail account name (including the @gmail.com part).

8. **Tap the Next button.**

9. **Type the account's password.**

   If you need assistance using the onscreen keyboard to type special characters, refer to Chapter 4.

10. **Tap the Next button.**

    The phone configures the account. You may be asked to provide further information, depending on the account type. That information is available from the service provider. For example, for a corporate account, contact your organization's IT department for details.

11. **Tap the Add Another Account button to add another account, choose Go to Inbox to review your mail, or press the Home button to visit the Home screen.**

    In other words, you're done.

In addition to your email, other information is copied to the Fire phone from the online service. This information includes contacts, calendar appointments, and other information, depending on the service:

- ✔ See Chapter 9 for details on using email on your Fire phone.

- ✔ Chapter 11 covers social networking on your phone. Refer there for specific information on adding Facebook, Twitter, and other accounts.

Goodbye, Phone

You have many means at your disposal to dismiss your Fire phone. Primarily, you can lock the phone or turn it off completely. You can also just sit and wait and eventually it locks itself automatically. This section describes the details.

Also, please appreciate my great restraint in avoiding using the term *putting out the Fire* in this section.

Locking the phone

To lock your phone, press and release the Power button. The touchscreen turns off and the phone is locked:

- ✔ Your Fire phone will probably spend most of its time locked.
- ✔ You can lock the phone while you're making a call: Simply press and release the Power button. The call stays connected, but the display is disabled.
- ✔ Likewise, you can lock the phone while listening to music. The music continues to play when the phone is locked.

- ✔ You can adjust the volume (by using the Volume button) while the phone is locked.
- ✔ Locking doesn't turn off the phone. Calls still come in, music plays, and alarms trigger.

Controlling the lock timeout

If you ignore your phone for a while, or if it just becomes painfully bored, it automatically locks. The normal delay length is about one minute, although you can adjust that value by obeying these steps:

1. **At the Home screen, swipe up the screen to view the App Grid.**
2. **Open the Settings app.**
3. **Choose Lock Screen.**
4. **Choose Change the Automatic Lock Time.**

   You see a screen similar to Figure 2-4.

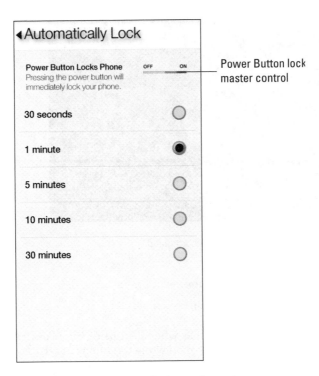

Figure 2-4: Select an automatic timeout interval.

5. **Select a timeout interval.**

   The standard value is one minute.

6. **Press the Home button to return to the Home screen.**

The lock timer measures inactivity. When you don't touch the screen or press a key, the timer starts ticking. A few seconds before the timeout value you set (refer to Step 5), the touchscreen dims. Then the phone locks. If you touch the screen before then, the timer is reset.

The lock timeout is similar to Sleep mode on a computer. As on a computer, when the Fire phone is locked, it uses less power and the screen is off.

Turning off the phone

To turn off your phone, obey these steps:

1. **Press and hold down the Power button.**

   When you see the Power Off/Restart menu, shown in Figure 2-5, you can release the key.

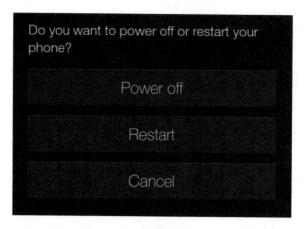

Figure 2-5: The Power Off/Restart menu.

2. Tap the Power Off button.

The phone turns itself off.

The phone doesn't receive calls when it's turned off. Likewise, any alarms or reminders you've set won't sound while the phone is off:

✔ Calls received while the phone is off are routed instead to voice mail. See Chapter 5 for more information on voice mail.

✔ The phone can be charged while it's off.

✔ Use the Restart option to turn the phone off and then on again. This option is helpful for fixing minor annoyances. Also see Chapter 23 for troubleshooting info.

+++++ 3 ·+++++

Fire Control

*F*ifty years ago, they had it wrong. Back then, it was a common belief that the more knobs, dials, and buttons something had, the more advanced it was. Technology of the future was all about throwing switches. Reality is far different, of course.

Your Fire phone is pretty advanced, yet it's terribly short of buttons. Therefore, another, less obvious way must be available to control the device. That less obvious way is the touchscreen, but also an accelerometer, which monitors how you hold the phone. This chapter explains how to use both of these gizmos to control your Fire phone.

Basic Operations

To get the most from your Fire phone, you must understand some basic operations. This involves an introduction to the various unconventional ways the device works. You need to not only become familiar with some interesting techniques but also know the wacky names applied to them.

Manipulating the touchscreen

My guess is that you've probably met the Fire phone's touchscreen already. It's pretty friendly and fun to use. What may not be friendly, fun, or familiar are the terms applied to the various actions you can perform on the touchscreen. Here's the list:

Tap: In this simple operation, you touch the screen. Generally, you're touching an object such as an icon or a control. You might also see the term *press* or *touch*.

Long-press: Touch the screen and hold down your finger. Some operations, such as selecting an item, begin with the long-press.

Swipe: When you swipe, you start with your finger in one spot and then drag it to another spot. Usually, a swipe is up, down, left, or right, which moves something in the direction you swipe your finger. A swipe can be fast or slow. It's also called a *flick* or a *slide*.

Double-tap: Touch the screen in the same location twice. A double-tap is used to zoom in on an image or a map, but it can also zoom out. Because of the double-tap's dual nature, I recommend using the pinch and spread operations instead.

Pinch: A pinch involves two fingers, which start out separated and then are brought together. The pinch is used to zoom out on an image or a map. This move may also be called a *pinch close*.

Spread: In the opposite of a pinch, you start with your fingers together and then spread them. The spread is used to zoom in. It's also known as a *pinch open*.

Rotate: Use two fingers to twist around a central point on the touchscreen, which has the effect of rotating an object on the screen. If you have trouble with this operation, pretend that you're turning the dial on a safe.

You can't manipulate the touchscreen while wearing gloves, unless they're gloves specially designed for use with electronic touchscreens, such as the gloves that Batman wears. Amazon sells them, of course.

Working with gestures

The Fire phone features some one-handed operations that will either delight or frustrate you. The key thing to remember is that alternative ways are available to perform the same tricks, as described in this section.

The gestures work by abruptly moving the phone in a specific direction. The phone's accelerometer picks up the motion and performs specific functions or shortcuts.

Four gestures are available:

Auto-Scroll: Tilt the top of the phone toward you or away from you to scroll the screen up or down, respectively. You can also swipe the screen instead of using this gesture.

Peek: Tilt the phone slightly to the left or right. As you do, details appear that are otherwise hidden, such as the status bar, shown in Figure 3-1. You may see other information as well, depending on what's on the screen. The items that appear offer helpful hints or additional information. A non-gesture technique for this feature isn't available.

Status bar

Flat

Peek
(tilted to the right)

Figure 3-1: The peek gesture.

Swivel: Flick your wrist as you hold the phone, like you're trying to shake something off the top edge. You can swivel either left or right. The effect is that you see the Quick Actions and notifications. See the later section "Reviewing Quick Actions and notifications" for more information.

Tilt: Abruptly lift the phone's left or right edges. If you tilt the left edge up, you see the Navigation panel. Tilting the right edge up displays Delighters and Shortcuts. See the later section "There's No Place Like Home Screen" for details on these features.

A fifth gesture is also used, though it doesn't involve moving the phone:

Back: Swipe the touchscreen from the bottom upward. This gesture returns you to the previous screen, dismisses an onscreen notice, hides the onscreen keyboard, or performs other actions that signify moving "back."

Also see the next section, on rotating the phone. This action isn't really a gesture; however, it's a feature that also uses the accelerometer.

Changing the orientation

In addition to providing gestures, the Fire phone's accelerometer is used by various apps to determine whether you've reoriented the phone from an upright to a horizontal position. You can test this feature by opening an app, such as the Silk Browser. Heed these steps:

1. **Start the Silk Browser app.**

   Tap the Silk Browser app icon on the Home screen. If you don't see the Home screen, press the Home button, and then look for the icon near the bottom. If you don't see it at the bottom, press the Home button again and look for the app icon on the App Grid.

   After the web browser app starts, it displays a web page. If not, browse to a web page so that you have visual content on the screen. Using the phone's web browser is covered in Chapter 10.

2. **Tilt the phone to the left.**

   As shown in Figure 3-2, the web page switches itself to the horizontal, or landscape, orientation. For some apps, it's truly the best way to see things.

3. **Tilt the phone upright again.**

   The web page redisplays itself in its original, upright mode.

The rotation feature may not work for all apps, especially games that present themselves in one orientation only. The Home and lock screens do not rotate.

The screen rotation feature might also be disabled. Refer to Chapter 21 for information on enabling or disabling this feature.

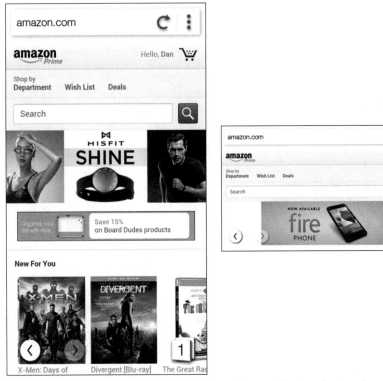

Vertical orientation   Horizontal orientation

Figure 3-2: Vertical and horizontal orientations.

Navigating from here to there

The most common way to get from one place to another on your Fire phone
is to tap an icon or a button. An icon is an image, and a button is text. You tap
either one and the phone displays another screen or returns you to the previous screen:

- To get back to where you were, swipe the touchscreen from bottom to
  top. This technique is known as the Back gesture.

- Another navigation technique is to press the Home button. Doing so
  always displays the Home screen.

Both the Back gesture and pressing the Home button work no matter what
else you're doing on the phone.

The Back gesture also works to dismiss the onscreen keyboard. See
Chapter 4.

Setting the volume

The Volume button is found on the left side of the phone. Press the top part of the button to raise the volume. Press the bottom part to lower the volume.

As you press the Volume button, a panel appears on the touchscreen to illustrate the relative volume level, as shown in Figure 3-3. You can manipulate the panel's controls to set the volume, as shown in the figure.

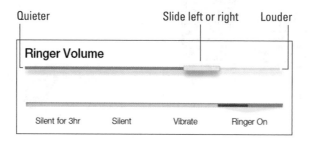

Figure 3-3: Volume and sound controls.

In addition to sliding the control by using your finger, you can tap one of the four sound options (refer to Figure 3-3):

Silent for 3hr: Choose this setting to silence the Fire phone for three hours, after which the ringer is on again. This option is perfect for watching movies or other situations where you may forget to unsilence the phone.

Silent: The phone doesn't make any sound, nor does it vibrate.

Vibrate: The phone vibrates on an incoming call or during a notification or an alert. Alarms still sound when the phone is in this mode.

Ringer On: The phone makes all sorts of noise!

If you press the bottom (or "down") Volume button all the way, the phone enters Vibrate mode. Press the Volume down button one more notch and it enters Silent mode.

The Volume button controls the phone's current sound, no matter what the source. For example, when you're on a call, the volume controls set the call's sound level. When you're listening to music or watching a video, the volume controls set the media volume.

Individual volume settings are available for various noisy things the phone does. See Chapter 21 for information on setting those individual levels.

There's No Place Like Home Screen

The Home screen is the location from which you begin almost all your Fire phone activities. It's the first screen you see when you unlock the phone. It's so important that it has its own button, right below the touchscreen. Obviously, the Home screen is some kind of big deal.

Exploring the Home screen

The Home screen's main turf is occupied by the Carousel. It shows a list of apps you've recently opened, music you've listened to, books you've read, and other activities you've pursued on the phone. The most recent activity is shown upfront, such as the Silk Browser shown in Figure 3-4.

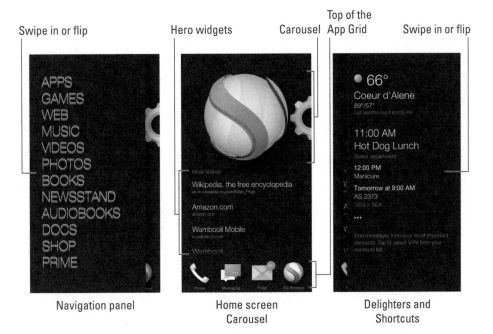

Figure 3-4: The Home screen.

To work the Carousel, swipe the screen from right to left. More-recent items are shown first. The list can be quite long, depending on how much you've used your phone.

Below each humongous app icon, you find hero widgets. These widgets relate to the icon above, such as recent web pages, photos taken, music played, and so on. The hero widgets might also include suggestions of apps to purchase or books to read, or they may simply list related info, such as weather for nearby cities.

To the left and right, you find hidden panels that you can view by either swiping the screen inward or using the flip gesture.

On the left is the *Navigation panel.* It contains items related to the app you're viewing, but on the Home screen it lists categories of things the phone does.

On the right side is the Delighters and Shortcuts panel. It lists items related to what you're viewing.

Most apps display information on the Navigation (left) and Delighters and Shortcuts (right) panels, but not every app takes advantage of this feature. Some games, for example, don't use the panels:

- ✔ The bottom of the Home screen shows the top row of apps, which is really part of the App Grid. See the later section "Starting an app" for details.

- ✔ See the earlier section "Working with gestures" for information on the flip gesture.

Peeking at the status bar

At the top of the screen dwells the status bar. You can't see it unless you use the peek gesture: Tilt the phone slightly left or right and the status bar shows up (refer to Figure 3-1).

The status bar offers details on the phone's condition: You see the time, Wi-Fi signal strength (if connected), cellular signal strength, cellular network, and battery charge percentage plus a battery graphic:

- ✔ You can also view the status bar when reviewing notifications. See the next section.

- ✔ The Fire phone can be configured to display the status bar all the time. See Chapter 21 for display settings and options.

Reviewing Quick Actions and notifications

The Notification panel is a place you can frequently visit to check out notifications and access Quick Actions.

Notifications are alerts, updates, and informative items that tell you what's going on in your online life or with the phone specifically. You can find new email alerts, appointment reminders, social networking updates, and other options all in one spot.

Quick Actions are commands or shortcuts for things you do often with your phone. You can enter Airplane mode, set Wi-Fi options, turn on Bluetooth, set the screen brightness, and have quick access to other popular features.

Both the notifications and Quick Actions dwell on the Notification panel. You can access that panel at any time: Swipe the screen from top to bottom. You can also use the swivel gesture to display the panel, which is shown in Figure 3-5.

Dismiss all notifications

Figure 3-5: Quick Actions and notifications.

Touch a notification to deal with it. What happens next depends on the notification, but most often the app that generated the notification appears. In the case of email messages, you're taken to the inbox associated with the named account, such as Yahoo! (shown earlier, in Figure 3-5).

Dismiss an individual notification by sliding it to the right or left. To dismiss all notifications, touch the Clear button, illustrated in Figure 3-5. Be aware that some notifications are ongoing and cannot be dismissed, such as the USB Connected notification. Also, some event notifications and appointment reminders appear again until they've been dealt with in the Calendar app.

When you're done looking, slide up the Notification panel again: Swipe the screen from bottom to top, or use the swivel gesture:

- Use the peek gesture to view the text below the Quick Action icons, as shown earlier, in Figure 3-5. Refer to the earlier section "Working with gestures" for more information on the peek gesture.

- The Settings Quick Actions icon provides instant access to the Settings app, a popular place to visit for changing features and customizing your Fire phone.

- Some apps, such as Facebook and Twitter, don't display notifications unless you're logged in. See Chapter 11.

The World of Apps

One of the key skills necessary to using your phone is the ability to run apps. The apps are like programs on a computer. An app is software that carries out specific duties, helps you organize things, or accesses information — or an app can be just for fun. Knowing how to deal with apps is vital to being a successful, happy Fire phone user.

Starting an app

To start an app, find its icon and tap. Apps that you've recently opened can be found on the Carousel: Swipe the Home screen from right to left to view those recent apps.

All the apps on your phone are found on the App Grid, shown in Figure 3-6. To view the App Grid, press the Home button to visit the Home screen. Then press the Home button again, or swipe the touchscreen up, from bottom to top.

To start an app from the App Grid, tap its icon. You may have to swipe the screen up or down to view the variety of available apps; the App Grid can be several pages long.

Master control

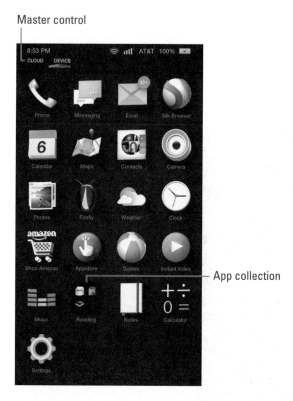

App collection

Figure 3-6: The App Grid.

When an app starts, it takes over the screen, doing whatever wondrous thing that app does:

- *App* is short for *app*lication. It's another word for *program* or *software*.

- New apps are obtained at the Appstore. See Chapter 17 for details.

- Also see Chapter 22 for information on the App Collection icon (refer to Figure 3-6) as well as other details on organizing your apps.

- The top row of apps on the App Grid always appears at the bottom of the Home screen.

 - When the Cloud/Device master control is set to Device, the App Grid shows all apps installed on your phone. When the control is set to Cloud, you see items you've obtained from the Appstore, whether they're installed on the phone or not.

Switching apps

The apps you run on your phone don't quit when you dismiss them from the screen. For the most part, they stay running. To switch between running apps, or any app you've recently opened, press the Home button twice in a row. You see the Quick Switch screen, shown in Figure 3-7.

Swipe left or right

Figure 3-7: The Quick Switch list.

Tap an icon from the Quick Switch list to switch back to that app. You can swipe the list left or right to peruse more apps. Or if you don't find an app to run, dismiss the list by pressing the Home button again, or swipe the screen from bottom to top — the Back technique.

Tap the Home button twice quickly to see the Quick Switch list. If you tap too slowly, you see the App Grid. When you press the Home button too long, you activate voice commands. See Chapter 24 for information.

Quitting an app

Unlike on a computer, you don't need to quit apps on your Fire phone. To leave an app, touch the Home button to return to the Home screen. You can also swipe the screen up to back out of any app.

Some apps may offer a Quit command or an Exit command. If so, choose that command to quit the app or leave the activity.

If necessary, the Fire phone automatically shuts down apps you haven't used in a while. You can directly stop apps that have run amok, which is described in Chapter 22.

Recognizing common icons

Many apps you use on the Fire phone use similar icons. These icons represent common actions or commands, and their use is consistent across many apps. Table 3-1 lists the most common icons and their functions.

Various sections throughout this book give examples of using the icons. Their images appear in the book's margins where relevant.

Table 3-1		Common Icons
Icon	*Name*	*What It Does*
✚	Add	Adds or creates an item
✕	Close	Closes a window or clears text from an input field
🗑	Delete	Removes one or more items from a list or deletes a message
✓	Done	Dismisses an item, a notice, or a message
✎	Edit	Lets you edit an item, add text, or fill in fields
⋮	Menu	Displays an app's menu or list of commands
🎤	Microphone	Lets you use your voice to dictate text

(continued)

Table 3-1 *(continued)*

Icon	Name	What It Does
	Refresh	Fetches new information or reloads
	Search	Searches for a tidbit of information
	Settings	Adjusts options for an app
	Share	Shares information stored on the phone via email, social networking, or other Internet services
	Star	Flags a favorite item, such as a contact or web page

Text Creation and Editing

In This Chapter

▶ Typing on the onscreen keyboard

▶ Getting at special characters

▶ Using word suggestion shortcuts

▶ Tracing text on the keyboard

▶ Dictating text with voice input

▶ Selecting, cutting, copying, and pasting text

*I*t may seem odd, especially given that your Fire phone is missing a physical keyboard, but you'll create a lot of text on the phone. Though you could write The Great American Novel, odds are that most of your work with text involves short tidbits, names, passwords, email, text messages, and comments on a social networking site. Those activities require that you somehow create text. This chapter explains how it's done on a device as revolutionary as the Fire phone.

Behold! The Onscreen Keyboard

Don't worry about finding the phone's onscreen keyboard. It finds you. Any time text input is required, up pops the keyboard, ready for typing action. It's pretty amazing, and it may take some getting used to, especially if you've never typed on a touchscreen.

Exploring the onscreen keyboard

The onscreen keyboard appears on the bottom part of the touchscreen. It shows up whenever text input is required, such as when you're up early, frantically writing an apology email for that drunk email you sent the previous night.

Figure 4-1 illustrates the Fire phone keyboard. Some keys may change, depending on what you're typing at the time, as illustrated in the figure.

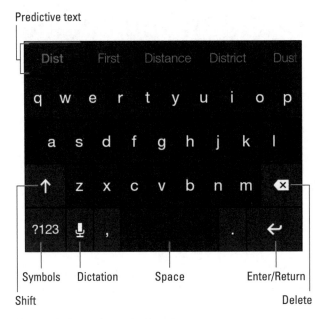

Figure 4-1: The onscreen keyboard.

In Figure 4-1, the onscreen alphabetic keyboard is shown. You see keys from A through Z in lowercase. You also see the Shift key for producing capital letters, and the Delete key, which works to backspace and erase.

The Enter key changes its look depending on what you're typing. Five variations are shown in Table 4-1, along with a description of what each one does:

Table 4-1		Key Variations
Symbol	*Name*	*What It Does*
↵	Enter	Just like the Enter or Return key on a computer keyboard, this key ends a paragraph of text. It's used mostly when filling in long stretches of text or when multiline input is needed.
Go	Go	This action key directs the app to proceed with a search, to accept input, or to perform another action.

Symbol	Name	What It Does
Q	Search	You see the Search key when you're searching for something. Touching the key starts the search.
Next	Next	This key appears when you're typing information into multiple fields. Touching this key switches from one field to the next, such as when typing a username and password.
Done	Done	This key appears whenever you've finished typing text in the final field of a screen that has several fields.

> ✔ The large key at the bottom center of the onscreen keyboard is the Space key.

> ✔ The keys to the left and right of the Space key may change, depending on the context of what you're typing. For example, a key labeled with @ or .com (dot com) may appear to assist in typing a web page or an email address. Other keys may change as well, although the basic alphabetic keys remain the same.

> ✔ To display the onscreen keyboard, touch any text field or spot on the screen where typing is permitted.

> ✔ To dismiss the onscreen keyboard, swipe the screen from bottom to top (the Back shortcut).

> ✔ The keyboard reorients itself when you rotate the phone. The onscreen keyboard's horizontal orientation is wide, so you might find it easier to use.

Typing one character at a time

The onscreen keyboard is pretty easy to figure out: Touch a letter to produce the character. It works just like a computer keyboard in that respect. As you type, the key you touch is highlighted. The phone may give a wee bit of feedback in the form of a faint click or vibration.

Some special keys generate more than one character at a time. One you'll notice is the .com ("dot-com") key, which appears when you need to type a web page or email address. Tapping the .com key causes those letters (four of 'em) to be typed at once:

> ✔ It helps to *type slowly* until you get used to the onscreen keyboard.

> ✔ When you make a mistake, touch the Delete key to back up and erase.

> ✔ A blinking cursor on the touchscreen shows where new text appears, which is similar to how typing text works on a computer.

✔ Tap the Shift key to produce an uppercase letter. The first letter on a line, or after a period, is capitalized automatically.

✔ To type in all caps, tap the Shift key twice. The Shift key changes to reflect All Caps mode, as shown in the margin. Tap the Shift key again to exit this mode.

✔ When you type a password, the character you type appears briefly, but for security reasons, it may be replaced by a black dot. The Show Password check box may appear, which disables this feature.

✔ People generally accept the concept that composing text on a phone isn't perfect. Don't sweat it if you make a few mistakes as you type text messages or email, though you should expect some curious replies about unintended typos.

Accessing special characters

You're not limited to typing only the symbols you see on the alphabetic keyboard (refer to Figure 4-1). Many more symbols are available, which you can see by touching the Number and Symbol key, labeled ?123, as shown in the margin. Touching this key gives you access to additional keyboard layouts, as shown in Figure 4-2.

Show more symbols

Numbers and Symbols

Alpha keyboard

Show numbers and symbols

More Symbols

Figure 4-2: Number and symbol keyboards.

To see additional symbols, tap the ~\< key. That keyboard variation is also shown in Figure 4-2.

To return to the standard alpha keyboard (refer to Figure 4-1), touch the ABC key.

To access accented and other special characters, long-press a key on the main, alphabetic keyboard. For certain keys, such as the A key shown in Figure 4-3, a palette of similar characters appears. Tap one of the characters to insert it into your text.

Long-press

Figure 4-3: Special symbol pop-up palette thing.

If you accidentally type a special character, tap the Delete key to erase it:

- ✔ Not every alphabetic character sports a special pop-up palette.

- ✔ Extra characters are available in uppercase as well; press the Shift key before you long-press on the onscreen keyboard.

- ✔ See Chapter 21 for more information on accessing special characters by modifying the phone's keyboard settings.

Predicting your next word

The Fire phone tries its best to guess which word you'll type next. The suggestions appear above the onscreen keyboard. As you type, the suggestions become more specific until the word you want appears. Tap that word to insert it into your text.

In Figure 4-4, I've typed the word *I*. The keyboard lists suggestions above the keyboard — suggestions that would make sense in context. Sometimes dozens of suggestions appear, in which case you can swipe the list to the left to view them all.

Predictive text

Text typed so far

Figure 4-4: Predictive text in action.

When a word is highlighted, tapping the Space key automatically inserts that word.

When the desired word doesn't appear, continue typing: The predictive-text feature begins making suggestions based on what you've typed so far. Touch the correct word when it appears, or if the word is highlighted, tap the Space key.

Dealing with spelling errors

When you type a word that the phone doesn't recognize, it's underlined, as shown in Figure 4-5. Tap the word to see a list of suggestions. Tap a suggestion to replace the misspelled word.

Misspelled word or typo

Figure 4-5: Adding a word to the dictionary.

Occasionally, a word may be spelled correctly, but unknown to the phone. In that case, you might be prompted to add the word to the phone's dictionary.

Yes, the phone has a dictionary.

Choose the Add Word to Dictionary option so that the phone doesn't flag the unknown word, similar to the one shown earlier, in Figure 4-5.

See Chapter 24 for more information about the phone's dictionary.

Using trace typing

If you truly crave typing speed, consider tracing your words instead of doing the old hunt-and-peck. Trace typing allows you to create text by swiping your finger over the onscreen keyboard, like mad scribbling but with a positive result.

For example, to type the word *hello,* drag your finger over the letters *H, E, L, L,* and *O* (in that order) without lifting your finger from the keyboard. Figure 4-6 illustrates how to type in this manner.

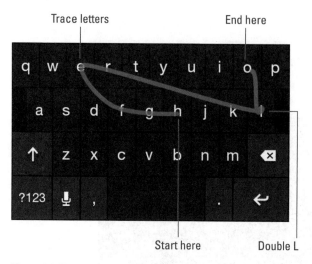

Figure 4-6: Trace typing the word *hello.*

✔ To type a capital letter, drag your finger up above the onscreen keyboard and then back down to swipe over the rest of the letters.

✔ Double letters are produced by swiping a tiny circle over the letter.

✔ The gesture typing feature may not be active when you need to type a password or for specific apps on the phone. When it doesn't work, use the onscreen keyboard one letter at a time.

Voice Typing

When you tire of using your finger to create text, you can always dictate your brilliance. The phone does an excellent job of interpreting your utterances, transforming the sound waves into text on the screen. The feature is called Voice Input.

 To type with your voice, tap the Microphone key on the onscreen keyboard, shown in the margin. After touching that key, you see a special window at the bottom of the screen, similar to the one shown in Figure 4-7. Dictate your text; speak directly at the phone.

Figure 4-7: Voice input in action.

As you speak, the Microphone icon animates. That means it's listening to your voice, interpreting what you're saying. Tap the Done button to pause input, or just keep blabbing:

  ✐ You can speak common punctuation symbols, such as "Comma," "Period," "Question mark," and "Exclamation point." You can also say "New line" to start text on a new line (like pressing the Enter key).

  ✐ You cannot dictate capital letters. If you're a stickler for such things, you have to go back and edit the text. See the next section.

  ✐ Dictation may not work without an Internet connection.

Text Editing

My guess: You didn't get a Fire phone so that you can edit text. Maybe you did, but text editing on a phone is something done mostly to augment the weakness that's inherent with an onscreen keyboard. Even so, you can do just about any type of text editing on your phone as you can do in a word processor.

Moving the cursor

The first part of editing text is to move the cursor to the correct spot. The *cursor* is that blinking, vertical line where text appears. After the cursor is in the proper spot, you can type, edit, or paste, or simply marvel that you were able to move the cursor hither and thither.

To move the cursor, simply touch the spot on the text where you want it to be. To help your precision, a cursor tab appears below the text, as shown in the margin. Further, you may see a tiny magnification bubble appear above the cursor, allowing for even more precision.

After you move the cursor, you can continue to type, use the Delete key to back up and erase, or paste in text copied from elsewhere.

 You may see a pop-up button above the cursor tab, showing a Paste command. That button is used to paste text, as described in the later section "Cutting, copying, and pasting text."

Selecting text

Selecting text on your phone works just like selecting text in a word processor: You mark the start and end of a block. That chunk of text appears highlighted on the screen. That process sounds simple — and it is, after you know the Fire phone text-selection secret.

Start selecting by long-pressing the text or double-tapping a word. Upon your success, the word is selected, as shown in Figure 4-8.

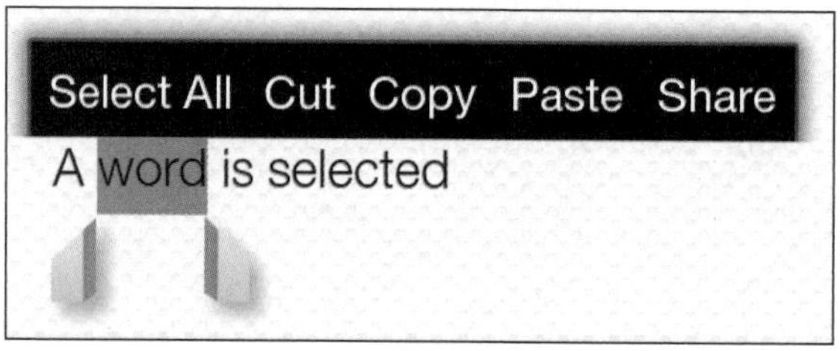

Select All   Cut   Copy   Paste   Share

A word is selected

Figure 4-8: A word is selected.

Drag the start and end markers around the touchscreen to mark a block of text.

A list of commands appears above the selected text, as shown in Figure 4-8. These commands are Select All, Cut, Copy, Paste, and Share. (Paste may not appear if nothing has been cut or copied.)

The Select All command selects all text in the text input area.

Cut, Copy, and Paste are described in the next section.

When you choose the Share command, you see a list of apps. Choose an app to send that bit of text to the app. For example, you could select text and share it with the Facebook app to include the text in a post. Or you could share the text with the Messaging app to include it in a text message.

To cancel text selection, touch anywhere on the screen outside of the selected block:

  ✔ Refer to other chapters throughout this book for information on using the Share command.

  ✔ Text selection on a web page works similarly to selecting text elsewhere. The primary difference is that the Cut and Paste commands are absent.

Cutting, copying, and pasting text

Selected text is primed for cutting or copying, which works just like it does in your favorite word processor: After you select the text, choose the Cut or Copy command shown above the selected text (refer to Figure 4-8).

To reproduce the cut or copied text, move the cursor to the location where you want the text to appear. Choose the Paste command that appears above the cursor tab, as shown in the margin:

  ✔ If the Paste command doesn't appear, the copied text cannot be pasted into the current app. That happens when text copied from one app may not be compatible with text in another app.

  ✔ Just like on your computer, cut or copied text on your phone is stored in a clipboard. You can continue to paste in text until new text is cut or copied.

Part II

The Phone Part of Smartphone

Learn how to dial the phone by using your voice — visit www.dummies.com/
extras/amazonfirephone.

In this part . . .

- Understand how to make phone calls
- Explore voice mail
- Deal with multiple calls
- Play with ringtones

Phone Calls

In This Chapter

▶ Calling someone

▶ Connecting with a contact

▶ Calling popular people and favorite friends

▶ Getting a call

▶ Dismissing calls

▶ Checking for missed calls

▶ Dialing into voice mail

*I*n the warm, inviting sea of amazing things the Fire phone does, the solid ground that is Phone Call Island is easy to overlook. In fact, you may have had a similar experience to my own: While playing with one of the phone's delightful features, I was interrupted by a phone call. I thought, "Oh, yeah: The thing's a phone, after all."

Peel back all the fancy graphics, the Internet, the camera, Firefly, and everything else that the Fire phone can do and you're left with a basic task: Placing and receiving phone calls.

You Make the Call

You would think that the phone part of the Fire phone would hold a high rank. It turns out that making a phone call simply involves using a Phone app. That seems kind of degrading, but then again, you can do more with the device than make phone calls.

The Phone app may feature an orange circle with a number affixed to it, like a "2 for 1" sticker on fruit at the grocery store. The number indicates either missed calls or pending voice mail messages. See the later sections "Dealing with a missed call" and "Retrieving your messages."

Dialing a number

Oh, pish: You don't dial a phone any more. Sure, go back into the hills and maybe you'll find a rotary phone. Today, numbers are punched. On the Fire phone, that process works like this:

1. **Open the Phone app.**

   If you've recently started the Phone app, swipe the Home screen's Carousel to locate its icon, and then tap that icon. Otherwise, press the Home button and then swipe the screen upward to view the App Grid. Tap the Phone icon to launch the app.

2. **If necessary, display the dialpad.**

   Touch the Dialpad icon at the bottom of the screen to view the dialpad, as illustrated in Figure 5-1.

Figure 5-1: The Phone app.

3. **Type the number to call.**

   Tap the keys on the dialpad to punch in the number. If you make a mistake, touch the Delete icon to back up and erase. To erase the entire number, long-press the Delete icon.

   As you dial, you hear the traditional touch-tone sound as you type the number.

4. **Tap the Call button to place the call.**

   As the phone attempts to make the connection, the screen changes to show the number you dialed, similar to Figure 5-2. When the recipient is in the phone's address book, the contact's name, photo, and other information may also appear.

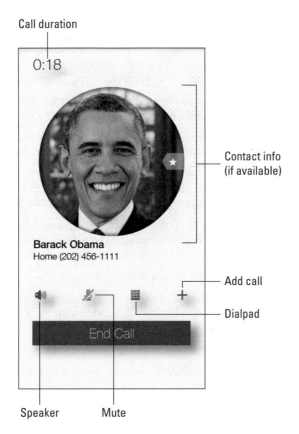

Figure 5-2: A successful call.

5. **When the person answers the phone, talk.**

Obviously, at this point you must stop looking at the point, place it against the side of your head, and initiate conversation.

Use the phone's Volume buttons (on the side of the device) to adjust the speaker volume during the call.

Don't worry about the phone's microphone being too far away from your mouth; it picks up your voice just fine.

6. **To end the call, touch the End Call icon.**

You hear a faint beep, confirming that the call has been disconnected.

If no one answers, you can try again. To redial the same number twice, simply tap the Call button. The previously typed number appears on the screen; tap the Call button to place the call:

🡒 If you're using earphones, press the phone's Power/Lock key during the call to turn off the display and lock the phone. I recommend turning off the display so that you don't accidentally mute or end the call.

🡒 You can connect or remove the earphones at any time during a call. The call is neither disconnected nor interrupted when you do so.

🡒 You can't accidentally mute or end a call when the phone is placed against your face; a sensor in the phone detects when it's close to something, and the touchscreen is automatically disabled.

🡒 To mute a call, touch the Mute icon, shown in Figure 5-2. Touch the icon again to unmute. Muting is a great way to put a call "on hold."

🡒 Touch the Speaker icon to be able to hold the phone at a distance to listen and talk, which allows you to let others listen and share in the conversation.

🡒 Don't hold the phone to your ear when the speaker is active.

🡒 If you're wading through one of those nasty voice mail systems, touch the Dialpad icon, labeled in Figure 5-2, so that you can "Press 1 for English" when necessary.

🡒 See Chapter 6 for information on using the Add Call icon.

🡒 When using a Bluetooth headset, connect the headset *before* you make the call. The Speaker icon (refer to Figure 5-2) is replaced by the Bluetooth icon whenever you use a Bluetooth headset to answer a call. Tap that icon to view a menu that lets you control how to hear the call.

🡒 If you need to dial an international number, press and hold down the 0 (zero) key until the plus sign (+) appears. Then input the rest of the international number. Refer to Chapter 20 for more information on making international calls.

✔ You hear an audio alert whenever the call is dropped or the other party hangs up. The disconnection can be confirmed by looking at the phone, which shows that the call has ended.

✔ You cannot place a phone call when the phone has no service; check the signal strength by viewing the status bar. (Refer to Chapter 3 for information.) Also see Chapter 18 for more information on signal strength.

✔ You cannot place a phone call while the phone is in Airplane mode. See Chapter 20 for information.

Dialing a contact

Your phone has an address book. One of the items that makes the address book useful is how it collects and stores people's phone numbers. To take advantage of the phone numbers stored in the Fire phone's address book, follow these steps:

1. **Start the Contacts app.**

   It's found on the App Grid, although if you've used it recently, check the Carousel on the Home screen.

2. **Scroll the list of contacts to find the person you want to call.**

   If the list is long, tap the Search icon and type a few letters of the contact's name.

3. **Touch the contact to display their information.**

4. **Tap the phone number you want to call.**

   That number is dialed.

At this point, dialing proceeds as described in the preceding section:

✔ To get to the address book from the Phone app, tap the Contacts icon, shown in Figure 5-1.

✔ See Chapter 7 for more details on how to use the Contacts app.

Calling a VIP

Not everyone is a Hollywood celebrity. Not even Hollywood celebrities have anything to do with the motion picture industry. In your own life, you have favorites, or Very Important People (VIPs) whom you call frequently.

To quickly view your own VIP list, display the right panel in the Phone app, the Delighters and Shortcuts. You'll see your address book's VIPs, similar to the ones shown in Figure 5-3.

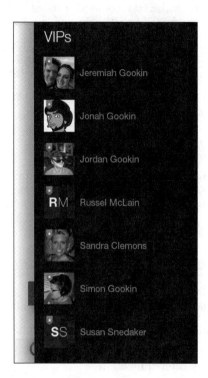

VIPs

Jeremiah Gookin

Jonah Gookin

Jordan Gookin

RM Russel McLain

Sandra Clemons

Simon Gookin

SS Susan Snedaker

Figure 5-3: VIPs on the Delighters and Shortcuts panel.

Tap a VIP entry to view information, and then choose a phone number, as described in the preceding section:

- ✔ See Chapter 7 for information on how to make one of your contacts a VIP.
- ✔ Refer to Chapter 3 for information on using the tilt gesture to quickly display the Delighters and Shortcuts panel in the Phone app.

Multitasking while on a call

You can do other things while you're making a call: Press the Home button to change your schedule, jot down a note, or do whatever. Activities such as these don't disconnect you, although your cellular provider may not allow you to do other things with the phone while you're on a call.

While the phone is on a call, you see the Tap to Return to Call notice atop the screen. Touch that notice to return to the call after doing something else. You return to the connected screen, similar to the one shown in Figure 5-2. Continue yapping.

See Chapter 3 for information on reviewing notifications.

It's For You!

Things have changed from the old days. Not only can you carry your phone with you and receive calls anywhere, but the phone also does a superior job of telling you who's calling. You see the number. You see contact information, if it's available. And you see options beyond merely answering or hanging up.

Receiving a call

An incoming call on your Fire phone is heralded by a ringtone. The phone might also vibrate. On the touchscreen, you see information about who's calling, similar to what's shown in Figure 5-4.

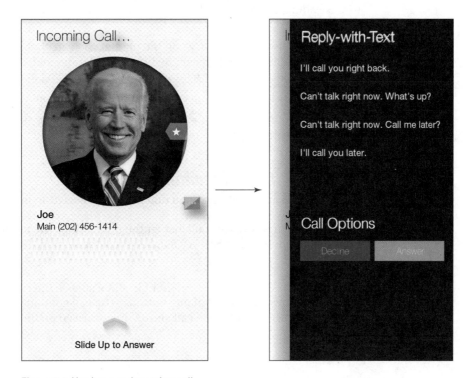

Incoming Call...

Joe
Main (202) 456-1414

Slide Up to Answer

Reply-with-Text

I'll call you right back.

Can't talk right now. What's up?

Can't talk right now. Call me later?

I'll call you later.

Call Options

Decline   Answer

Figure 5-4: You have an incoming call.

To answer the call, swipe the screen from bottom to top. If the Answer button is visible, tap it to answer the call.

After answering, place the phone to your ear and start yapping.

Touch the End Call button to hang up when you're done yapping. If the other party hangs up first, the call ends automatically:

- Tilt the phone, or swipe in from right to left to view the Reply with Text shortcuts, or to access the Decline and Answer buttons.

- In Figure 5-4, the phone is locked for an incoming call. If you're using the phone when a call comes in, the Decline and Answer buttons appear below the incoming-caller info.

- When wearing earphones, answer the call by pressing the button on the noodle. See Chapter 1 for more information on the earphones.

- If you're using a Bluetooth headset, you touch the control on the headset to answer the phone. See Chapter 18 for more information on Bluetooth.

- The sound you hear when the phone rings is known as the *ringtone*. You can configure your phone to play a number of ringtones, depending on who is calling, or you can set a universal ringtone. Ringtones are covered in Chapter 6.

- If you receive a call while you're on the phone, you can choose to answer the call separately, place the original caller on hold, or create a conference call. See Chapter 6 for information on juggling multiple calls.

- See Chapter 21 for information on setting the incoming call volume.

- See the "Rejecting a call with a text message" section, later in this chapter, for information on the Reply with Text feature.

Dispensing with an incoming call

Several options are available when you don't want to receive an incoming call.

The first option is to ignore the call; just let the phone ring. The missed call shows up on the phone's Call History list. See the later section "Dealing with a missed call."

The second option is to ignore the call but blissfully silence the ringing. To do so, press the Power/Lock or Volume buttons. The call continues to ring through, but you can't hear it. The call shows up as missed on the phone's Call History list.

The third option is to dismiss the call: Tap the Decline button. If you don't see that button, slide the screen from right to left, as illustrated in Figure 5-4. The phone stops ringing. Calls you choose to ignore don't show up as missed calls on the call history.

A final option is to ignore the call and reply with a text message. See the next section.

Declined, ignored, and missed calls are all redirected to voice mail. See the later section "Leave Me a Message" for details.

Rejecting a call with a text message

Rather than just dismiss a call, you can opt to dismiss *and* reply with a text message. That's a quick way to let someone know you're not just banishing them to voice mail. It means that you care!

To dismiss a call with a text message, tap the wee icon found on the Incoming Call screen, illustrated in Figure 5-4. The Delighters and Shortcuts panel appears, from which you can choose a preset text reply; tap one and you're done.

To edit text message replies or to create your own, heed these steps:

1. **Open the Settings app.**

2. **Choose Phone.**

3. **Choose Edit Reply-with-Text Messages.**

4. **Tap a message to edit its content.**

5. **Touch the OK button to confirm your changes.**

Only four quick responses are available to edit. As this book goes to press, you cannot create additional replies:

  ✔ Not every phone is a cell phone and can receive the text message reply. Sending a text message to your grandma's landline phone just won't work.

  ✔ See Chapter 8 for more information on text messages.

Dealing with a missed call

Missed calls are flagged by a tiny circle affixed to the Phone app's icon. Inside the circle is a number that shows the total number of missed calls, although the number can also indicate voice mail messages. In Figure 5-1, you see the circle on the History icon on the Phone app's main screen.

To discover who called and when, start the Phone app and tap the History icon. You see a list of recent calls. Use the Peek gesture to see which calls were incoming, outgoing, or missed.

Touch a Missed call entry to immediately return the call:

- You can return any call by choosing its entry in the call log or history list.
- To remove a call from the list, long-press it. Choose Delete Call.

Leave Me a Message

When you miss or dismiss a call, it's immediately banished to that unearthly realm known as voice mail. It's a service run by your cellular provider that provides a way for people yearning for your human contact to temporarily sate their frustrations. Or, to be specific, for them to leave you a message.

Setting up carrier voice mail

Even if you believe your voice mail to be set up and configured, consider churning through these steps, just to be sure:

1. **Open the Phone app.**

2. **Tap the Voicemail icon.**

   It's found in the lower-right corner of the screen; refer to Figure 5-1.

   If voice mail has been set up, either the phone dials into the voice mail system or a voice mail app runs. Otherwise:

3. **Tap the Call Voicemail button.**

4. **During the call, tap the Speaker button and keep the dialpad on the screen so that you can work through the prompts.**

5. **Work through the prompts.**

   Obey whatever directions are necessary to complete voice mail setup for your phone's voice mail service.

Set your name, a voice mail password, a greeting, and various other steps as guided by your cellular provider's cheerful robot.

Some cellular services provide a voice mail app, such as Visual Voicemail from AT&T. Voice mail setup is concluded by configuring this app, which handles your voice mail on the phone.

Retrieving your messages

When you have a voice mail message looming, the New Voicemail notification icon appears on the lock screen, similar to the one shown in Figure 5-5. And when the message comes in, a tiny notice briefly appears on the screen (which is not shown in Figure 5-5).

Pending voice mail

Scheduled appointment

Figure 5-5: A new voice mail notification on the lock screen.

When using the phone, you may also see an orange circle appears with the number of voice mail messages on the Voicemail icon of the Phone app's main screen.

To listen to your messages, tap the Voicemail icon on the Phone app's main screen (refer to Figure 5-1). The phone dials into your carrier's voice mail system, or you may see an app, such as the Visual Voicemail app, shown in Figure 5-6.

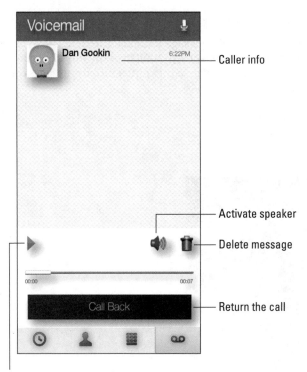

Play message

Figure 5-6: Visual Voicemail on AT&T.

To deal with your carrier's voice mail system, respond to the prompts by using the Phone app's dialpad. Type your PIN and then proceed to listen to and manage messages.

For Visual Voicemail, choose a message from the list, which is similar to how email operates on the phone. Tap the Play icon to listen to the message, or work the other controls as illustrated in Figure 5-6. The Call Back button appears on the screen, which you can use to return the call.

6

Phone Options Galore

In This Chapter

▶ Handing multiple incoming calls

▶ Switching between calls

▶ Setting up a conference call

▶ Configuring call forwarding options

▶ Changing the phone's ringtone

▶ Setting a contact's ringtone

*B*ack in the 1980s, the phone companies started offering new and won-derful features. Before cellular phones were popular, cordless phones were all the rage. Then came nifty features, such as Caller ID, call waiting, and call forwarding. It was the dawn of a new age.

Your Fire phone is certainly able to keep up with the times, especially when the times were happening 30 years ago. The Phone app is capable of more than just placing or receiving calls. This chapter covers some of those additional, bonus phone feats.

Multiple Call Mania

Expensive government studies have shown that human beings can hold only one conversation at a time. These studies have failed to mention that the Fire phone allows you to handle more than one call at a time. It's a psychological condition that scientists have labeled *multiple call mania*.

Receiving a new call when you're on the phone

You're on the phone, chatting it up. Suddenly, someone else calls you. What happens next?

Your phone alerts you to the new call, perhaps by vibrating or making a sound. Look at the touchscreen to see what's up with the incoming call, similar to what's shown in Figure 6-1.

Incoming call info

Options   Reply with text message

Figure 6-1: Suddenly, there's an incoming call!

You have several options:

- ✔ **Answer and hold.** Tap the Answer Hold Current Call button to answer the incoming call. The call you're on is placed on hold.

- ✔ **Answer and end.** Tap the Answer End Current Call button to disconnect the current call and take the new call.

- ✔ **Dismiss the incoming call.** Tap the Decline button and the incoming call is rejected, sent to voice mail.

- ✔ **Do nothing.** The call eventually goes into voice mail.

When you choose to answer the call and the call you're on is placed on hold, you return to the first call when you end the second call. Or you can manage the multiple calls, as described in the next section.

Juggling two calls

After you answer a second call, as described in the preceding section, your phone is working with two calls at a time. In this situation, you can speak with only one person at a time; juggling two calls isn't the same thing as participating in a conference call.

Figure 6-2 illustrates the multi-call screen on the Fire phone. The current call appears in the center of the screen; the call on hold is on top. To swap the calls, tap the caller ID atop the screen, as shown in the figure.

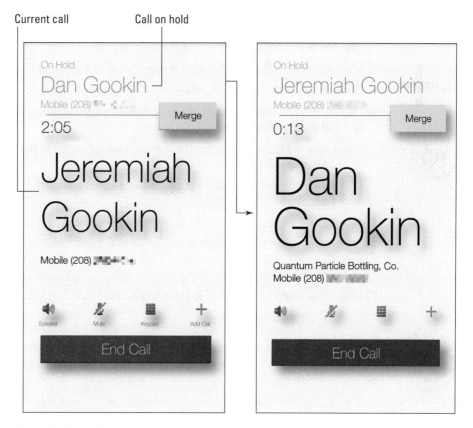

Figure 6-2: The multi-call screen.

Each time you swap, you're talking with the other person. To talk with them both at the same time, tap the Merge button.

After one call ends, the conversation returns to the other caller. You can then proceed to talk — discuss the weather, the local sports team, whatever — until you hang up or yet another call interrupts you.

The number of different calls your phone can handle depends on your carrier. For most subscribers in the United States, your phone can handle only two calls at a time. In that case, a third person who calls you either hears a busy signal or is sent directly into voice mail.

Making a conference call

Unlike someone interrupting a conversation by making an incoming call, a *conference call* is one you set out to make intentionally: You make one call and then *add* a second call. Touch an icon on the phone's touchscreen and then everyone is talking. Here's how it works:

1. **Phone the first person.**

   The call connects and you exchange pleasantries.

2. **After the first call is established, touch the Add Call icon.**

   The first person is put on hold and the Contacts list is displayed.

3. **Choose the second person from the phone's address book, or tap the Keypad icon to dial the second number.**

   When viewing the address book, tilt the phone or swipe in from the right to display the VIPs panel.

   After the call connects, say your pleasantries and inform the party that the call is about to be merged.

4. **Touch the Merge button.**

   The two calls are now joined: The touchscreen says "Conference Call" and the other caller's IDs are listed. Everyone you've dialed can talk to and hear everyone else.

5. **Touch the End Call icon to end the conference call.**

   All calls are disconnected.

When several people are in a room and want to participate in a call, you can always put the phone in Speaker mode: Touch the Speaker icon on the Ongoing Call screen.

Forward Calls Elsewhere

When you don't want to answer an incoming call, you can dismiss it or ignore it. You can also choose not to get the call in the first place by using a feature known as call forwarding.

For example, you can send all your calls to the office while you're on vacation. Then you have the luxury of having your cell phone and still making calls but freely ignoring anyone who calls you.

To set call forwarding options on the Fire phone, obey these steps:

1. **Open the Settings app.**

2. **Choose Phone.**

3. **Choose Forward Incoming Calls.**

   A screen detailing several handy phone features appears.

4. **Choose Call Forwarding.**

5. **Slide the master control to the On position.**

   Call forwarding is now active, but you need to set the forwarding number.

6. **Type the call forwarding number.**

   If you've already activated call forwarding, a forwarding number may be preset. Otherwise, tap the Call Forwarding Number option and use the onscreen keypad to type a phone number.

   Include the area code in the phone number.

7. **Touch the OK button to set call forwarding.**

   All incoming calls are redirected to the number you specified in Step 6.

You can still use the phone with call forwarding active. Calls can be placed, but none will be received.

The phone gives no indication that call forwarding is active, so you have to remember to disable it when you're done. To disable call forwarding, repeat Steps 1 through 4, but in Step 5 slide the master control to the Off position.

Fun with Ringtones

Ringtones can be lots of fun. They uniquely identify your phone's jingle, especially when you forget to mute your phone and you're hustling to turn the thing off because everyone in the room is annoyed by your *Baby Baby Baby* ringtone.

Selecting the phone's ringtone

To choose a new ringtone for your phone, or to simply confirm which ringtone you're using, follow these steps:

1. **Open the Settings app.**

2. **Choose Sounds & Notifications.**

3. **Choose Change Your Ringtone.**

   The Sound entry controls the phone's ringtone. The current ringtone should be shown, such as Olympic.

4. **Tap a ringtone from the list that's displayed.**

   Scroll the list. Tap a ringtone to hear its preview.

5. **Tap the Done button to accept the new ringtone.**

   The ringtone is assigned.

The ringtone plays whenever a call comes in.

When you choose None as the ringtone, no sound signals an incoming call. The touchscreen activates to display information about the call, but the phone otherwise doesn't alert you. That is, unless you have vibration turned on. See Chapter 21.

Also see Chapter 8 for setting text messaging ringtones.

Setting a contact's ringtone

It's possible to set individual ringtones for your contacts. That way, you can easily distinguish between regular phone calls and calls from your best friend forever. To make such a change, heed these directions:

1. **Open the Settings app.**

2. **Choose Sounds & Notifications.**

3. **Choose Select Ringtones for Specific People.**

   The phone's address book is displayed, listing all your contacts.

4. **From the list, choose the contact to which you want to assign a ringtone.**

5. **Select a ringtone from the list.**

   It's the same list that's displayed for the phone's ringtones.

6. **Touch the Done button to assign the ringtone to the contact.**

Whenever the contact calls, the phone rings using the ringtone you've specified.

To remove a specific ringtone for a contact, repeat the steps in this section but in Step 5 choose Default Ringtone. (It's found at the top of the list of ringtones.) This choice sets the contact's ringtone to be the same as the phone's ringtone.

You can also set a ringtone when you edit an individual contact. See Chapter 7 for information on editing contacts.

The People You Know

*Y*ou might still be able to find one, somewhere in the recesses of an office-supply or stationery store. Even so, the traditional address book doesn't sell as well as it once did. Phone books, too, have become kind of passé. At my house, someone drops off a hefty phone book or some yellow pages and it goes immediately into the recycle bin. Gone are the days when a clutch of phone numbers was written on the inside of a kitchen cabinet.

Replacing the traditional methods of storing names and numbers is the smartphone. Your Amazon Fire phone comes with a Contacts app. It serves as the phone's address book, storing names, numbers, addresses email and physical, plus other interesting information about the people you know.

The Contacts App

The address book is used by many other apps on the phone. These include Email, Messaging, social networking apps, as well as the obvious Phone app. That makes the address book a vital part of using your Fire phone:

✔ The Fire phone doesn't ship with any preset contacts. To add contacts, add accounts to your phone, as described in Chapter 2. Also see the section "Make New Friends," later in this chapter.

✔ See Chapter 11 for more information on social networking.

Accessing the phone's address book

To peruse your phone's address book, you use the Contacts app. Tap the Contacts icon on the App Grid or, if you've accessed that app recently, look for it on the Carousel.

Figure 7-1 shows the Contacts app, along with the Navigation panel and the Delighters and Shortcuts panel.

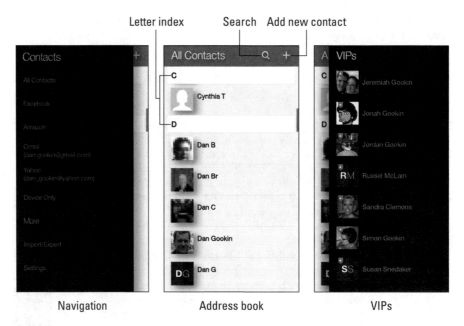

Letter index　　　Search　Add new contact

Navigation　　　　　Address book　　　　　VIPs

Figure 7-1: The phone's address book.

Scroll the list by swiping your finger on the touchscreen.

Tap the letter index (refer to Figure 7-1) to see an A-to-Z index. Then you can tap a letter to visit contacts whose names start with that letter. (Also see the next section, on sorting the address book.)

Use the Search icon to quickly locate any contact by typing all or part of their name. Tap the *Cancel* text to clear the search:

✔ To view all contacts available to your phone, choose All Contacts from the Navigation panel, as shown in Figure 7-1. To view contacts associated with a specific account, choose that account.

✔ The Contacts app pulls in contact information from online accounts associated with your phone. You can also add accounts individually, which is described in the later section "Creating a new contact from scratch."

✔ Some contacts may be duplicated. To remove this redundancy, see the later section "Joining identical contacts."

✔ No correlation can be made between the number of contacts you have and how popular you are in real life.

Sorting the address book

The Contacts app displays your people in a certain order, such as alphabetically by first name. You can change the order to whatever you like by following these steps:

1. **Open the Contacts app.**

2. **Display the Navigation panel.**

   Swipe in from the left edge of the screen, or use the Tilt gesture to see the panel.

3. **Choose Settings.**

4. **Choose Contact Settings.**

5. **Choose Sort Order of Contact Name to specify how the contacts are sorted in the address book: First Last or Last First.**

   The First Last option means that the contacts are sorted by first name, so *Dan Gookin* would appear under D. The Last First option would put *Dan Gookin* under G.

6. **Choose Display Order of Contact Name to specify whether contacts appear First Last or Last First.**

   The First Last option lists names with the first name first and then last name. The Last First option lists last names first.

The address book is updated, displayed per your preferences.

Viewing a contact

After you locate a contact in the address book, tap that entry to view details. You see additional information, similar to what's shown in Figure 7-2.

Return to address book

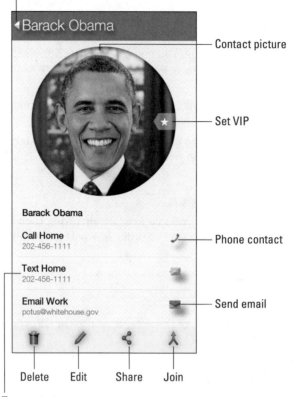

Contact picture

Set VIP

Phone contact

Send email

Delete   Edit   Share   Join

Text contact

Figure 7-2: More details about a contact.

The list of activities you can do with the contact depends on the information shown and the apps installed on the phone. Here are some options:

Place a phone call. To call the contact, touch one of the contact's phone entries, such as Home or Mobile.

Send a text message. Touch the Text item (refer to Figure 7-2) to open the Messaging app and send the contact a message. See Chapter 8 for information about text messaging.

Locate the contact on a map. When the contact has a home or business address, you can touch the contact's View Address item to summon the Maps app. Refer to Chapter 13 to see all the fun stuff you can do with Maps.

Some tidbits of information that show up for a contact have no associated action. For example, the phone won't sing *Happy Birthday* whenever you touch a contact's birthday information.

Touch the triangle at the top of the screen, or swipe from bottom to top (the Back action) to return to the Contacts app's main screen:

- Not every contact has a picture, and the picture can come from a number of sources (Gmail or Facebook, for example). See the section "Adding a contact's picture" for more information.

- A contact without a picture shows initials, such as JC for Julius Caesar. A Facebook contact without a picture shows the generic Facebook human icon.

- Some contacts are *joined*. That means the information you see comes from multiple sources, such as Gmail or Facebook. See the later section "Joining identical contacts" for information on joining contacts, as well as the section "Splitting contacts" for information on splitting improperly joined contacts.

Make New Friends

Having friends is great. Having more friends is better. You'll find myriad ways to add new friends and place new contacts into your phone. This section lists a few of the more popular and useful methods.

Adding contacts from your accounts

The best way to sweep a boatload of fresh contacts into the Fire phone is to add one of your online accounts. This process is outlined in Chapter 2: By adding your Gmail or Yahoo! or another online account to the phone, you instantly incorporate that account's contacts into your phone.

The navigation panel in the Contacts app lists your current accounts. In Figure 7-1, you see that my Facebook, Amazon, Gmail, and Yahoo! accounts have been associated with the phone. All my contacts from those accounts become part of the phone's address book. That's the easiest way to bring in your contacts:

- The contacts associated with an online account are created by using that account, or whatever device is connected to that account.

- A contact entry displays the associated account: Swipe to the bottom of the contact's Information screen to see which account is associated with that contact.

Creating a new contact from scratch

Sometimes it's necessary to create a contact when you meet another human being in the real world. In that case, you have more information to input, and it starts like this:

1. **Open the Contacts app.**

2. **Touch the Add icon to start building the new contact.**

   A new Contact screen appears with lots of fill-in-the-blanks items.

3. **Fill in the contact's information.**

   Tap a text field to summon the onscreen keyboard and begin filling in the contact's information. The more information you provide, the more useful the contact entry.

   After filling in some items, you may see the Add New prompt. Use it to add multiple phone numbers, email addresses, and so on.

   Use the Menu button to specify whether a phone number or email address is Home, Mobile, Work, or whatever — providing that you know the information.

   At the bottom of the screen, you find the Add More Fields button. Tap that button to add more details for the contact, such as a website.

4. **Touch the Done icon to save the new contact.**

The new contact is created. If the contact was created under an online account, it's immediately synchronized with that account. See the nearby sidebar "What's the 'default account'?" for information on which accounts are used to save new contacts.

What's the "default account"?

New contacts are saved in the default account, but what's the default account? And isn't the word *default* bad? I mean, no one wants to default on a loan, right?

Default is an ancient technological term that means "the option chosen automatically." I suppose that *default* is easier to type. Anyway, for the Contacts app, the *default account* is the one in which new accounts are created or stored. It can be any of the accounts associated with the

phone, or it can be just the phone itself when Device Only is chosen as the default account.

To determine which account is the default, choose the Settings command from the Navigation panel. Choose Contact Settings and then tap the item Create New Contacts In. You see a list of accounts, one of which is selected as the default. To set a new default account, choose one from the list that's presented.

Importing contacts from your computer

Your computer's email program is doubtless a useful repository of contacts you've built up over the years. You can export these contacts from your computer's email program and then import them into your Fire phone. The process isn't the simplest thing to do, but it's a quick way to build up your phone's address book.

The key is to save or export your computer email program's records in the *vCard* (.vcf) file format. These records can then be imported into the phone and read by the Contacts app. The method for exporting contacts varies depending on the email program:

- **In the Windows Live Mail program,** choose Go⇨Contacts, and then choose File⇨Export⇨Business Card (.VCF) to export the contacts.

- **In Windows Mail,** choose File⇨Export⇨Windows Contacts, and then choose vCards (Folder of .VCF Files) from the Export Windows Contacts dialog box. Click the Export button.

- **On the Mac,** open the Address Book program, and choose File⇨Export⇨ Export vCard.

After the vCard files are created, connect the phone to your computer and transfer the vCard files from your computer to the phone. Directions for making this type of transfer are found in Chapter 19.

After the vCard files have been copied to the phone, you import them into the Contacts app. Follow these steps:

1. **In the Contacts app, display the Navigation panel.**

   Swipe the screen from left to right, or use the Tilt gesture, to see the panel.

2. **Choose Import/Export.**

3. **Choose the Import from Phone Storage command.**

   The vCard(s) you copied to the phone are digested and inserted into the address book.

If the default account for the Contacts app is an online account, such as Gmail or Yahoo!, the imported contacts are synchronized with that account as well. See the earlier sidebar "What's the 'default account'?" for details on this default account nonsense.

Address Book Management

If you believe that your phone's address book is all finished, then you haven't met any new friends lately. Or perhaps none of the people you know will ever move or change their phone numbers or email addresses. Such a thing could happen, but probably won't. Therefore, a modicum of address book management is necessary.

Changing contact info

To make minor touch-ups on any contact, start by locating and displaying that person's information in the Contacts app. Touch the Edit icon and start making changes.

Change or add information by touching a field and typing on the onscreen keyboard. You can edit information as well: Touch a field to change whatever you want.

Some information cannot be edited. For example, fields pulled in from social networking sites can be edited only by that account holder on the social networking site.

When you're done editing, touch the Done button.

Adding a contact's picture

To add a picture to a contact, you can snap a picture and save it, grab a picture from the Internet, or use any image already stored in the phone's photo album. The image doesn't even have to be a picture of the contact — any image will do.

After the contact's photo or any other suitable image is stored on the phone, follow these steps to update the contact's information:

1. **Locate and display the contact's information.**

2. **Edit the contact's information.**

   Touch the Edit icon.

3. **Touch the Edit Image command.**

   The command is found next to the contact's image, or initials if the contact doesn't have an image.

4. **Choose the Add Photo command.**

   If the Take Photo command is available, you can use the Fire phone's camera to quickly snap a picture. See Chapter 14 for more information on using the camera.

5. **If you see the Complete Action Using prompt, choose the Photos app. Tap the Just Once option.**

   Refer to Chapter 24 for information on the Always/Just Once type of choice.

6. **Choose a suitable image.**

   Browse the album to find an image.

7. **Tap the Choose icon to select that image.**

   The Choose icon is shown in the margin.

8. **Touch the Save icon to set the image for the contact.**

   The image is assigned, and it appears whenever the contact is referenced on your phone.

The contact's image appears when the person calls, in the text messaging app, as well as other instances when the contact is referenced in your phone:

✓ Pictures can also be added by accessing your various online accounts and editing the contacts there. Gmail and Facebook accounts may change their images if the contact decides to add or change their own image for those services.

✓ Some images in the Gallery may not work for contact icons. For example, images synchronized with your online photo albums may be unavailable.

✓ To remove or change a contact's picture, follow Steps 1–3 in this section, but choose the Remove Photo command to get rid of the existing image.

Making a VIP

VIP is an acronym for Very Important Person. It's really overused. I find it degrading, because I'd like to believe that everyone is important, but not everyone can be a VIP.

On your phone, a *VIP contact* is someone you stay in touch with most often. The person doesn't have to be someone you like — just someone you (perhaps unfortunately) phone often, such as your parole officer.

To create a favorite, display a contact's information and touch the Star icon. You don't even need to edit the contact; when the star is highlighted, the contact is flagged as one of your VIPs.

VIP contacts appear on the Delighters and Shortcuts panel when you're viewing the Contacts app, but also in the Phone app. To quickly access a VIP, choose the person from the tab:

✓ To remove a contact from the VIP list, touch the contact's star again. Removing a VIP status doesn't delete the contact.

✓ A contact has no idea whether he's a VIP, so don't believe that you're hurting his feelings by not making him a favorite.

Joining identical contacts

The Fire phone can pull in contacts from multiple online accounts, including Facebook, Gmail, Twitter, and others. Because of these many sources, you may discover duplicate contact entries in the phone's address book. Rather than fuss over which contact to use, you can join them. Here's how:

1. **Wildly scroll the address book until you locate a duplicate.**

   Well, maybe not *wildly* scroll, but locate a duplicated entry. Because the address book is sorted, the duplicates appear close together (though that may not always be the case).

2. **Select one of the duplicate contacts.**

   When you see two identical address book entries, one after the other, you have duplicates. Even if you don't see them, choose a contact because the phone will find similar or related entries.

3. **Tap the Join icon.**

   After choosing the command, you see a list of suggested contacts, which the phone guesses could be identical. You might also see the entire list of contacts in case the phone is stumped. Your job is to find the duplicate contact.

4. **Choose the duplicate contact from the list.**

   The contacts are merged, appearing as a single entry in the Edit screen.

5. **Save the merged contact; tap the Save icon.**

   The contacts are joined.

Joined contacts aren't flagged as such in the address book, but you can easily identify them: When you're looking at the contact's information, a joined contact looks like a single long entry, often showing two sources or accounts from which the contact's information is pulled.

Splitting contacts

The topic of separating contacts has little to do with parenting, although separating bickering children is the first step to avoiding a fight. Contacts in the address book might not be bickering, but occasionally the phone may automatically join two contacts that aren't really the same person. When that happens, you can split them by following these steps:

1. **Display the improperly joined contact.**

   As an example, I'm Facebook friends with other humans named Dan Gookin. My phone accidentally joined my address book entry with another Dan Gookin.

2. **Touch the Menu icon.**

   The Menu icon is found on the individual contact's screen. You do not need to edit the contact to locate this command. And if you don't see the icon (in the lower-right corner), the contact isn't joined.

3. **Choose the Split command.**

4. **Touch the OK button to confirm that you're splitting the contact.**

You don't need to actively look for improperly joined contacts — you'll just stumble across them. When you do, feel free to separate them, especially if you detect any bickering.

Removing a contact

Every so often, consider reviewing your phone's contacts. Purge the folks whom you no longer recognize or you've forgotten. It's simple: View the forlorn contact and touch the Trash icon, similar to the one shown in the margin. Touch the OK button to confirm. Poof! They're gone:

✔ If the contact might be synchronized with an online account, the contact is also removed there.

✔ You may not be able to delete contacts associated with specific accounts, such as your social networking friends. To remove those contacts, you need to go to the source, such as Facebook or Twitter.

✔ Removing a contact doesn't kill the person in real life.

Part III
Stay Connected

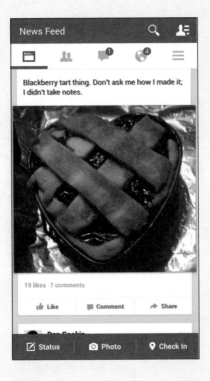

Learn how to save web pages for offline viewing at www.dummies.com/extras/amazonfirephone.

In this part . . .

- ✔ Use the address book
- ✔ Try text messaging
- ✔ Send Gmail and email
- ✔ Discover the web on a cell phone
- ✔ Connect with social networking
- ✔ Dig into text, voice, and video chat

8

Msg 4 U

In This Chapter

▶ Creating a text message
▶ Getting a text message
▶ Forwarding a text message
▶ Texting pictures
▶ Managing your text messages
▶ Changing the text message tone

*Q*uicker than a phone call, with more brevity than an email, the text message has become the preferred form of communications for a majority of people. My kids send thousands of text messages a month but make only a dozen, brief phone calls. You may find yourself attracted to the trend as well: Text messages are short, quick, and discrete. They may also be the only way you can communicate with certain family members. And as a bonus, spelling and grammar are completely optional.

The Joy of Texting

Everyone calls it *texting,* but the official name is *SMS,* which stands for Short Message Service. By using the Messaging app on your Fire phone, you can send and receive text messages to any other smartphone, just like all those cool kids who hang out in coffee shops, not talking with one another but texting like they were paid to do it:

▷ Don't text while you're driving.

▷ Don't text in a movie theater.

▷ Don't text in any situation where it's distracting.

✔ Once upon a time, cellular providers levied a per-message fee on text messages. You were charged both for messages sent and received above a certain monthly quota. Today, unlimited text messaging is offered with just about every cell plan, but check your monthly statement to ensure that's the case.

Composing a text message

On the Fire phone, the Messaging app is responsible for handling text messaging chores. Here's how it works:

1. **Open the Messaging app.**

   Unless you've messed with the App Grid, the Messaging app is found on the top row, which is conveniently accessible from the Home screen.

   If the app icon features a number in an orange circle, that number indicates unread text messages. See the later section "Receiving a text message."

2. **If you don't see the main Messaging screen, swipe the screen from bottom to top to back up.**

   The main messaging screen is shown in Figure 8-1.

3. **Tap the Compose button to start a new conversation.**

   Or you can choose a person you want to text from the list of ongoing conversations (refer to Figure 8-1).

4. **If you're starting a new conversation, type a contact name or cell phone number into the To field.**

   When the number you type matches one or more existing contacts, those contacts are displayed. Tap a contact to send a message to that person; otherwise, continue typing the phone number.

   You can add multiple recipients, if you like. Just keep adding contacts or phone numbers. The message is sent to everyone.

   Use the Add Contacts button, shown in Figure 8-2, to peruse the phone's address book, where you can choose and add contacts.

5. **Type your text message.**

   Apparently, you commit a grave sin if you try to capitalize or punctuate.

   You can tap the Microphone button on the keyboard to dictate your message.

6. **Tap the Send button to send the message.**

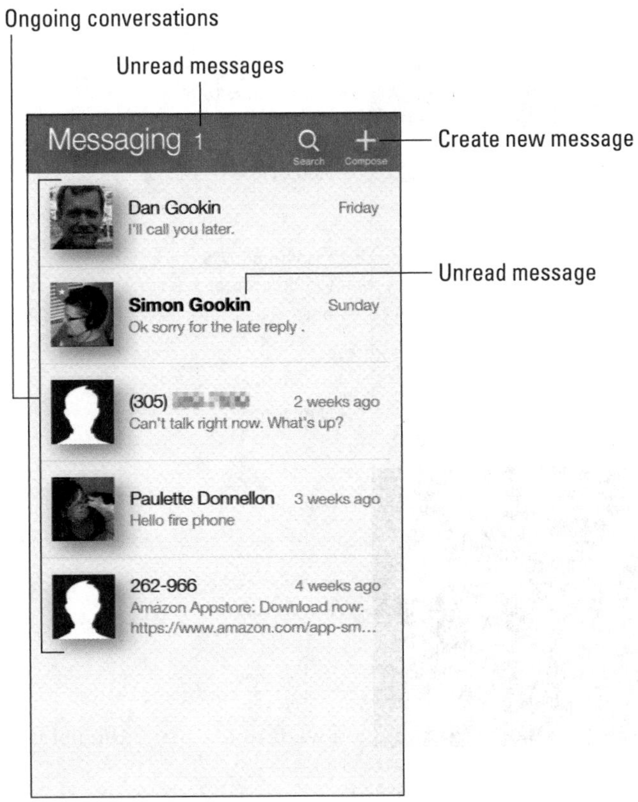

Ongoing conversations

Unread messages

Messaging 1   Q   +   — Create new message
                Search Compose

Dan Gookin   Friday
I'll call you later.

                                        — Unread message

Simon Gookin   Sunday
Ok sorry for the late reply .

(305)   2 weeks ago
Can't talk right now. What's up?

Paulette Donnellon   3 weeks ago
Hello fire phone

262-966   4 weeks ago
Amazon Appstore: Download now:
https://www.amazon.com/app-sm...

Figure 8-1: Conversations in the Messaging app.

Another way to send a text message is to view a contact's information in the
Contacts app. Choose the Text Mobile (or other Text entry) when viewing the
contact's information. After you touch that item, the Messaging app opens
and you can compose the message:

✔ You can send text messages only to cell phones. Aunt Mabel cannot
   receive text messages on her landline that she's had since the 1960s.

✔ When you receive a group message (one that has several recipients),
   your reply is sent to everyone.

✔ Continue a conversation at any time: Open the Messaging app, peruse
   the list of existing conversations, and touch one to review what has been
   said or to pick up the conversation.

✔ Do not text and drive. Do not text and drive. Do not text and drive.

To field

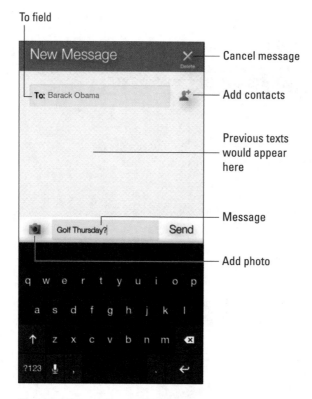

Cancel message

Add contacts

Previous texts would appear here

Message

Add photo

Figure 8-2: Composing a new text message.

Receiving a text message

Whenever a new text message comes in, the message appears briefly at the top of the Fire phone's touchscreen. The Messaging icon appears on the touchscreen, shown in Figure 8-3, which tells you that a new text (or more) is waiting.

To view the message, pull down the Notification panel. Touch the messaging notification, and that Conversation window immediately opens.

You can also peruse text messages by opening the Messaging app and tapping the highlighted conversation shown earlier, in Figure 8-1.

Text messages waiting

Figure 8-3: Oh, boy! Texts!

Whether to send a text message or an email

Sending a text message is similar to sending an email message. Both involve the instant electronic delivery of a message to someone else. And both methods of communication have their advantages and disadvantages.

The primary limitation of a text message is that it can be sent only to another cell phone.

Email is available to anyone who has an email address, whether or not the person uses a cell phone.

Text messages are pithy; short and to the point. They're informal, more like quick chats. Indeed,

the speed of reply is often what makes text messaging useful. Like sending email, however, sending a text message doesn't guarantee a reply.

An email message can be longer than a text message. You can receive email on just about any Internet-connected device. Email message attachments (pictures, documents) are handled better and more consistently than text message (MMS) media.

Finally, email is considered a wee bit more formal than a text message. But if you're after formal, make a phone call or send a letter.

Common text message abbreviations

Texting isn't about proper English. Indeed, many of the abbreviations and shortcuts used in texting, such as LOL and BRB, are slowly becoming part of the English language.

The weird news is that these acronyms weren't invented by teenagers. Sure, the kids use them, but the acronyms have their roots in the Internet chat rooms of yesteryear. Regardless of a shortcut's source, you might find a shortcut handy for typing messages quickly. Or maybe you can use this reference for deciphering an acronym's meaning. You can type acronyms in either uppercase or lowercase letters.

2	To, also
411	Information
BRB	Be right back
BTW	By the way
CYA	See you
FWIW	For what it's worth
FYI	For your information
GB	Goodbye
GJ	Good job
GR8	Great
GTG	Got to go
HOAS	Hold on a second
IC	I see
IDK	I don't know
IMO	In my opinion
JK	Just kidding
K	Okay
L8R	Later

LMAO	Laughing my [rear] off
LMK	Let me know
LOL	Laugh out loud
NC	No comment
NP	No problem
NRN	No reply needed (necessary)
OMG	Oh my goodness!
PIR	People in room (watching)
POS	Person over shoulder (watching)
QT	Cutie
ROFL	Rolling on the floor, laughing
SOS	Someone over shoulder (watching)
TC	Take care
THX	Thanks
TIA	Thanks in advance
TMI	Too much information
TTFN	Ta-ta for now (goodbye)
TTYL	Talk to you later
TY	Thank you
U2	You too
UR	You're, you are
VM	Voice mail
W8	Wait
XOXO	Hugs and kisses
Y	Why?
YW	You're welcome
ZZZ	Sleeping

Forwarding a text message

It's possible to forward a text message, but it's not the same as forwarding email. Instead of forwarding the entire conversation, you can forward only a single text snippet — a cartoon bubble. Here's how it works:

1. **Open a conversation in the phone's texting app.**

2. **Long-press the text entry (the cartoon bubble) you want to forward.**

3. **From the menu that appears, choose the Forward command.**

   From this point on, forwarding the message works like sending a new message from scratch: You see the New Message window, similar to the one shown earlier, in Figure 8-2, but with the forwarded text filled in for you.

4. **Type the recipient's name (if the person is a contact), or type a phone number.**

5. **Tap the Send button to forward the message.**

Multimedia Messages

Even though the term *texting* sticks around, a text message can contain media; usually a photo. Such a message ceases to be a mere *text* message and becomes a *multimedia message*:

- ✔ Multimedia messages are handled by the same Messaging app you use for text messaging.

- ✔ Not every mobile phone can receive multimedia messages. Rather than receive the media item, the recipient may be directed to a web page where the item can be viewed on the Internet.

- ✔ The official name for a multimedia text message is Multimedia Messaging Service, which is abbreviated MMS.

Attaching media to a text message

The most consistent way to compose a multimedia message is to attach existing media — something you've already saved on your phone — to the outgoing message. Obey these steps:

1. **Compose a text message as you normally do.**

2. **Display the Delighters and Shortcuts panel.**

   Swipe in from the right edge of the screen, or use the Tilt gesture to see a list of recent photos.

3. **Choose a photo from those listed.**

4. **If you like, compose a message to accompany the media attachment.**

   Tap the Reply text below the photo to type the message.

5. **Touch the Send button to send the media text message.**

In just a few, short, cellular moments, the receiving party will enjoy your multimedia text message:

✔ Tap the Camera icon (refer to Figure 8-2) to see a pop-up menu of media-attachment options. Choose Capture a Photo or Capture a Video to use the Fire phone's camera to instantly record media, which can then be attached and sent in a multimedia message.

 ✔ Another way to send a multimedia message is to start with the source, such as a picture or video stored on your phone. Use the Share icon (shown in the margin), and choose Messaging to share the media item in an MMS. The various Share commands on your phone are covered throughout this book.

✔ To attach a video, first open the phone's photo album. Choose the video, and then share it via the Messaging app. The phone automatically resizes videos that are too large for multimedia messages.

Receiving a multimedia message

A multimedia attachment comes into your phone just like any other text message does. You may see a thumbnail preview of whichever media was sent, such as an image. To preview the attachment, touch it.

TIP

Opt out of text messaging

You don't have to be a part of the text messaging craze. Indeed, you can opt out of text messaging altogether. Simply contact your cellular provider and have them disable text messaging on your phone. They will happily comply, and you'll never again be able to send or receive a text message.

People opt out of text messaging for a number of reasons. A big one is cost: If the kids keep running up the text messaging bill, simply disabling the feature is often easier than continuing to pay all the usage surcharges. Another reason is security: Although cell phone viruses are rare, the scammers love sending malicious text messages. If you opt out, you don't have to worry about any SMS security risks.

To do more with the multimedia attachment, long-press it and then select an option from the menu that's displayed. For example, to save an image attachment, long-press the image thumbnail and choose the Save command.

You might not be able to preview or save some types of attachments.

Text Message Management

You don't have to manage your messages. I certainly don't. But the potential exists: If you ever want to destroy evidence of a conversation, or even do something as mild as change the text messaging ringtone, it's possible. Heed my advice in this section.

Removing messages

Although I'm a stickler for deleting email after I read it, I don't bother deleting my text message threads. That's probably because I have no pending divorce litigation. Well, even then, I have nothing to hide in my text messaging conversations. If I did, I would follow these steps to delete a conversation:

1. **Long-press the conversation you want to remove.**

   Choose the conversation from the main screen in the Messaging app.

2. **Choose the Delete command.**

   The conversation is gone.

You cannot undo the Delete command, and there is no "Are you sure?" prompt. When it's gone, it's gone.

Setting the text message ringtone

The sound you hear when a new text message floats in is the text-message notification ringtone. It might be the same sound you hear for all notifications, though it can be changed to something unique. If so, follow these steps to set the Messaging app's ringtone:

1. **Open the Settings app.**

2. **Choose Sounds & Notifications.**

3. **Choose Change Your Ringtone.**

4. **Tap the Phone item at the top of the screen.**

   You see the App Notifications screen.

5. **Choose the Messaging app from the list.**

   You may have to scroll down a ways to find the app.

   On the Messaging screen, you see several options for setting notifications in the Messaging app. Ensure that both Notifications and Banners are on, which helps alert you to new messages. The Vibrate option is also good to have, which tells you something's up when the phone is silenced.

6. **Choose Sound.**

7. **Pluck a ringtone from the list.**

 8. **Touch the Done icon.**

9. **Press the Home button to return to the Home screen.**

You can also set text message ringtones for individual contents. See the later section . . . oh! Here it is:

Setting individual contact ringtones

To distinguish between your bestest friends and only your mildly acceptable friends, you can assign individual text messaging ringtones to contacts. To do so, secretly follow these steps:

1. **Open the Settings app.**

2. **Choose Sounds & Notifications.**

3. **Choose Select Test Message Tones for Specific People.**

   The phone's address book is displayed.

4. **Select a contact for that special messaging ringtone.**

   Scroll the list to find your buddy.

5. **Choose a ringtone from the list.**

6. **Tap the Done icon.**

   The special ringtone is assigned.

7. **Repeat Steps 4 through 6 to assign additional contact ringtones.**

The specific ringtone plays when that contact sends you a text message.

You can use the Contacts app to view special ringtones for individual contacts. Look for the heading Text Ringtone (and Call Phone Ringtone, if you've assigned specific incoming call ringtones as well). The ringtones can be changed by editing the contact. See Chapter 7 for information on editing contacts.

You've Got Mail

I received a letter in the mail the other day. The opening sentence read, "I don't do email." Years ago, no such explanation was necessary; writing letters was a standard part of human communications. It was a formal assignment in grammar school. Today, it's a curiosity, almost an anachronism.

Taking the place of writing letters is electronic mail, written as *email*. It's the preferred form of digital communications, although text messaging is nipping at its heels. On your Fire phone, the Email app is used to handle the email task. It's capable of sending and receiving mail, dealing with attachments, and doing all the standard email stuff.

Email on the Go

Email on the Fire phone is handled by the logically named Email app. That single app coordinates all your email accounts — as long as you've added the accounts to your phone. Once configured, email shows up, ready for reading, replying, forwarding, and all the other email gerunds I can't think of right now:

> ✒ You can add any email account to your Fire phone, from web-based email to corporate email to traditional ISP email. See Chapter 2 for information on adding email accounts.

✔ Although you can use the Silk web browser app to visit your web email accounts, such as Gmail or Yahoo! Mail, use instead the Email app to pick up your messages.

✔ Web-based email accounts are known as *IMAP* accounts, after the protocol thingamajig that fetches the mail. Traditional email accounts, such as those you'd receive from an ISP such as Comcast or Cox, are known as *POP3* accounts. The Email app handles both.

Exploring the Email app

Start the Email app on your phone. The app is found on the App Grid, although if you've checked email recently, the app can be found quickly by using the Carousel on the Home screen.

When you open the Email app, you're taken to the inbox. In Figure 9-1, you can see the combined inbox, which lists email from all your various accounts. You can also choose an individual account's inbox from the Navigation panel.

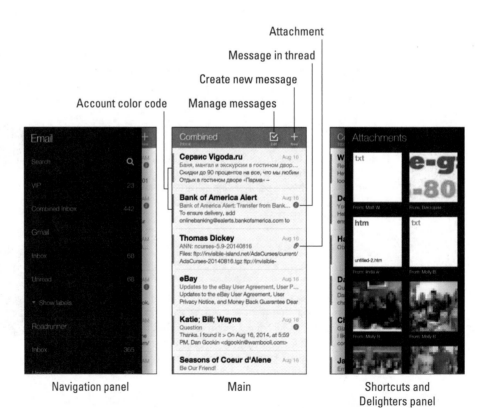

Navigation panel   Main   Shortcuts and Delighters panel

Figure 9-1: The Email app.

The messages in the combined inbox are color-coded. In Figure 9-1, you see green flags for my main email account and a red flag for my personal account. Each account uses a different color, which is reflected in the inbox:

- Swipe the screen to peruse older messages. Newer messages appear atop the list.

- The wee-number-in-a-circle (refer to Figure 9-1) indicates any related messages, replies, or follow-ups. They're all included in the single message entry shown in the inbox.

- The Paperclip icon shows that the message contains an attachment. See the later section "Message Attachments."

- The VIP inbox can be chosen from the Navigation panel to view email from your VIP contacts. The messages are culled from all your email accounts. See Chapter 7 for information on creating VIP contacts.

Getting a new message

New email arrivals are heralded by a notification. You may see the New Email icon on the lock screen or pull down the Notification panel to peruse the quantity of freshly delivered messages for each of your online accounts.

You can tap a notification on the Notification panel to instantly launch the Email app and peruse messages for that account or simply visit the Email app to examine a particular inbox or the combined inbox.

Touch a message in the inbox to display it full-screen, similar to what's shown in Figure 9-2. Swipe the message up or down to read.

● You access message commands by choosing the icons at the bottom of the
● screen. The icons change, depending on the message and phone's orientation.
● For example, in Figure 9-2 you don't see the Archive, Move, or Label icons. Sometimes a menu icon appears (as shown in the margin), from which you can choose additional commands.

Tap the Respond icon to view a menu of replying options, as shown in Figure 9-2. Here are your choices:

Reply: Choose this command to reply to a message. A new message window appears with the To and Subject fields reflecting the original sender(s) and subject.

Reply All: Choose this command to respond to everyone who received the original message, including folks on the Cc line. Use this option only when everyone else must get a copy of your reply.

Forward: Choose this command to send a copy of the message to someone else.

Return to inbox

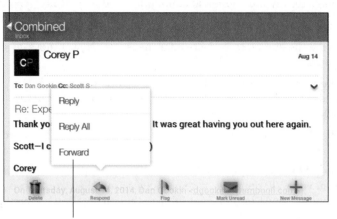

Respond menu

Figure 9-2: Reading a message.

You don't have to reply to any message. In fact, swipe the screen left or right to continue reading your email: Swipe left-to-right to view older messages; swipe right-to-left to view newer messages:

✔ When you're reading a message, the Shortcuts and Delighters panel displays previous messages from that same contact.

✔ The email you receive on the phone is echoed to other devices that also check your email, such as a laptop or desktop computer. This duplication may cause an issue for POP3 email accounts, such as those from an ISP like Comcast or Cox. See the later section "Configuring the server delete option" for details on how to avoid email coordination problems.

Composing an electronic message

Creating a new email epistle in the Email app works similarly to creating a new message on a computer. The key is to touch the New Message icon, similar to the one shown in the margin. This icon is found on the Inbox screen, and it might also show up when reading messages.

The New Message screen is shown in Figure 9-3. This layout should be familiar to you if you've ever written email on a computer.

Fill in the To, Subject, and message content fields. As you type in the To field, matching contacts from the phone's address book appear. Choose one from the list. As with any email message, you can send your message to multiple recipients.

Subject

Send message

Tap to expand

Discard

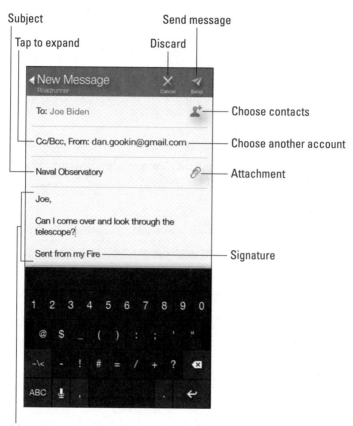

To: Joe Biden — Choose contacts

Cc/Bcc, From: dan.gookin@gmail.com — Choose another account

Naval Observatory — Attachment

Sent from my Fire — Signature

Message text

Figure 9-3: Writing a new email message.

Tap the Cc/Bcc item to display those fields.

When you have more than one email account configured for the Email app, you can select which account to use for sending the message. Touch your email address in the new message window, and then select another account.

To send the message, touch the Send icon:

✔ To cancel a message, touch the Cancel icon. Choose Save Draft to save the message for later, or choose Discard Draft to dispose of the email.

✔ You can rescue saved drafts by opening the Drafts folder for a specific email account; choose the folder from the Navigation panel. You can then edit the message and tap the Send icon to whisk it off.

✏ Copies of the messages you send in the Email app are stored in the Sent mailbox. Display the Navigation panel, and then choose the Show Folders command for a specific email account. Choose the Sent folder from the list that's displayed.

✏ Messages are sent from the default account. See the later section "Setting the default account" for details.

Sending email to a contact

A quick and easy way to compose a new message is to find a contact in the phone's address book. Heed these steps:

1. **Open the Contacts app.**

2. **Locate the contact to whom you want to send an electronic message.**

3. **Touch the contact's email address.**

4. **Compose the message.**

   The To field is already filled in for you.

At this point, creating the message works as described in the preceding sections.

Message Attachments

The key to understanding email attachments on your phone is to look for the Paperclip icon. When you find that icon, you can either deal with an attachment for incoming email or add an attachment to outgoing email.

Receiving an attachment

You'll find an attachment lurking at the bottom of a received message. It appears as a large square with a preview inside — if the document can be previewed. Otherwise, the square is labeled with the document type. Figure 9-4 shows how a text attachment appears.

To deal with the attachment, touch it. In most cases, the attachment opens using a given app on your phone. The app that's used depends on the type of attachment. For example, a PDF attachment might be opened by the OfficeSuite app:

Figure 9-4: An email attachment.

✏ As with email attachments received on a computer, the only problem you may have is that the phone lacks the app required to deal with the attachment. When an app can't be found, you have to either suffer through not viewing the attachment or simply reply to the message and direct the person to resend the attachment in another file format.

✏ You may see a prompt displayed when several apps can deal with the attachment. Choose one and touch the Just This Once button to view the attachment. Also see Chapter 24 for information on the Always/Just This Once prompt.

Sending an attachment

The best way to email an attachment is to use the Share icon, shown in the margin. That's the accepted way to send files via email on a mobile device, such as the Amazon Fire phone. Here's the general procedure:

1. **Visit the app that created the attachment.**

   For example, to send a photo, open the Photos app.

2. **View the specific item you want to attach.**

   In the Photos app, view an image full-screen. In the Maps app, view the information card about a location.

3. **Tap the Share icon.**

   A list of apps appears.

4. **Choose Email.**

5. **Compose the message.**

The item is attached to the message, so at this point, writing the email works as described earlier in this chapter.

The computer way of attaching a file to a message is to first use the Email app to write the message. Tap the Paperclip (Attach) icon and then choose a command representing what you want to attach. For example, choose Attach a Photo to fetch a picture from the phone's photo album as an attachment.

When you send the message, the attachment rides along with it. In mere Internet moments, the message and attachment are made available to the recipient(s):

✔ It's possible to attach multiple items to a single email message. To add another attachment, tap the Attach icon again.

✔ The variety of items you can attach depends on which apps are installed on the phone.

✔ You can locate some attachments by opening the Docs app. From the Home screen, choose Docs from the Navigation panel. When the Docs app opens, swipe its Navigation panel and choose Email Attachments. You see a list of saved document attachments.

Email Configuration

You can have oodles of fun and waste oceans of time confirming and customizing the email experience on your Fire phone. Two of the more interesting things you can do are to modify or create an email signature and specify whether messages retrieved by the Email app can be made available later for pickup by a computer.

Managing your messages

You can deal with a horde of email messages all at once by selecting them for editing. Then you can perform specific tasks with the group of messages. You can delete the lot, flag them, or mark them as read or unread. It all starts by marking the messages. Follow these steps:

1. **Display an inbox of messages in the Email app.**

2. **Tap the Edit icon.**

Refer to Figure 9-1 for its location.

3. **Tap to place check marks in the boxes, which selects the message(s).**

4. **Choose an icon from the bottom of the screen.**

   Your choices are

   Delete: Remove the selected messages. A confirm prompt does not appear.

   Flag: Mark the message with a flag icon, making it easier to find later.

   Mark Read: Change the status of an unread message to read.

   Mark Unread: Change the status of a read message to unread. This option is good for picking up email elsewhere at a later time.

   The action you choose affects the selected messages.

5. **Tap the Cancel icon when you're done working with the messages.**

   This icon doesn't appear when you delete the messages.

Deleted messages are found in the Trash folder for the account. To view that folder, display the Navigation panel and choose the email account. Tap the Show Folders item under the account's heading, and then choose Trash.

Creating a signature

I highly recommend that you create a custom email signature for sending messages from your phone. Here's my signature:

```
DAN
This was sent from my Fire phone.
Typos, no matter how hilarious, are unintentional.
```

To create a signature, obey these directions:

1. **In the Email app, display the Navigation drawer.**

2. **Choose Settings.**

3. **Choose one of your email accounts.**

4. **Choose Signature.**

5. **Type or dictate your signature.**

6. **Touch OK.**

You need to repeat Steps 3 through 5 for each of your email accounts. A separate signature exists for each one.

Setting the default account

The Email app automatically sets one of your email accounts as the primary, *or default,* account. That's the account from which all messages are automatically sent.

To determine which account is the default, in the Email app choose the Settings command from the Navigation panel. Under the Accounts heading, you see your various email accounts listed and color-coded. The primary account is labeled as Default.

To change the default account, choose another account from the list. Tap the Default Account item and choose another account:

  ✔ It doesn't really matter which account is the default, although as you use your phone, you may find that some accounts are more reliable than others.

  ✔ Also, you can change which account is used to send messages by long-pressing the account name on the New Message screen. See the earlier section "Composing an electronic message."

Configuring the server delete option

Messages fetched by your phone from traditional email accounts typically remain on the email server. This is true for traditional email accounts, but not true for webmail accounts, such as Gmail or Yahoo! Mail.

The issue with traditional email accounts is that, unlike a computer's email program, the Email app doesn't delete messages after it picks them up. The advantage is that you can retrieve the same messages later using a computer. The disadvantage is that you can end up retrieving mail you've already read and replied to.

You can control whether the Email app removes messages after they're picked up. Follow these steps:

  1. **In the Email app, swipe the Navigation panel all the way to the bottom.**

  2. **Choose the Settings command.**

  3. **Choose your Email account from the list of accounts.**

   It must be an ISP type of email account, also known as a *POP3* account.

  4. **Choose the Incoming Settings item.**

5. **Below the item Delete Email from Server, choose the option When I Delete from Inbox.**

   If this option isn't available, the account isn't a POP3 account, and the messages you work with aren't affected.

6. **Touch the Done button.**

After you make or confirm this setting, messages you delete in the Email app are also deleted from the mail server. The message won't be picked up again — not by the phone, another mobile device, or any computer that fetches email from that same account:

✔ Mail you retrieve using a computer's mail program is deleted from the mail server after it's picked up. That behavior is normal. Your phone cannot pick up mail from the server if a computer has already deleted it.

✔ Deleting mail on the server isn't a problem for webmail. No matter how you access your account, from your phone or from a computer, the inbox lists the same messages.

Fire Web Browsing

*I*t's been said that viewing the web on a cell phone is like seeing the Grand Canyon through a keyhole. The web was designed to be viewed on a computer with a nice, roomy monitor. Your Fire phone has a relatively diminutive screen, which does make it a tad undersized for viewing the web. Don't let that stop you.

Thanks to the Silk app, your phone is more than up to the task of surfing the web. You can do just about anything with the phone that can be done by viewing the web on a computer. Things do work a tad bit differently, however, which is why I wrote this chapter:

✔ If possible, activate the phone's Wi-Fi connection before you venture out on the web. See Chapter 18 for more information on Wi-Fi.

✔ Many places you visit on the web can instead be accessed directly and more effectively by using specific apps. Netflix, Facebook, Twitter, and even Amazon itself have apps you can use that make the online experience better than by using a web browser.

The Silk Browser

I finally get it. The web is made of silk; spiders use their spinnerets to create silk, with which they fashion a web. And of course, the World Wide Web is the number-one attraction on the Internet. So, obviously, the Fire phone's web browser is named Silk. It all makes sense.

You probably are quite familiar with the web — the Internet one, not the spider variety, although (like me) you've probably walked into a few now and then. Anyway. I probably don't need to explain how a web browser works. You already know. What you may not know is how web browsing works on the Fire phone. Therefore, some Fire phone Silk browser app orientation is in order.

Surfing the web

The Silk Browser app — or Silk, for short — is shown in Figure 10-1. The main screen shows the web page you're viewing, along with various onscreen controls. The Navigation panel lists browser features. The Delighters and Shortcuts panel shows page suggestions, which are dependent upon the web page being viewed.

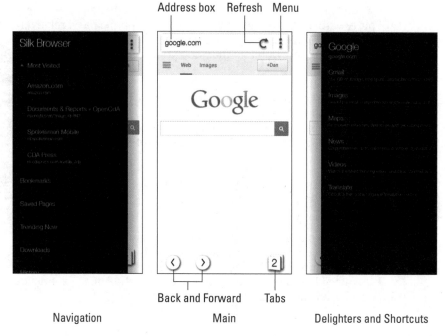

Navigation   Main   Delighters and Shortcuts

Figure 10-1: The Silk app beholds the Google home page.

Here are some handy phone web-browsing tips:

✔ Pan the web page by dragging your finger across the touchscreen. You can pan up, down, left, and right.

✔ Double-tap the screen to zoom in or zoom out.

✔ Pinch the screen to zoom out, or spread two fingers to zoom in.

✔ Place the phone in landscape orientation to make teensy text more readable.

Visiting a web page

To visit a web page, type its address in the address box (refer to Figure 10-1). You can also type a search word, if you don't know the exact web page address. Touch the Go button on the onscreen keyboard to search the web or visit a specific web page.

If you don't see the address box, swipe your finger from top to bottom on the touchscreen. The address box appears.

Touch links on a web page to visit the relevant link. If you have trouble touching a specific link, zoom in on the page:

✔ To reload a web page, tap the Refresh icon. Refreshing updates a website that changes often. You can also refresh to reload a web page that may not have completely loaded the first time.

✔ To stop a web page from loading, touch the Stop (X) icon that appears to the right of the address box.

✔ Many web pages load a special mobile version when they detect your phone's Silk web browser. You can request the desktop (nonmobile) version of the page by tapping the Menu icon and choosing the Request Another View command. Choose Desktop and tap the OK button.

Improving web page visibility

Two conventional things you can do to make a web page more readable are

✔ Use the phone in horizontal orientation.

✔ Zoom in (double-tap the screen or spread your fingers).

A third, unconventional method presents itself for certain web pages. It's Easy Reading mode, illustrated in Figure 10-2.

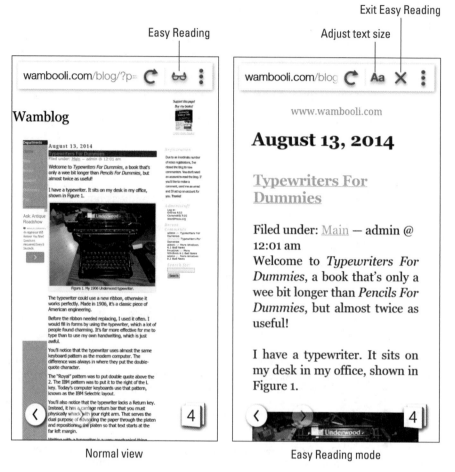

Figure 10-2: Easy Reading mode.

You can't force Easy Reading mode; it simply shows up. Tap the Spectacles icon (refer to Figure 10-2) and the web page reformats itself with larger text, plus a text-size-adjustment icon.

To exit Easy Reading mode, tap the Cancel icon, illustrated in Figure 10-2.

Browsing back and forth

Two icons appear at the bottom left of the Silk browser screen, looking like less-than and greater-than characters. These are the Back and Forward icons, respectively.

To return to a previous web page, tap the Back icon.

Tap the Forward icon to return to a page you were visiting before you touched the Back icon.

Reviewing your browser history

To review the web pages you've visited, check out the browser's History: Choose the History command from the Navigation panel. You see a list of web pages you've visited today, yesterday, and days before.

Tap an entry in the history list to revisit that web page.

To remove an entry from the History, long-press the item. From the menu that appears, choose the Delete command. It's gone!

If you need to purge more than a single entry, tap the Edit icon atop the History screen, similar to the one shown in the margin. Tap in the boxes that appear next to the various entries to place check marks. Or you can tap the Select All icon at the bottom of the screen. Tap the Delete icon to purge the selected entries.

Recently visited web pages appear on the Carousel beneath the Silk app.

Creating a bookmark

Bookmarks are those electronic breadcrumbs you can drop as you wander the web. Need to revisit a website? Just look up its bookmark. This advice assumes, of course, that you bother to create (I prefer *drop*) a bookmark when you first visit the site.

To bookmark a web page in the Silk app, obey these steps:

1. **Visit the web page you adore or somehow feel compelled to bookmark.**

2. **Tap the Menu icon.**

   It's found in the upper-right corner of the screen, similar to the one shown in the margin.

3. **Choose the Add Bookmark command.**

   The Add Bookmark window appears, as shown in Figure 10-3.

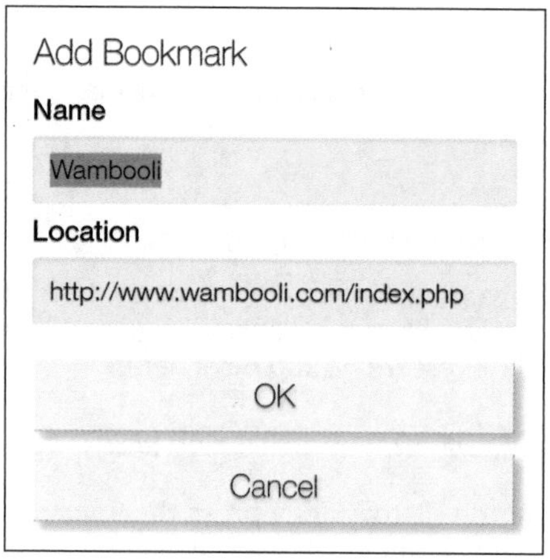

Add Bookmark

Name

Wambooli

Location

http://www.wambooli.com/index.php

OK

Cancel

Figure 10-3: Adding a bookmark.

4. **Edit the Name field to make the entry shorter and more descriptive.**

   Especially when the web page's title is long, cut it down to something more descriptive. Shorter names look better in the Bookmarks window.

5. **Touch the OK button to add the bookmark.**

View your bookmarks by visiting the Bookmarks screen. See the next section.

Using bookmarks

To view the bookmarks, choose the Bookmarks command from the Navigation panel. You see a scrolling list of bookmarks showing a web page thumbnail, the bookmark name, and the address. Touch a bookmark to visit that page.

To open a bookmark in a new tab, long-press the bookmark entry and choose the Open in New Tab command.

To remove a bookmark, long-press its entry on the Bookmarks screen. Choose the Remove Bookmark command. Tap OK to confirm.

Managing multiple web pages in tabs

The Silk browser uses a tabbed interface. Each web page appears on a tab, and several pages can be open in multiple tabs. The number of tabs in use is shown in the bottom corner of the screen. Tapping that Tabs icon displays a list of open tabs, as shown in Figure 10-4.

Add new tab

Touch to switch   Close tab

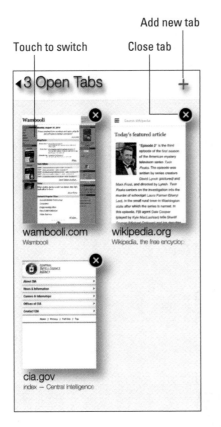

Figure 10-4: The Silk app's tab interface.

Touch a web page thumbnail to switch to that tab. Tap the thumbnail's X icon to close the tab.

To open a link in a new tab, long-press the link and choose the Open in New Tab command. A new tab is created, showing the web page.

To open a bookmark in a new tab, long-press the bookmark and choose the Open in New Tab command.

You can also open a link or bookmark on a background tab. That simply means that a new tab is opened but not currently visible on the screen.

Close a tab by touching its Close (X) button, as shown in Figure 10-4. When you close the last tab, the home page appears. It lists your most visited web pages.

Finding text on a web page

To locate text on a web page, touch the Menu icon and choose the Find in Page command. Type the search text into the Find on Page box. As you type, found text is highlighted on the screen, as shown in Figure 10-5.

Figure 10-5: Locating text on a web page.

Use the up and down chevrons to the left of the search box to page through the document.

Tap the Cancel (X) icon to exit Find in Page mode after you've finished searching.

Sharing a web page

There it is! That web page you just *have* to talk about to everyone you know. The gauche way to share the page is to copy and paste it. Because you're reading this book, though, you know the smart way to share a web page. Heed these steps:

1. **Go to the web page you desire to share.**

   Actually, you're sharing a *link* to the page, but don't let my obsession with specificity deter you.

2. **Touch the Menu icon and choose the Share Page command.**

   A smattering of app icons are displayed. The variety and number of apps depend on what's installed on your phone.

3. **Choose a method to share the page.**

   For example, choose Email to send the link by email, or choose Facebook to share the link with your friends.

4. **Do whatever happens next.**

   Whatever happens next depends on how you're sharing the link: Compose the email, write a comment on Facebook, or whatever. Refer to various chapters in this book for specific directions.

Download It from the Web

One of the most misused terms in all of computerdom is *download*. Officially, a *download* is a transfer of information over a network from another source to your phone. For the Silk browser app, the network is the Internet, and the other source is a web page:

- ✔ Most people use the term *download* when instead they mean *transfer* or *copy*. Those people will be dealt with.

- ✔ New apps are installed on your phone by using the Appstore app, covered in Chapter 17. That's a type of downloading, but it's not the same as the downloading described in this section.

- ✔ The opposite of downloading is *uploading*. That's the process of sending information from your gizmo to another location on a network.

Grabbing an image from a web page

The simplest thing to download is an image from a web page. It's cinchy: Long-press the image. You see a pop-up menu, from which you choose the Save Image command:

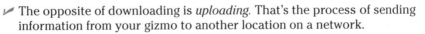

✔ The image is copied and stored on your phone. You can view the image by using the Photos app. Look in the Download album.

✔ Refer to Chapter 14 for information on the phone's photo album.

Downloading a file

When a link opens a document on a web page, such as a Microsoft Word document or an Adobe Acrobat (PDF) file, you can download that file to your phone. Touch the file link to download. If that doesn't work, long-press the file link and choose the Save Link command:

✔ The phone is smart, and it does attempt to open or display links you touch.

✔ To review any documents saved by using the Save Link command, choose the Downloads command from the Silk app's Navigation panel.

✔ Downloaded items generate the Download notification. Display the phone's Notification panel to review the Download notification(s). Tap a notification to view the specific item.

✔ Manage the download list by long-pressing any entry on the Downloads screen. Choose the Open or Delete command to view or remove the item, respectively.

Social Networking Friends and Followers

Social networking is that 21st century phenomenon that proves many odd beliefs about people. For example, it's possible to have hundreds of friends and never leave your house. You can jealously guard your privacy against the wicked intrusions of the government and Big Brother, all while letting everyone on the Internet know that you've just "checked in" to Starbucks and are having an iced mocha Frappuccino. And you can share your most intimate moments with humanity, many of whom will "like" the fact that your grandmother is in the hospital or that your cat was run over by the garbage collection service.

One of your Fire phone's duties is to keep you connected with your social networking universe. To make that happen, the phone works well with services such as Facebook and Twitter. Getting things set up and working is the key to unlocking your digital social life.

Facebook Phone Time

Of all the social networking sites, Facebook is the king. It's the online place to go to catch up with friends, send messages, express your thoughts, share pictures and video, play games, and waste more time than you ever thought you had.

Setting up your Facebook account

The best way to use Facebook is to have a Facebook account. You can sign up for an account using the phone, but the best way is to sign up at www. facebook.com by using a computer. Register for a new account by setting up your username and password.

Don't forget your Facebook username and password!

Eventually, the Facebook robots send you a confirmation email. You reply to that message, and the online social networking community braces itself for your long-awaited arrival.

Now you're ready to access Facebook on your Fire phone. To get the most from Facebook, however, you need the Facebook app. Keep reading in the next section.

Getting the Facebook app

You can access Facebook on the web by using the Silk web-browsing app, but I highly recommend that you use the Facebook app instead. If you can find the app on the App Grid, great! Otherwise, you need to obtain a free copy.

To get the Facebook app, go to the Appstore and search for the Facebook app. Download the app. If you need specific directions, see Chapter 17, which covers using the Appstore.

Running Facebook on your phone

The first time you run the Facebook app, you're asked to sign in. Do so: Type the email address you used to sign up for Facebook, and then type your Facebook password. Touch the Log In button.

If you're asked to sync your contacts, do so. I recommend choosing the option to synchronize all your contacts, which adds all your Facebook friends to the phone's address book.

Eventually, you see the Facebook News Feed, similar to what's shown in Figure 11-1.

When you need a respite from Facebook, press the Home button to return to the Home screen.

The Facebook app continues to run until you either sign out or turn off the phone. It may also time-out after a period of inactivity.

Figure 11-1: The Facebook app.

To sign out of Facebook, choose the Settings icon (refer to Figure 11-1), and swipe to the bottom of the screen. Tap the Log Out command. Touch the Confirm button:

- Use the Like, Comment, or Share buttons below a News Feed item to like, comment on, or share something. You can see the comments only when you choose the Comment item.

- The News Feed is updated when you swipe down the screen.

- Notifications for Facebook appear in the notifications drawer: Pull down the notifications drawer from the top of the screen to quickly review any Facebook updates or comments.

Setting your status

The primary thing you live for on Facebook, besides having more friends than anyone else, is to update your status. It's the best way to share your thoughts with the universe, far cheaper than skywriting and far less offensive than a robocall.

To set your status, follow these steps in the Facebook app:

1. **Touch the Status button at the bottom of the screen.**

   Refer to Figure 11-1 for the Status button's location. If you don't see it, ensure that you're viewing the News Feed.

   The Write Post screen appears. It's where you type your Facebook musing, similar to the one shown in Figure 11-2.

Figure 11-2: Updating your Facebook status.

2. **Type something pithy, newsworthy, or typical of the stuff you read on Facebook.**

   When you can't think of anything to post, take off your shoes, sit down, and take a picture of your feet against something else in the background. That seems to be really popular.

3. **Touch the Post button.**

And the world is enriched by you sharing your experience.

Uploading a picture to Facebook

One of the many things your Android phone can do is take pictures. Combine that feature with the Facebook app and you have an all-in-one gizmo designed for sharing the various intimate and private moments of your life with the ogling Internet throngs.

 The picture posting process starts by touching the Photo icon in the Facebook app. Refer to Figures 11-1 and 11-2 for popular Photo icon locations on the main screen and the Write Post screen. After you touch the Photo icon, the photo selection screen appears. You have two choices:

✔ Select an image from pictures shown on the screen. These images are ones found on the phone. Touch an image, or touch several images to select a bunch, and then proceed with the steps listed later in this section.

✔ Take a picture by using the phone's camera.

If you elect to use the phone's camera to take a picture, touch the Camera icon on the photo selection screen. (It's in the lower-left corner.) You then find yourself thrust into Facebook's Camera app, shown in Figure 11-3. This is not the same app as the Camera app, covered in Chapter 14.

Use the onscreen controls to take the picture. Or you can shoot a quick video. When you're done, touch the Gallery icon. Refer to Figure 11-3 for the location of the Gallery icon as well as other onscreen controls.

To proceed with uploading the image, follow these steps:

1. **Touch an image in the phone's photo album to select it.**

2. **Optionally, tap the image to add a tag.**

You can touch someone's face in the picture and then type the person's name. Or choose from a list of your Facebook friends to apply a name tag to the image.

 3. **Use the Rotate icon to reorient the image, if necessary.**

The icon is shown in the margin. Please don't try to annoy me on Facebook by posting improperly oriented images.

4. **Touch the Compose icon.**

The Compose icon is shown in the margin.

Switch cameras
(Front/Back)

Flash control

Record video

Photo album

Take picture

Figure 11-3: Snapping a pic for Facebook.

5. **Add a message to the image.**

At this point, posting the image works just like adding a status update, similar to the one shown earlier, in Figure 11-2.

6. **Touch the Post button.**

The image is posted as soon as it's transferred over the Internet and digested by Facebook.

The image can be found as part of your status update or News Feed, but it's saved also to Facebook's Mobile Uploads album.

Facebook appears also on the various Share menus you find in other apps on the phone. Choose the Share command to send to Facebook whatever it is you're looking at. (Other chapters in this book give you more information about the various Share menus and where they appear.)

Configuring the Facebook app

The commands that control Facebook are stored on the Settings screen. To see that screen, choose the More icon atop the screen, shown as Settings and Stuff in Figure 11-1. Choose the App Settings command to behold a host of Facebook app settings. Two commands worthy of your attention are Refresh Interval and Notification Ringtone.

Choose Refresh Interval to specify how frequently the app checks for new Facebook activities. If you find the one-hour value to be too long for your frantic Facebook social life, choose something quicker. Or, to disable Facebook notifications, choose Never.

The Notification Ringtone item sets the sound that plays when Facebook has a new update. Choose the Silent option when you don't want the app to make noise upon encountering a Facebook update.

Use the Back technique to return to the main Facebook screen: Swipe the screen from bottom to top.

You can manually update the Facebook app by tugging down the News Feed screen: Swipe the screen from about the midpoint to the bottom.

Tweet Suite

Twitter is a social networking site, similar to Facebook but with increased brevity. On Twitter, you write short spurts of text that express your thoughts or observations, or you share links. Or you can just use Twitter to follow the thoughts and twitterings, or *tweets,* of other people:

- ✔ A message posted on Twitter is a *tweet.*
- ✔ A tweet can be no more than 140 characters long. That number includes spaces and punctuation.
- ✔ You can post messages on Twitter and follow others who post messages. It's a good way to get updates and information quickly, from not only individuals but also news outlets and other organizations.

Setting up Twitter

The best way to use Twitter is to already have a Twitter account. Start by going to `http://twitter.com` on a computer and follow the directions there for creating a new account.

After you establish a Twitter account, you can use the Twitter app on your phone. The app may not be preinstalled, so obtain a copy from the Appstore. Refer to Chapter 17 for information on downloading apps to your phone. Search for the Twitter app from Twitter, Inc.

When you start the Twitter app for the first time, touch the Sign In button. Type your Twitter username or email address, and then type your Twitter password. After that, you can use Twitter without having to log in again — until you turn off the phone or exit the Twitter app.

Figure 11-4 shows the Twitter app's main screen, which shows the current tweet feed. The main screen may look subtly different if the Twitter app has been updated since the time this book went to press.

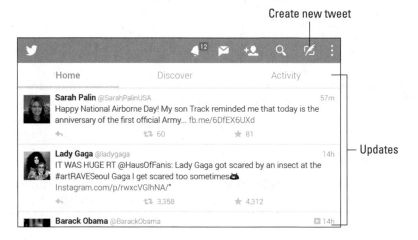

Figure 11-4: The Twitter app.

Tweeting

The Twitter app provides an excellent interface to the many wonderful and interesting things that Twitter does. Of course, the two most basic tasks are reading and writing tweets.

To read tweets, choose the Home category, which is shown in Figure 11-4. Recent tweets are displayed in a list, with the most recent information at the top. Scroll the list by swiping it with your finger.

To tweet, touch the Create New Tweet icon, shown in Figure 11-4. The New Tweet screen appears, as shown in Figure 11-5, so that you can compose your tweet.

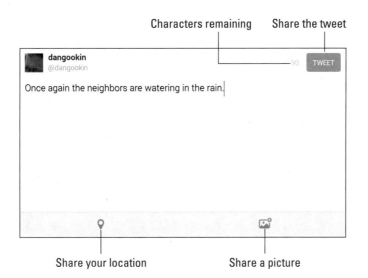

Figure 11-5: Creating a tweet.

Touch the Tweet button to share your thoughts with the twitterverse:

> ✔ You have only 140 characters for creating your tweet. That count includes spaces.

> ✔ The character counter in the Twitter app lets you know how close you're getting to the 140-character limit.

> ✔ The Twitter app appears on various Share menus in other apps. You use those Share menus to send to Twitter whatever you're looking at.

Even More Social Networking

The Internet is nuts over social networking. Facebook may be the king, but you'll find lots of landed gentry out for that crown. It almost seems as though a new social networking site pops up every week. Beyond Facebook and Twitter, other social networking and similar share sites include, but are not limited to

> ✔ Instagram

> ✔ LinkedIn

> ✔ Tumblr

I recommend first setting up the social networking account on a computer, similar to the way I describe it earlier in this chapter for Facebook and Twitter. After that, obtain an app for the social networking site using the

Google Play Store. Set up and configure that app on your Android phone to connect with your existing account:

- ✔ The HootSuite app can be used to share your thoughts on a multitude of social networking platforms. You can obtain it from the Appstore.

- ✔ See Chapter 17 for more information on the Appstore.

- ✔ As with Facebook and Twitter, you may find your social networking apps appearing on Share menus in various apps. That way, you can easily share your pictures and other types of media with your online social networking pals.

12

Skype the World

*T*he holy grail of communications has always been the video phone call. Back in the 1960s, people believed that video phone technology would be introduced in the 1970s and widely available by 1980. Along with our flying cars and food-in-pill-form, the video phone never materialized — until now!

Skype is used the world over as a free way to make Internet phone calls and to text-chat. Plus, Skype offers you the ability to video-chat with other Skype users. It's not really the video call nirvana that was promised decades ago, but it's one step in that direction. And it's something your Fire phone can do, thanks to the Skype app.

The Skype Setup

Using Skype requires a bit of work on your behalf, although it's nothing tedious, like anything you did in the eighth grade. Most importantly, you need to obtain the Skype app. Then you need to connect with Skype users. That's because Skype is useful only when you have friends and associates who also use Skype.

Obtaining the Skype app

Your Fire phone most likely didn't ship with the Skype app preinstalled. That's not a problem. You can easily obtain a free copy of Skype from the Appstore. Open the Appstore app and browse for Skype. Install the app. Refer to

Chapter 17 for information on using the Appstore and installing new apps for your phone.

Signing up for Skype

To use Skype, you need a Skype account. This is yet another online account, although you can use your Microsoft Live account to sign in to Skype. Figure 12-1 shows the Skype sign-in screen, as well as your options.

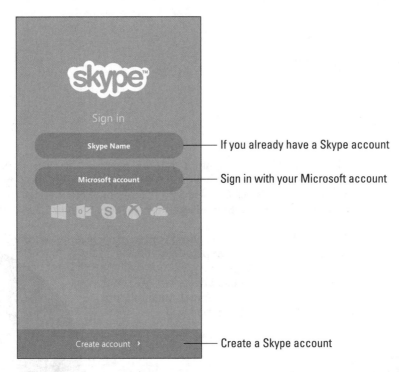

— If you already have a Skype account

— Sign in with your Microsoft account

— Create a Skype account

Figure 12-1: Welcome to Skype.

Choose a sign-in method, as shown in Figure 12-1. Or tap the Create Account button to set up a new Skype account. You can also set up an account by accessing Skype on a computer: Visit www.skype.com.

✔ Skype is free. Text chat is free. Voice and video chat with one other Skype user is also free. When you want to call a real phone or video-chat with a group, you need to boost your account with Skype Credit.

✔ If you want to video-chat with multiple people in Skype, it costs extra.

⮑ Don't worry about getting a Skype Number, which is available for a fee. That's used mostly for incoming calls and, well, that's why you have a phone.

Using Skype

When you start the Skype app for the first time, work through the initial setup screens. You can even take the tour. Be sure to have Skype scour the phone's address book for contacts you can Skype. This process may take a while, but if you're just starting out, it's a great help.

The Skype app's main interface is shown in Figure 12-2. It may change subtly with future app updates, but the major parts remain, as illustrated in the figure.

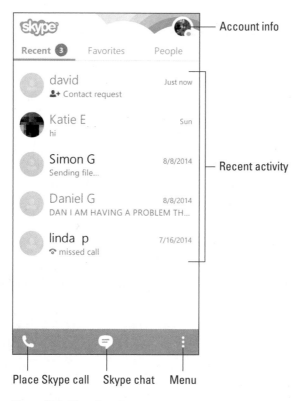

Figure 12-2: Skype's main screen.

The Recent tab (refer to Figure 12-2) lists your recent Skype activity, including chats, calls, contact requests, and other updates. The Favorites tab shows your favorite or frequent contacts. The People tab lists all of your Skype contacts.

Adding Skype contacts

Odds are probably good that many of your friends and associates already use Skype. You need to connect with them via Skype before you can communicate.

To add Skype contacts, follow these steps:

1. **Tap the Menu icon.**

   It's found in the lower-right corner of the Skype app's main screen, shown earlier, in Figure 12-2.

2. **Choose Add People.**

3. **Type the person's name, email, or phone number.**

   As you type, matches appear in a list. If a match represents the person you want, choose it.

4. **Tap the Search icon on the keyboard.**

   A contact request form appears.

5. **Type a brief message.**

   For example, "Please O please add me to your Skype contacts list!" Type something unassuming like that.

6. **Tap the Add to Contacts button.**

7. **Wait.**

The contact has to approve your request. After that happens, you can communicate with them on Skype.

Signing out of Skype

The Skype app stays active on your phone, even when you switch away from it to do something else. New messages come in, video-chat requests, and so on. That's good. When you want to sign out of Skype, follow these steps:

1. **Tap the Menu icon.**

   It's in the lower-right corner of the main Skype app screen, illustrated in Figure 12-2.

2. **Choose Sign Out.**

   That's it.

When you sign out of Skype, you can no longer receive chat requests. You need to sign in again, as described earlier in this chapter.

It's possible to have Skype installed on multiple devices, such as a tablet or computer, in addition to your Fire phone. If so, any Skype requests appear on all devices where you're actively signed in to Skype. You need to choose only one device to participate in Skype activities.

Skype in Action

The most popular thing to do in Skype is chat — particularly video-chat. That's only one aspect of the program. You can also text-chat and use Skype to place a phone call to a real phone — which is kind of silly, given that the Fire phone is a real phone. Even so, phone calling with Skype has its purpose, especially for international calling.

Chatting with another Skype user

Text-chatting with Skype works similarly to texting. The only difference is that the other person must be a Skype user. That makes it a bit more exclusive than text messaging, where the other person merely needs to have a cell phone.

To Skype-chat, follow these steps:

1. **Start the Skype app and sign in.**

   You don't need to sign in when you've previously run the Skype app. Like most apps on your phone, Skype continues to run until you sign out or turn off the phone.

2. **At the main Skype screen, touch the Favorites tab or People tab and choose a contact.**

   Or you can choose one of the contact icons shown on the main screen.

   You can also tap the Skype Chat icon on the main Skype screen. You need to type the name of one or more people to join you in the chat.

3. **Type some text in the text box.**

   The box is at the bottom of the screen. It says Type a Message Here, as shown in Figure 12-3.

4. **Touch the blue arrow icon to send the message.**

   As long as your Skype friend is online and eager, you'll be chatting in no time.

At the far right end of the text box, you find the Smiley icon. Use this icon to insert a cute graphic in your text.

Exit chat

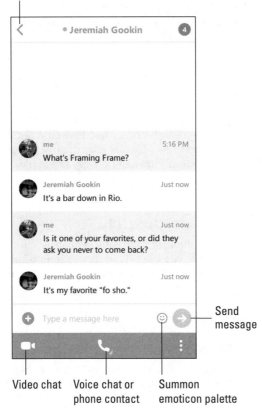

Send
message

Video chat   Voice chat or   Summon
             phone contact   emoticon palette

Figure 12-3: A Skype chat.

✔ New Skype chat requests generate a notification. Pull down the Notification panel to peruse chat requests. Tap a request to join in the conversation.

✔ To stop chatting, tap the left-pointing chevron in the upper-left corner of the screen. The conversation is retained in the Skype app, even after the other person has disconnected.

✔ For the chat to work, the other user must be logged in on Skype and available to chat.

Placing a Skype voice call

To take a text chat up a notch, tap the Phone icon at the bottom of the Skype chat screen, shown in Figure 12-3. Choose Skype Call to connect with the current chat user. At that point, you enter a voice call with the Skype user, similar to a phone call but over the Internet.

Figure 12-4 shows a Skype voice call in progress. It works similarly to a phone call, although you can chat only with other Skype users.

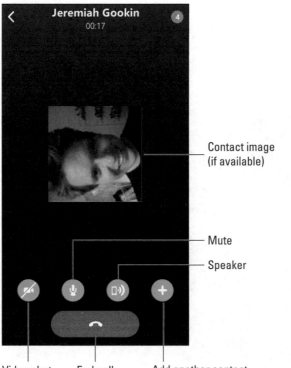

Contact image
(if available)

Mute

Speaker

Video chat   End call   Add another contact

Figure 12-4: A Skype voice call.

To end the Skype voice call, tap the End Call icon, shown in Figure 12-4.

In Figure 12-4, the Video Chat icon is disabled. That means the caller is unable to do video chat, either because the device he's using doesn't feature a camera or he's already in a video chat and cannot start another one.

Making a Skype video call

Placing a video call with Skype is easy: Start a text chat as described in the preceding section. After the conversation starts, touch the Video Call icon. The call rings through to the contact, and if that person wants to video-chat, they pick up in no time and you're talking and looking at each other.

When someone calls you on Skype, you see the Skype Incoming Call screen, similar to the one shown in Figure 12-5. Touch the Audio (handset) icon to answer as a voice-only call; touch the Video icon (if it's available) to answer using video. Touch the Decline icon to dismiss the call, especially when it's someone who annoys you.

Simon Gookin

Calling..

Video chat   Decline/Ignore

Answer voice only

Figure 12-5: An incoming Skype voice call.

The Incoming Call screen (see Figure 12-5) appears even when the phone is sleeping; the incoming call wakes up the phone, just as a real call would.

When you're in a Skype video conversation, the screen looks like Figure 12-6. Touch the screen to see the onscreen controls if they disappear. Touch the red Disconnect icon to end the call:

✔ Voice and video chat on Skype over the Internet are free. When you use a Wi-Fi connection, you can chat without consuming your cellular plan's data minutes.

✔ You can chat with any user in your Skype Contacts list by using a mobile device, a computer, or any other gizmo on which Skype is installed.

The other human

You

Mute

End video chat

Video settings   Switch to text chat

Figure 12-6: A Skype video call.

✔ If you plan to use Skype a lot, get a good headset.

✔ It's impossible to tell whether someone has dismissed a Skype call or simply hasn't answered. And Skype has no voice mail, so you can't leave a message:

Placing an international call

Because Skype uses the Internet, you can also use Skype to contact over-seas Skype users without incurring extra costs (well, beyond your normal data plan). You can, however, use Skype Credit in your Skype account to dial internationally, from the United States to a foreign country as well as from a foreign country to home.

You need Skype Credit to place an international call (or any call to a real phone). The easiest way to add credit is to visit Skype on the Internet using a computer: www.skype.com. Sign in to your account and surrender a credit card number to add a few pennies of credit. Although that may seem "expensive," remember that Skype's rates are far cheaper than placing a call by using your cellular provider.

To make an international call, log in to Skype as you normally would. At the main Skype screen, touch the Phone icon to summon the phone dialpad, shown in Figure 12-7.

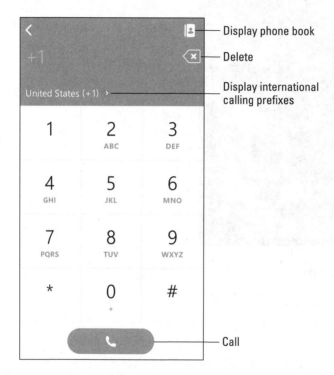

— Display phone book

— Delete

— Display international calling prefixes

— Call

Figure 12-7: Using Skype to place a phone call.

Punch in the number, including the plus sign (+) for international access. Touch the Call icon to make the call.

When you're finished with the call, touch the End icon. Say "Goodbye" first. Or say, "Adios, arrivederci, auf wiedersehen, au revoir, до свидания, 再見." Et cetera:

✔ To see the list of international-calling prefixes, touch the chevron by the text *United States (+1)*, as illustrated in Figure 12-7.

✔ Tapping the Phone Book icon (in the upper-right corner of the Skype dialpad screen) links to the Contacts app. Choose a contact to call from the address book to connect with them via Skype. In this instance, they don't need to be a Skype user, because Skype dials their phone directly.

Part IV
It Does Miraculous Things

In this part . . .

- ✔ Understand how to use the Maps app
- ✔ Work with the phone's camera
- ✔ Explore music on an Android phone
- ✔ Discover interesting apps
- ✔ Drool over getting even more apps

Explore Your World with Maps

So she told me, "Get lost!" I just laughed and showed her my Fire phone. "Honey, I can't get lost because I have a smartphone with GPS. It knows exactly where I am, it can get me to where I'm going, and it can find points of interest. For example, would you enjoy some fine Hungarian food right now?"

I suppose the answer was "No," because she slammed the door and I was left standing on the porch. Again. Fortunately, my Fire phone is always eager to get me places and find me things. Like a taxi. That all works, thanks to the Maps app.

Hello, Maps App

Back in the day, a map was something you purchased. It was a frustratingly folded sheet of paper. Finding locations was difficult. Finding yourself was impossible. Finding a Hungarian restaurant involved using the Phone Book. And by Phone Book, I don't mean *Amazon Fire Phone For Dummies*.

The Maps app is digital. It charts everything you need to find your way: freeways, highways, roads, streets, avenues, drives, bike paths, addresses, businesses, and points of interest.

Using the Maps app

Start the Maps app by choosing Maps from the App Grid, or it might be found on the Carousel if you've used it recently.

The first time you start the Maps app, or after an update, you might be prompted to agree to the terms and conditions. Do so.

The Maps app takes advantage of the phone's GPS radio. It communicates with GPS satellites to hone in on your current location. (See the later sidebar "Activate location technologies!") That location appears on the map, similar to the one shown in Figure 13-1. The position is accurate to within a given range, as shown by a circle around your location. If the circle doesn't appear, your location is either pretty darn accurate or you need to zoom in.

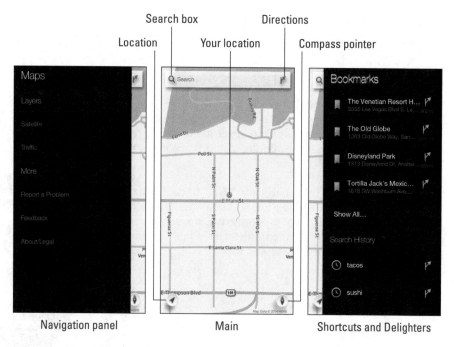

Figure 13-1: Your location on the map.

Here are some fun things you can do when viewing the basic street map:

Zoom in: To make the map larger (to move it closer), double-tap the screen. You can also spread your fingers on the touchscreen to zoom in.

Zoom out: To make the map smaller (to see more), pinch your fingers on the touchscreen.

Activate location technologies!

The Maps app works best when all the Fire phone's location technologies are activated. The operation is simple: From the Apps Grid, open the Settings icon. Choose the Location Services item. If you see the item Disable Enhanced Location Services, you're all set.

If you see the item Enable Enhanced Location Services, choose that item. On the Location screen, slide the master control by Location Services to the On position. Slide the master control by the Enhanced Location Services item to the On position.

Some apps access the phone's location technology. You can disable this feature, preventing some apps from knowing your location. To do so, open the Settings app, choose Location Services, and then Disable Enhanced Location Services. Swipe down the screen to peruse the apps that use location services. Slide the master control by a specific app to the Off position to prevent that app from knowing where you are.

Pan and scroll: To see what's to the left or right or at the top or bottom of the map, swipe your finger on the touchscreen. The map scrolls in the direction you swipe.

Rotate: Using two fingers, rotate the map clockwise or counterclockwise. Touch the Compass Pointer icon (refer to Figure 13-1) to reorient the map with north at the top of the screen.

Perspective: Tilt the phone in any direction to view the map in perspective. You can also touch the screen with two fingers and swipe up or down.

The closer you zoom in to the map, the more detail you see, such as street names, address block numbers, and businesses and other sites — but no tiny people.

Adding layers

You add details to the map by applying layers: A *layer* can enhance the map's visual appearance, provide more information, or add other fun features to the basic street map, such as the Satellite layer, shown in Figure 13-2.

Layers are accessed from the Navigation panel (refer to Figure 13-1). Two layers are available: Satellite and Traffic.

The Satellite layer shows details obtained from alien war machines in low orbit around Earth. That's what I learned on the Internet, although I suspect it's merely ground imagery from our own satellites.

The Traffic layer highlights road conditions, showing colors from green to deep red, depending on how fast things are moving.

Figure 13-2: The Satellite layer.

To remove a layer, choose it again from the navigation drawer; any active layer appears highlighted. When a layer isn't applied, the street view appears.

Where Are You?

By definition, when you're lost, you don't know where you are. Therefore, it doesn't help when you call someone to get you and they invariably ask, "Where are you?" You don't know. You're lost.

Fret not! The Maps app always knows where you are. Further, you can send that location to someone else. That way, you have an answer when they ask where you are.

Finding out where you are

The Maps app shows your location as a blue dot on the screen. But *where* is that? I mean, if you need to phone a tow truck, you can't just say, "I'm the blue dot on the orange slab by the green thing."

Well, you *can* say that, but it probably won't do any good.

To find your current street address, or any street address, long-press a location on the Maps screen. A pin is dropped at that location, similar to the one shown in Figure 13-3. You also see a card appear at the bottom of the screen. The card gives your approximate address.

Dropped pin   Get directions

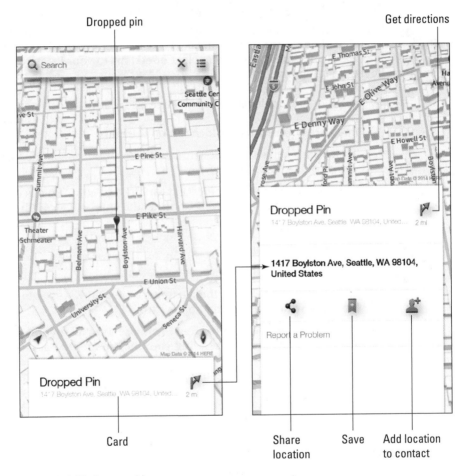

Card   Share   Save   Add location
                                             location   to contact

Figure 13-3: Finding an address.

If you touch the card, you see a screen with more details and additional information, as shown in Figure 13-3, on the right.

    ✔ This trick works only when your phone has Internet access. When Internet access isn't available, the Maps app is unable to communicate with the map servers.

    ✔ To make the card go away, touch anywhere else on the map.

✔ The time estimate under the Directions icon (see Figure 13-3) indicates how far away the address is from your current location. See the later section "Getting directions" for details.

Helping others find your location

You can use your Fire phone to send your current location to a friend. If your pal has a phone with smarts similar to those of your phone (rare but possible), he can use the coordinates to get directions to your location. Maybe he'll even bring Hungarian food!

To send your current location to someone else, obey these steps:

1. **Long-press your current location on the map.**

   To see your current location, touch the Location icon in the lower-right corner of the Maps app screen.

   After you long-press your location (or any location), a pin is dropped and you see a card displayed, showing the approximate address.

2. **Touch the card.**

3. **Touch the Share icon.**

   Refer to Figure 13-3 for this icon's location.

4. **Choose the app to share the message, such as the Messaging app, Email, or whichever useful app is listed.**

5. **Continue using the selected app to choose a recipient and otherwise complete the process of sending your location to that person.**

As an example, you can send your location by using the Messaging app. The recipient can touch the link in the text message to open your location in his phone's Maps app. When the location appears, the recipient can follow my advice in the later section "Getting directions" to reach your location. Don't loan him this book either — have him purchase his own copy. Thanks.

Find Stuff

The Maps app can help you find places in the real world, just as the Silk browser app helps you find places on the web. Both operations work basically the same way: Open the Maps app and type something to find in the Search text box (refer to Figure 13-1). You can type a variety of terms in the Search box, as explained in this section.

Looking for a specific address

To locate an address, type it in the Search box; for example:

```
1600 Pennsylvania Ave. NW, Washington, D.C. 20006
```

Touch the Search button on the keyboard, and that location is shown on the map. The next step is getting directions, which you can read about in the later section "Getting directions."

- ✔ You don't need to type the entire address. Oftentimes, all you need is the street number and street name and then either the city name or zip code.

- ✔ If you omit the city name or zip code, the Maps app looks for the closest matching address near your current location.

- ✔ Touch the X button in the Search box to clear the previous search.

Finding a business, restaurant, or point of interest

You may not know an address, but you know when you crave tacos or perhaps the exotic flavors of Topeka. Maybe you need a hotel or a gas station, or you have to find a place that fixes dentures. To find a business entity or a point of interest, type its name in the Search box; for example:

```
movie theater
```

This command flags movie theaters on the current Maps screen or nearby.

Have the Maps app jump to your current location, as described earlier in this chapter, to find locations near you. Otherwise, the Maps app looks for places near the area shown on the screen.

Or you can be specific and look for businesses near a certain location by specifying the city name, district, or zip code, such as

```
tacos 66612
```

After typing this command and touching the Search button, you see a smattering of taco supplies found near Topeka, Kansas, similar to those shown in Figure 13-4.

To see more information about a result, touch its card, such as the one for Tortilla Jack's in Figure 13-4. Or touch the Results List icon to see a whole swath of cards. After touching a card, you can view more details.

You can touch the Directions icon on the restaurant's (or any location's) Details screen to get directions; see the later section "Getting directions."

Search text   Results   Clear search   Results list   Close

Figure 13-4: Search results for tacos in Topeka.

- Every dot on the screen represents a search result (refer to Figure 13-4).

- Spread your fingers on the touchscreen to zoom in to the map.

- If you *really* like the location, save it for later. That directs the Maps app to store the location as one of your bookmarked places. The location is flagged with the Pin icon on the Maps app screen. See the next section.

Searching for favorite or recent places

Just as you can bookmark favorite websites on the Internet, you can bookmark favorite places in the real world by using the Maps app. The feature even has the same name: Bookmarks.

Create a bookmark in the Maps app by tapping the Bookmark icon on a location's card. It can be a random spot, as shown in Figure 13-3, or a specific place, such as a restaurant or bordello. The key is to display the location's card, which is where you'll find the Bookmark icon.

To review bookmarked places or browse recent map searches, display the Shortcuts and Delighters panel: Swipe in from the right side of the screen, or use the tilt gesture. Bookmarked locations appear atop the list. Swipe down the panel to view recent search items. Touch any item to instantly zoom to that location.

Locating a contact

The Maps app also provides information about a contact's location, as long as that information is available in the phone's address book. You can look up home, work, or other locations and even get directions.

The secret to finding a contact's location is to look in the Contacts app. Tap the contact's entry in the address book and look for the View Address item. It might instead be called View Home Address, View Work Address, and so on. After you touch that item, the Maps app starts and drops a pin at the given location. A card is displayed, providing further details as well as the Directions icon for navigation instructions:

- See Chapter 7 for more details about the phone's address book.
- See the later section "Getting directions" for information on using the Directions icon.

You can hone in on where your contacts are located by using the map. This trick works when you've specified an address for the contact — either home or work or another location. If so, your phone can easily help you find that location or even give you directions.

From Here to There

Finding a location on a map is only the first step. The next step is getting there. You can ask that old-timer at the gas station for directions. He'll say something like, "Go down the road a ways. When you come to where the old red barn used to be, turn left. Then when you see Granny Johnson's maple, turn right. It's just across from where old Cooter Williams buried his Mason jars."

That doesn't help.

Thanks to the Directions icon, you can easily obtain directions from your current location to a found location, or from between any two locations. You can also activate the phone's navigation feature to get turn-by-turn directions while viewing an interactive map. It's just like having a backseat driver, but one who knows where he's going and — *bonus* — has a Mute option.

Getting directions

One command that's associated with locations found in the Maps app is the one for getting directions. Look for the Directions icon, shown in the margin. That's your key to getting where you want to go. Here's how it works:

1. **Touch the Directions icon in a location's card.**

2. **Choose a method of transportation.**

   The available options are car, public transportation, and on-foot.

3. **Set a starting point.**

   Your current location is shown automatically, as illustrated in Figure 13-5. You can tap the X icon to clear that field and type another address.

Mode of transportation

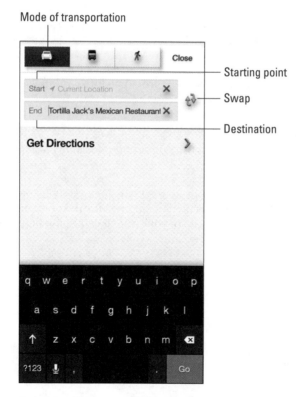

Starting point

Swap

Destination

Figure 13-5: Planning a trip.

The destination location is determined by the card you tapped in Step 1. Even so, you can tap that field to choose another destination.

4. **Ensure that the starting location and destination are what you want.**

   If they're backward, touch the Swap icon, which is labeled in Figure 13-5.

5. **Tap the text *Get Directions*.**

   One or more routes are listed on the screen, highlighted in blue, as shown in Figure 13-6.

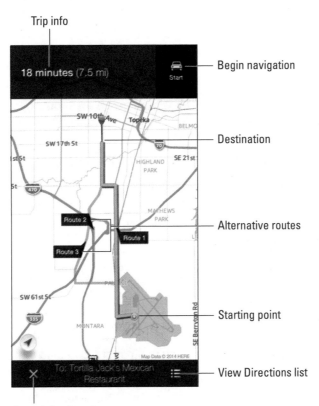

Figure 13-6: Plotting your course.

Here are some things you can do while viewing the route in the Maps app:

✔ Touch one of the routes to select a new route. The travel time and distance change to reflect the new route.

✔ Tap the Direction List icon to view the turn-by-turn directions.

✔ Touch the Start icon to begin navigation, as covered in the next section. (This icon is labeled Preview if your current location is not the starting location for the route displayed.)

The Maps app alerts you to any toll roads on the specified route. As you travel you can choose alternative, non-toll routes, if they're available. You're prompted to switch routes during navigation; see the next section.

Navigating to your destination

Maps and lists of directions are so 20th century. I don't know why anyone would bother, especially when your Fire phone features a digital copilot, in the form of voice navigation.

To use navigation, obey these steps:

1. **Choose a location on the map.**

   It must be a spot other than your current location. You can search for a spot, type a location, or long-press any part of the map.

2. **Tap the Directions icon.**

3. **Ensure that Current Location is chosen as the starting point.**

   If you don't see Current Location, touch the top entry and choose Current Location from the list.

4. **Touch the Get Directions command.**

5. **Tap the Start icon.**

   The first time you use this feature, you see Safety Guidelines. Read them if you must, and then tap the Continue button.

6. **Obey the directions as they're given.**

   The phone starts barking orders at you, and you're on your way.

While navigating, the phone displays an interactive map that shows your current location and turn-by-turn directions for reaching your destination. A digital voice tells you how far to go and when to turn, for example, and gives you other nagging advice, such as to sit up, be nice to other drivers, and call your mother once in a while.

 To exit navigation, touch the Close icon at the bottom of the screen. If you don't see this icon, tap the screen and it appears:

- ✔ The neat thing about the Navigation feature is that whenever you screw up, a new course is immediately calculated.

- ✔ When you tire of hearing the navigation voice, tap the Speaker icon at the bottom of the screen. If you don't see this icon, tap the screen and it appears.

REMEMBER

✓ The phone stays in Navigation mode until you exit. The Navigation icon appears on the phone's status bar whenever Navigation mode is active. Pull down the Notification panel and tap the item Turn by Turn Navigation to return to Navigation mode.

✓ While traveling, you can tap the List icon (shown in the margin) to review step-by-step directions as you go. Tap the X icon to dismiss the list and return to the Navigation screen.

WARNING!

✓ In Navigation mode, your phone consumes a *ton* of battery power. I highly recommend that you plug the phone into your car's power adapter (the "cigarette lighter") for the duration of the trip.

14

The Camera Chapter

▶ Taking a still picture

▶ Shooting video

▶ Deleting the image you just shot

▶ Turning on the flash

▶ Recording yourself

▶ Exploring Lenticular and Panorama

▶ Perusing the photo album

▶ Sharing pictures and videos

▶ Editing images

My guess is that cell phone technology is really tiny. A cell phone is the size of a bug. The manufacturers put that technology inside a box and said, "There's too much room! What else can we put in the box?" One of those items turned out to be a digital camera, one that's capable of taking both still images and recording video. "There!" the manufacturers exclaimed proudly, never bothering to think about whether a camera benefits a cell phone.

Actually, the key factor in having a camera in your phone is that now just about everyone has a camera wherever they go. No longer is it necessary to remember to bring the camera or to buy film or even to get the film developed. That way, should you see a UFO or Bigfoot, you're always ready. Perhaps that was another reason why they put a camera into the phone?

The Phone's Camera

A camera snob will tell you that no true camera has a ringtone. You know what? He's correct: Phones don't make the best cameras. Regardless, your Fire phone has a camera. It can capture both still and moving images. That task is carried out by using the Camera app:

- ✔ Press the Camera button to both unlock the phone and instantly start the Camera app. The button is found on the left side of the device.

- ✔ You can press the Camera button at any time to start the Camera app; the phone can be on or off.

- ✔ The Camera app doesn't provide any features for adjusting the image resolution or video quality. All images and videos are shot at the highest quality.

- ✔ The Fire phone's main, or rear, camera offers a resolution of 13MP (megapixels). It also features an LED flash. The front camera has a resolution of 2.1MP. Both cameras support a video resolution of 1080p, where the *p* stands for "*p*retty good."

Snapping a picture

After it's started, the Camera app takes over the phone, turning the touchscreen into a viewfinder. Figure 14-1 illustrates the Camera app's interface. It's set for taking still images, as shown by the Mode icon in the lower-left corner of the screen.

Shutter

Previous image   Focus square

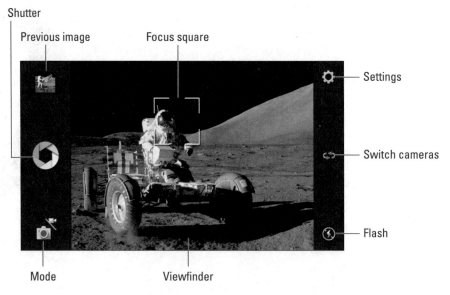

Settings

Switch cameras

Flash

Mode   Viewfinder

Figure 14-1: The Camera app.

To take a still image, follow these steps:

1. **Start the Camera app.**

   Pluck the app icon from the App Grid, or simply press the Camera button on the side of the phone.

2. **Ensure that the camera mode is set to Single Shot.**

   The Camera app shoots both still images and video. To snap a picture, tap the Mode icon. When the still camera (the SLR icon) appears up front, the Camera app is in Still Shot mode. Refer to Figure 14-1.

3. **Point the camera at the subject.**

4. **Tap the Shutter icon or press the Camera button.**

   The phone makes a noise and the picture is snapped.

After the image is snapped, it's saved and it appears in the thumbnail preview onscreen (refer to Figure 14-1). If you have the Image Review feature active, the image is previewed on the screen, where you can accept or reject it. See the later section "Deleting immediately after you shoot."

Pictures taken by the Camera app are stored in the Fire phone's internal storage. You can review the images by opening the Photos app, as described in the later section "Your Digital Photo Album."

✔ To focus the camera, tap the screen to adjust the focus square. The camera focuses on whichever item you choose, near or far.

✔ Your phone can take pictures in either landscape or portrait orientation. No matter how you take the picture, the image is stored upright. Even so, you can reorient images later; see the "Rotating pictures" section.

✔ You can take as many pictures as you like, as long as you don't run out of space for them in the phone's storage.

✔ If your pictures appear blurry, ensure that the camera lens on the back of the phone isn't dirty.

✔ Zooming in or out is done by using your fingers on the touchscreen: Spread to zoom in; pinch to zoom out.

✔ The phone doesn't use the Volume button to zoom! Some phones may use this technique, but on the Fire phone, pressing the Volume button snaps another photo.

Recording video

To capture moving pictures, or video, switch the camera mode to Video Recording: Tap the Mode icon, shown in Figure 14-1 and found in the lower-left corner of the screen. When the Video icon is shown "in front," the Camera app is set for Video mode.

In Video mode, the Shutter icon changes to the Record icon. Tap the Record icon to begin recording video. The Video Recording screen is shown in Figure 14-2.

Recording time   Stop recording

Snap still shot   Activate LED

Figure 14-2: Recording a video.

To stop recording, tap the Stop icon, shown in Figure 14-2. It replaces the Record icon while video is recording:

- ✔ An onscreen timer appears while video is recording. It informs you of the video's length.

- ✔ Tap the viewfinder while recording to adjust focus.

- ✔ To zoom in while recording, spread your fingers on the touchscreen. Pinch your fingers to zoom out.

- ✔ While recording, the Shutter icon appears in the lower-left corner of the screen. (Refer to Figure 14-2.) Tap that icon to grab a still image.

- ✔ Hold steady! The camera still works when you whip the tablet around, but wild gyrations render the video unwatchable.

Deleting immediately after you shoot

Sometimes you just can't wait to banish an image to bit hell. Either an annoyed person is standing next to you, begging that the photo be deleted, or you're just not happy and you feel the urge to smash into digital shards the picture you just took. Hastily follow these steps:

1. **Touch the image thumbnail that appears on the screen.**

   The thumbnail appears in the upper-left corner of the screen, as shown in Figure 14-1. When the phone is held vertically, the thumbnail is found in the lower-left corner.

2. **Tap the Delete icon.**

   If you don't see the icon, touch the screen so that the icon shows up.

3. **Touch the Delete button to confirm.**

   The image or video is gone.

If you want to immediately review every snapped image, activate the Image Review feature: Tap the Settings icon and slide the master control by Image Review to the On position.

With Image Review activated, you see an image preview appear just after you take the shot, similar to the one shown in Figure 14-3. Tap the Done icon to accept the image; tap Cancel to immediately delete it.

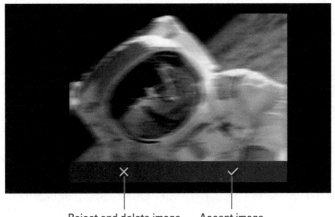

Reject and delete image   Accept image

Figure 14-3: Image Review in action.

The Image Review goes away after a moment, so be quick if you want to delete the image!

Also see the later section "Deleting photos and videos" for information on managing the phone's images.

Setting the flash

The Camera app features three flash settings for Single Shot mode. The current setting is shown on the screen, such as Flash Off in Figure 14-1. To change the flash setting, tap the Flash icon. It cycles through three different flash modes, illustrated in Table 14-1.

Table 14-1		Flash Settings
Icon	*Mode*	*Description*
	Auto Flash	Turns on the phone's flash in low-light situations, not when it's bright.
	Flash On	The flash always activates.
	Flash Off	The flash never activates, not even in low-light situations.

When you're shooting video, the flash can either be on or off. Tap the Flash icon (refer to Figure 14-2) to turn the LED lamp on or off:

- A good time to turn on the flash is when you're taking pictures of people or objects in front of something bright, such as a fuzzy kitten playing with a ball of yarn in front of an exploding gasoline truck.

- Using the flash, or *LED lamp,* while shooting video illuminates the subject in dark situations, but it also uses a lot of battery power. Be careful not to exhaust the phone's battery when using that feature.

Shooting yourself

That front-facing camera isn't just there so that the government can spy on you. It's actually for taking self-shots, called *selfies.* That makes it easier to video-chat, but it also avoids the awkward situation where you have to find a mirror to take your own picture.

To take your own mug shot, start the Camera app and switch to the front camera. Tap the Switch Cameras icon, illustrated earlier, in Figure 14-1. When you see yourself, you've done it correctly.

Smile. Click.

Touch the same icon again to switch back to the rear camera:

> ✓ You can shoot both still images and videos by using the front-facing camera. First change the Camera app's mode as described earlier in this chapter.

> ✓ The front camera does not have a flash.

Using special shooting modes

The Camera app sports two special shooting modes: Lenticular and Panorama. Both of these modes involve a little more work on your part, but the results are some interesting images that will instantly induce jealousy in other cell phone owners.

Both modes are chosen by tapping the Settings icon in the Camera app. Under the Camera Modes heading, choose Lenticular or Panorama. The next shot you take with the camera assumes that mode.

Lenticular mode captures multiple shots of a single subject. The result is a 3D-like image that takes advantage of the phone's Dynamic Perspective feature, similar to the lock screen image on the Fire phone. To take that image, you choose Lenticular and then take up to 12 shots of a single object. Each time you tap the Shutter button, move the camera slightly in one direction. A ghost image of the previous shot helps you keep things lined up.

The Panoramic mode lets you take a very wide or very tall shot. Enter that mode, and then position the camera to the far left or right (or top or bottom) of the subject, such as a wide vista or a tall building. Tap the Shutter icon, and then use the onscreen guide to help you capture the rest of the image. Tap the Stop icon to stop at any time, or just wait until the image stops by itself:

> ✓ Tap the X icon on the screen to exit from Lenticular mode or Panorama mode.

> ✓ Lenticular and panoramic images appear in the Photos app, along with all other images taken by the Fire phone camera.

> ✓ The Lenticular images you capture react to the phone's movements, allowing you to view the image in a quasi-3D manner.

Your Digital Photo Album

The pictures and videos you take with your phone don't simply disappear after you touch the Camera app's Shutter icon. Although you can generally preview a previously shot picture or video, the place you go to look at the gamut of visual media is the app named Photos. It's the phone's digital photo album.

Visiting the Photos app

Start the Photos app by locating its icon on the App Grid. You might also find a copy riding the Carousel on the Home screen.

The main screen in the Photos app lists all photos stored in the camera. You can narrow down the images displayed by choosing a category from the Navigation panel, shown in Figure 14-4.

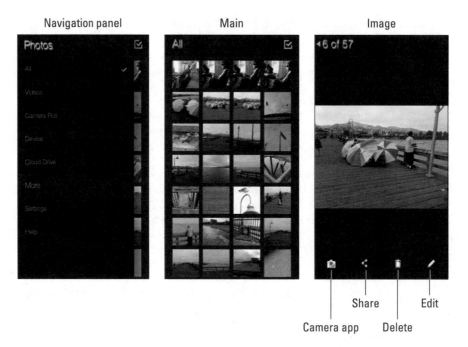

Navigation panel   Main   Image

Share   Edit

Camera app   Delete

Figure 14-4: The Photos app.

Tap an individual image to view it on a screen by itself. The icons, shown in Figure 14-4, may disappear after a while; touch the screen to bring them back.

When viewing an image, you can reorient the phone; pinch or spread your fingers on the screen to zoom.

Videos appear with the Play icon on the screen. Touch that icon to play the video. As the video is playing, touch the screen again to see the controls to pause the video:

 ✔ The Camera Roll album contains pictures you've shot using the phone's camera.

✓ The Device album contains images downloaded from the Internet, as well as images synchronized with a computer. Choose Device from the Navigation panel, and then tap an album to view its contents.

Finding your photos in the cloud

Photos snapped on the Fire phone are automatically synchronized with the Amazon cloud. That's fancy talk for Internet storage, which is something that comes with your phone.

To view the contents of your online photo album, choose Cloud Drive from the Photos app's Navigation panel. You see a list of online albums, including the Fire Camera Roll. You can peruse those albums and images from the Photos app, or you can view them on the Internet.

To view your Amazon Cloud photos on the Internet, use a computer's web browser to visit Amazon.com. Under the Your Account menu, choose Your Cloud Drive. Sign in by using your Amazon account when prompted. You see your cloud storage, similar to what's shown in Figure 14-5. Click the Pictures folder to view your Amazon Fire phone images.

Also see Chapter 19 for more information on cloud storage and your phone.

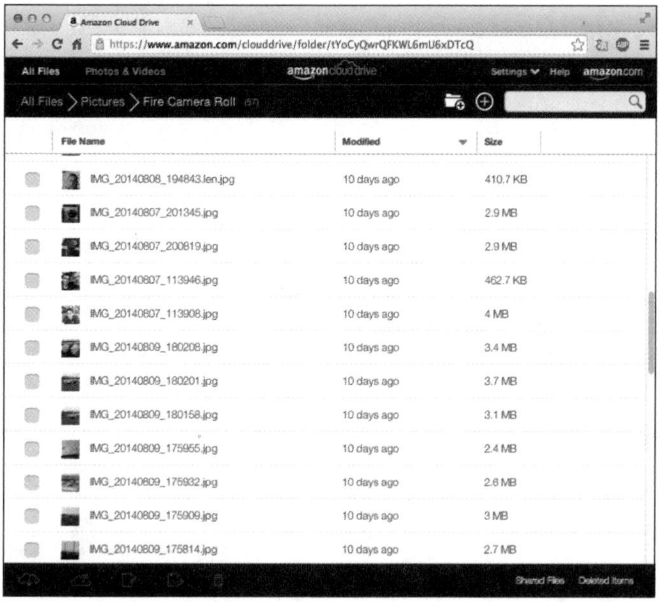

Figure 14-5: The Amazon Cloud drive.

Sharing pictures and videos

The key to getting images out of the phone and into the world is to look for the Share icon, shown in the margin. Touch that icon while viewing an image (refer to Figure 14-4, on the far right), and peruse the apps shown on the list to choose a sharing method. Here are some of your choices:

Bluetooth: Send the picture or video to another device via the Bluetooth connection. That other device might be a printer, for example, in which case you can print the picture. See Chapter 18 for details on sharing with Bluetooth.

Email: Attach the image to a new message you compose using the Email app.

Facebook: Share the photo on the Facebook app.

Messaging: Send the photo or video along in a multimedia text message. The image or video is automatically resized, although some videos are too large to send in this manner.

Additional options may appear on the Share screen, depending upon which apps are installed on your phone.

Image Management

The Photos app is more than just a photo album. It also sports features that let you perform some minor image surgery. This section discusses a few of the more interesting options.

Cropping an image

When the camera has captured more of an image than you desire to keep, you crop out the unwanted portions. This is the same thing teenagers did ages ago to remove unwanted former boyfriends and girlfriends from their pictures. Rather than use a pair of scissors, you use the Crop command in the Photos app. It works like this:

1. **Summon the image you want to crop.**

   You must view the image on the screen by itself.

2. **Tap the Edit icon.**

   If you don't see that icon, tap the screen and it shows up.

3. **Choose Crop.**

4. **Work the crop rectangle.**

   You can drag the rectangle around to choose which part of the image to crop. Drag an edge of the rectangle to resize the left and right or top and bottom sides. Or drag a corner of the rectangle to change the rectangle's size proportionally. Use Figure 14-6 as your guide.

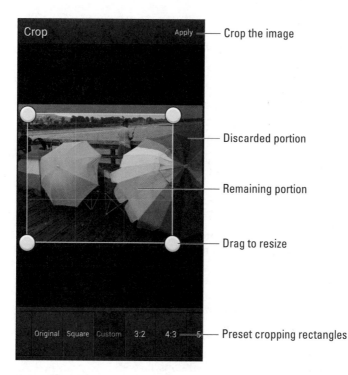

   Crop — Apply ——— Crop the image

   ——— Discarded portion

   ——— Remaining portion

   ——— Drag to resize

   Original Square Custom 3:2 4:3 5 ——— Preset cropping rectangles

Figure 14-6: Working the crop thing.

5. **Touch the Apply button when you've finished cropping.**

   The portion of the image within the rectangle is saved as a new image; the rest is discarded.

6. **Tap the Done button to exit the image editor.**

The original image is retained after you crop, so don't be afraid of botching up something.

Rotating pictures

Which way is up? It depends on how you orient yourself. If an image refuses to position itself in the orientation you prefer as "up," you can change it. Follow these steps:

1. **Display the image you want to crop.**

2. **Tap the Edit icon.**

    Touch the screen briefly if you don't see that icon.

3. **Choose the Orientation command.**

4. **Tap the Rotate or Flip buttons to position the image the way you prefer.**

5. **Touch the Apply button to save your changes.**

6. **Tap the Done button to exit image editing.**

The rotated or flipped image is saved as a new copy; the original image remains as it was.

Deleting photos and videos

It's entirely possible, and often desirable, to remove unwanted, embarrassing, or questionably legal images and videos from the phone's photo album. It's cinchy:

To delete an image, follow these steps:

1. **View the image you want to destroy in the Photos app.**

2. **Touch the Delete icon.**

3. **Place a check mark by the item Also Delete from Your Cloud Drive if you want to remove that copy as well.**

    If you leave that item unchecked, a copy of the photo remains on the cloud drive, and it shows up in the Photos app again.

4. **Touch the Delete button to confirm.**

    Poof! It's gone.

Well, it's gone unless you decided to keep the Cloud Drive copy. In that case, the image shows up when All photos are viewed or when the Cloud Drive item is chosen from the Navigation panel.

You can't undelete an image you've deleted. There's no way to recover such an image using available tools on the phone.

15

Music to Go

*P*ortable music is nothing new. Historians tell us how the Roman emperor Nero would wander the streets followed by an orchestra towed on an elaborate ox cart. Smartly dressed businessmen of the 1920s would hoist phonographs on their shoulders and parade about, enjoying their music. And starting in *this* century, smartphone designers decided that it would be cool if their mobile phones also played music. It all makes sense.

Listen to the Music

Your Fire phone is ready to entertain you with music whenever you want to hear it. Simply plug in the headphones, summon the Music app, and choose tunes to match your mood. It's truly blissful — well, until someone calls you and the phone ceases being a musical instrument and returns to being the ball-and-chain of the digital era.

Browsing the music library

The Music app is illustrated in Figure 15-1. If you're displeased with the quantity of available music or you don't see any music, refer to the later section "More Music for Your Phone."

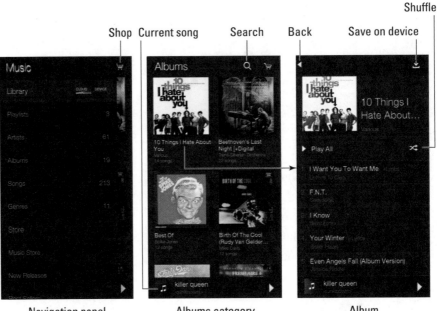

Figure 15-1: The Music app.

To view your music library, choose a category from under the Library heading found on the Navigation panel, as shown in Figure 15-1. Your music library appears on the main Play Music screen. Swipe through the list to peruse your choices. Tap an album to view its songs, or view all the songs by choosing the Songs category.

The phone's music library is found in one of two places: stored on the Amazon music cloud or on the device itself, saved in internal storage. A master control on the Navigation panel determines which location's music you view in the Music app. You cannot view both locations at one time.

Playing a tune

To listen to music on your phone, you first find a song in your music library, as described in the preceding section. After you find the song, you touch its title. The song plays on another screen, similar to the one shown in Figure 15-2.

While the song is playing, you're free to do anything else with the phone. To access the song from the Music app, look for it at the bottom of the screen (refer to Figure 15-1). Or, any time you're using the phone, pull down the Notification panel and choose the playing song from the list.

Repeat   Play/Pause   Shuffle

Lyrics

Figure 15-2: A song is playing.

After the song has finished playing, the next song in the list plays.

The next song doesn't play if you have the Shuffle icon activated (refer to Figure 15-2). In that case, the Play Music app randomly chooses another song from the same list. Who knows which one is next? Shuffle is on when it's colored orange.

The next song might not play either when you have the Repeat option on: The three Repeat settings are off (white), on (orange), and repeat once (the number 1). To change settings, simply touch either the Shuffle icon or Repeat icon.

To stop the song from playing, touch the Pause icon (labeled in Figure 15-2):

✔ Some songs have the Lyrics feature on the Shortcuts and Delighters panel, as shown in Figure 15-2. Sing along with your favorite tunes — especially when you're out of earshot from any other living thing.

✔ The volume is set by using the Volume key on the side of the phone: Up is louder, down is quieter.

- Determining which song plays next depends on how you chose the song that's playing. If you chose a song by artist, all songs from that artist play, one after the other. When you choose a song by album, that album plays. Choosing a song from the entire song list causes all songs in the phone to play.

- To choose which songs play after each other, create a playlist. See the "Organize Your Tunes" section, later in this chapter.

- After the last song in the list plays, the phone stops playing songs — unless you have the Repeat option on, in which case the song or list plays again.

Keeping music on the phone

Music accessed by the Music app exists not on the phone, but on the cloud. Specifically, music is stored on the Internet, available by way of Amazon's cloud music service. The Music app merely provides a window to your songs. It all works fine, providing you have an Internet connection. When you don't, you can save music from the cloud to your phone.

The technical term for saving music from the cloud to your phone is *download*. To make that happen, look for the Download icon, shown in the margin. Tap that icon to download a song or an album. If you don't see the icon, long-press the song and choose the Download command:

- Music downloaded to the phone is available to play at any time.

- To review the music saved on the phone, display the Music app's Navigation panel and slide the master control to Device. Only music kept on the phone appears in the Music app.

- Music available via the Amazon cloud music service can be downloaded to the phone *and* is available online. The only difference is that the downloaded copy is always available, whether you have an Internet connection or not.

- See the later section "Deleting music" for information on removing the downloaded copy of a song. Doing so doesn't remove the song from the cloud.

Being the life of the party

You need to do four things to make your Fire phone the soul of your next shindig or soirée:

- Connect it to external speakers.

- Use the Shuffle command.

- Set the Repeat command.

- Provide plenty of drinks and snacks.

The external speakers can be provided by anything from a custom media dock or a stereo to the sound system on the Times Square Jumbotron. As long as the device has a standard line input, you're good.

Oh, and you need an audio cable. Get one with a mini-headphone connector for the phone's headphone jack and an audio jack that matches the output device. Look for such a cable at Radio Shack or any store where the employees wear name tags.

After you connect your phone to the speakers, start the Music app. Choose the party playlist you've created, per the directions elsewhere in this chapter. If you want the songs to play in random order, touch the Shuffle icon.

You might also consider choosing the Repeat command so that all songs in the list repeat:

- ✐ To play all songs saved on your phone, choose the Songs category and touch the first song in the list.

- ✐ See the later section "Organize Your Tunes" for information on creating playlists. Build one playlist for your book club and another one for your theater friends.

- ✐ Enjoy your party, and please drink responsibly.

More Music for Your Phone

How much music is enough? That's for you to find out!

More music flows into your Fire phone in a number of ways. Amazon would like for you to purchase music at its online music store. Doing so makes Amazon's stockholders rejoice. Another way, and one that causes less rejoicing, is to copy music from a computer to the Amazon music cloud. That's the 21st century equivalent of kids in the 1950s swapping 45s as opposed to spending their hard-earned nickels at the music store.

Buying music at the Music Store

Amazon is more than happy to sell you all the music you can stuff into your Fire phone. And it's not just about money: Occasionally, music goes on sale or is offered at no cost. You must keep a keen eye out for such things, so visit the Music Store frequently!

To visit the Music Store, choose the Music Store item from the Navigation panel. Or, if you see the Shop icon on the screen, tap it (refer to Figure 15-1). The Music Store's main screen looks similar to the one shown in Figure 15-3.

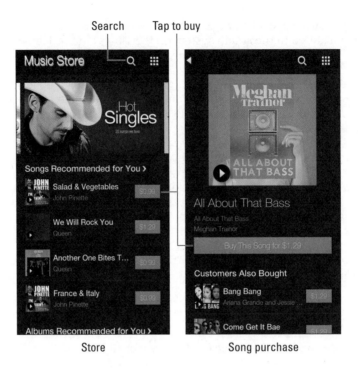

Search   Tap to buy

Store   Song purchase

Figure 15-3: The Music Store.

Browse the Music Store by swiping the screen and perusing what's available.

 Use the Search icon to locate specific songs, artists, or genres.

Tap a song or an album to view its specific screen, similar to the one shown on the right in Figure 15-3.

 Use the Play icon to preview 30 seconds of a song.

To purchase a song or an album, tap the Buy button. The button may also simply list the price. After tapping, the button changes color and says only *Buy.* Tap the button again to make the purchase.

The purchase is made immediately, based upon your mobile device's 1-Click settings. See Chapter 17 for information on reviewing or changing this setting.

 The music you buy isn't copied to your phone. It shows up, but it plays over the Internet. That means you can hear it only when the phone has an Internet connection. To ensure that the music is always available, see the earlier section "Keeping music on the phone."

 ✔ All music sales are final.

 ✔ You can review your music purchases by visiting the Purchased or Recently Added to Cloud playlists. See the later section "Reviewing your playlists."

 ✔ Eventually, Amazon sends you an email summary of your music purchases.

 ✔ I recommend downloading music while the phone is connected to a Wi-Fi network. That way, you don't run the risk of suffering a data surcharge on your cellular plan. See Chapter 18 for information on activating Wi-Fi.

"I hear it and I want to buy it!"

You can use the Firefly app on your phone to quickly identify any song playing in your immediate vicinity. And I mean *song* playing, as opposed to people singing or playing musical instruments. This music-identification feature works best with music you can purchase (hint-hint).

To identify any music that's playing, first tell everyone to shut up. Start the Firefly app, or press and hold the Camera/Firefly button on the side of the phone. Eventually Firefly starts, as shown in Figure 15-4. Tap the Music icon.

Tap to listen

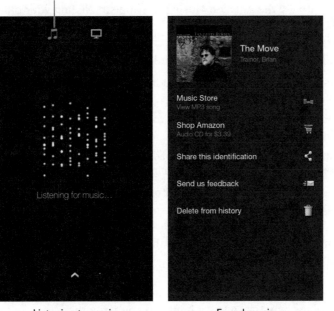

Listening to music   Found music

Figure 15-4: Using Firefly to find music.

In mere moments, the song is identified and you have the ability to purchase it — right then and there!

See Chapter 17 for more Firefly fun.

Copying music from your computer to the cloud

Gone is the household stereo system. Taking its place is the computer, which acts as a combination tuner, amplifier, and turntable. You've probably copied over a goodly chunk of your CDs to the computer — maybe even records that you've digitized. If so, you can share your digital music library with your Fire phone.

The best way to get music out of your computer and into your phone is to upload your computer's music library to the Amazon cloud in the Internet. This option has the bonus of making the music available to all devices that can access the Internet, as long as they have an Amazon cloud app installed.

To upload your music, obey these steps:

1. **Visit** www.amazon.com **on your PC or Macintosh.**

2. **Under the Your Account menu, choose Your Music Library.**

   If you're prompted to log in, do so.

   Eventually the Amazon Music page appears, listing your online music. The tunes you see are effectively the same that you find on the Fire phone in the Music app.

3. **Click the Import Your Music link.**

   As this book goes to press, that link is found on the left side of the screen, at the bottom.

4. **Obey the onscreen directions to download the Amazon Music Importer utility.**

   An installer program is downloaded. Open that program, and then follow its directions to set up and configure the Amazon Music Importer.

5. **Use the Importer to import all or selected music to the Amazon Music Library.**

   I clicked the Import All button, which takes more time, but it makes the entire PC library of music available online.

6. **Click the Close button when you're done.**

The songs you upload appear instantly on the computer's web browser screen. They may take a few minutes to appear in the Music app's library on your Fire phone, but they'll be there!

TECHNICAL STUFF

Copying music directly to the phone

A more direct, albeit less sane, method of getting music from your computer to the phone is to copy it directly: Hook the computer to the phone by using a USB cable, as described in Chapter 19. Use the file copying techniques presented in that chapter to copy over your tunes. This trick works for both the PC and Macintosh computers.

Be forewarned: The Fire phone doesn't recognize the Windows Media Player music file format, known as WMA, for Windows Media Audio. If you can, copy only MP3 files from the computer to the phone. And if you're really

nerdy, create album folders beneath the Music folder on the phone. Copy the individual music files into their associated albums. (If that doesn't make sense, don't worry about it.)

Accessing directly copied music requires knowing a special trick: Open the Music app, and display the Navigation panel. Slide the master control from Cloud to Device and you'll find your manually copied music. This extra step makes that copied music a bit more difficult to access because it's not mixed in with the cloud music. I suppose Amazon is trying to tell you something.

Organize Your Tunes

Yes, I've purchased an entire album just because I liked one song. That happens less today, thanks to online music stores. Even so, putting together collections of your own favorite songs, or songs you like to listen to at certain times or in certain moods, is something everyone does. To accommodate that activity in the Music app, you use the Playlist tool.

Reviewing your playlists

To view any playlists that you've already created or that have been preset on the phone, display the Music app's Navigation panel and choose Playlists. You see a list of playlists, similar to what's shown in Figure 15-5.

To see which songs are in a playlist, touch a playlist. To play the songs in the playlist, touch the first song in the list.

Building playlists

The Music app features two automatic playlists — one for songs you've purchased and another for songs recently added to the cloud. Beyond that, the playlists you see are those you create. Here's how it works:

1. **Choose Playlists from the Navigation panel in the Music app.**

2. **Tap the Create New Playlist button.**

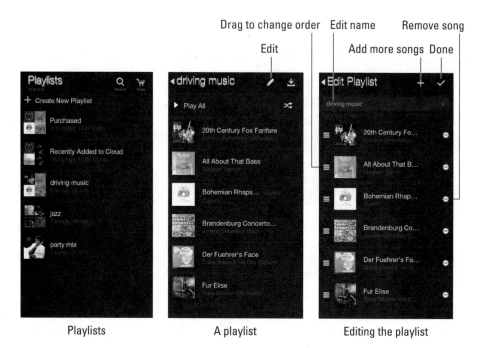

Figure 15-5: Playlists in the Play Music app.

3. **Type a name for the playlist, and then tap the Save button.**

   Keep the name short and descriptive.

   After naming the playlist, you see the Add to *Playlist* screen, where *playlist* is the name of the playlist, such as *1990s,* shown in Figure 15-6.

   All songs available to your phone appear on the screen. Swipe the tabs left and right to display the songs by artist, album, song, or genre, as shown in Figure 15-6.

4. **Tap the Plus icon (+) by a song to add it to the playlist.**

5. **Repeat Step 4 over and over to build the playlist.**

6. **Tap the Done button to create the playlist.**

   The playlist appears on the list of playlists, under the name you chose in Step 3.

You can edit the playlist to modify it at any time. Select the playlist and tap the Edit button, shown earlier, in Figure 15-5. Remove songs by tapping the Minus icon (–) next to the song; add more songs by tapping the Plus icon atop the screen. Rearrange the order by dragging up or down the tabs on the left end of a song. Refer to Figure 15-5 for details.

Songs list   Add song

Scroll categories   Done

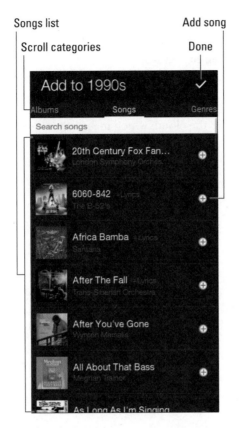

Figure 15-6: Adding songs to a playlist.

✐ You can have as many playlists as you like on the phone and stick as many songs as you like into them. Adding songs to a playlist doesn't noticeably affect the phone's storage capacity.

✐ Removing a song from a playlist doesn't delete the song from the music library; see the next section.

✐ To delete a playlist, long-press its entry on the Playlists screen. Choose the Delete from Cloud command. Tap the Delete button to confirm, and the playlist is gone. This action doesn't delete any of the playlist's songs. For that process, see the next section.

Deleting music

To remove music from your phone, heed these directions:

1. **Long-press the song or album.**

2. **Choose the command Delete from Cloud or Remove from Device.**

When the Remove from Device command appears, the item was either purchased online or copied directly to the phone.

3. **Tap the Delete button to confirm.**

The confirmation doesn't appear when you choose the Remove from Device command.

The song is removed from the cloud, which means that it's pretty much gone forever — unless you send another copy to the cloud, as described elsewhere in this chapter.

When you delete a purchased song, it's only removed from the device. The song is still available in the cloud and can be copied to the phone again, if you choose to do so.

Fire Phone Radio

Although they're not broadcast radio stations, some sources on the Internet — *Internet radio* sites — play music. To listen to these services, you need the proper app, which is obtained for free from the Appstore. I can recommend these apps:

- Spotify Music
- TuneIn Radio
- Pandora Radio

Spotify provides access to millions of popular songs based on genre, artist, label, and so on. You can browse by category or choose to listen to a channel based on your mood. Spotify lets you create custom playlists that you can share with others. It offers integration with the social networking sites Facebook and Twitter.

The TuneIn Radio app gives you access to hundreds of Internet radio stations broadcasting around the world. They're organized by category, so you can find just about whatever you want. Many of the radio stations are also broadcast radio stations, so odds are good that you can find a local station or two, which you can listen to on your phone.

Pandora Radio lets you select music based on your mood and then customizes, according to your feedback, the tunes you listen to. The app works like the Internet site www.pandora.com, in case you're familiar with it. The nifty thing about Pandora is that the more you listen, the better the app finds music you like:

✔ These apps are free, but paid versions might also be available. The paid versions offer wider selections and no advertising.

✔ It's best to listen to Internet radio when your phone is connected to the Internet via a Wi-Fi connection. Streaming music can use a lot of your cellular data plan's data allotment.

✔ Internet music of the type delivered by the apps mentioned in this section is referred to by the nerds as *streaming music*. That's because the music arrives on your phone as a continuous download from the source. Unlike music you download and save, streaming music is played as it comes in and isn't stored long-term.

Other Things It Does

*T*he first few primitive cell phones featured mini-programs. Today these programs are called *apps,* but they're nothing new. I remember a Tetris game I played on one of my first cell phones. The phone also had an address book, a scheduler, and even an alarm clock. Back then, such things were imaginative and impressive.

Today, the myriad apps that come with a cell phone are still imaginative and impressive. They demonstrate the versatility of the device. A piece of technology such as the Fire phone is about more than making phone calls. This chapter covers many of the useful and, occasionally, necessary things the phone can do with its various apps.

Time to Wake Up

Thanks to your cellular provider, the Fire phone keeps constant, accurate track of the time. The time is displayed on the lock screen and the status bar and in the Clock app. But the Clock app is more than just a tick-tock clock; it has several useful time-related features.

Figure 16-1 illustrates the Clock app's Alarms screen. You see two alarms set — one for 4:20 AM Wednesday and another for 5:50 AM on weekdays. The current time is also displayed.

Current time   Create new alarm

Alarm clock   Timer   Alarm set

World clocks   Stopwatch

Figure 16-1: The Clock app.

You create alarms by tapping the Add button and then working the onscreen controls to set the alarm time and the days of the week (repeat value), and to choose an annoying sound to play when the alarm triggers.

Other features of the Clock app include a world clock, which displays the time in various major cities around the globe; a timer, which I use to remind me when to move forward the laundry; and a stopwatch, which I'd use if I ever bothered to run laps:

✔ Alarms must be set, or else they won't trigger. Set an alarm by sliding its master control to the On position.

✔ When an alarm is set, the Alarm icon appears on the status bar. The icon is your clue that an alarm is set and ready to trigger.

✔ Turning off an alarm doesn't delete the alarm.

  ✔ To delete an alarm, long-press it and choose the Remove command.

  ✔ The alarm doesn't work when you turn off the phone. The alarm triggers, however, when the phone is locked. The alarm also sounds when you've silenced the phone.

  ✔ So tell me: Do alarms go *off,* or do they go *on?*

Become a Math Wiz

The Calculator is perhaps the oldest of all traditional cell phone apps. It's probably also the least confusing and frustrating app to use — providing you don't orient the phone horizontally.

Figure 16-2 illustrates the Calculator app, shown in both vertical (OMG, how simple!) and horizontal (I need an Excedrin) views.

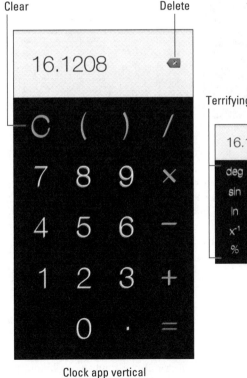

Clock app vertical

Clock app horizontal

Figure 16-2: The Calculator app.

I use the calculator most often to determine the tip at a restaurant. In Figure 16-2, I calculated an 18 percent tip on a tab of $89.56. That's kind of silly, seeing how the Delighters panel in the Clock app has a tip calculator, shown in Figure 16-3.

Check amount:	$89.56
Tip %:	18%
Split:	4
Tip/person:	$4.03
Total/person:	$26.42

```
7    8    9

4    5    6

1    2    3

     0    C
```

Figure 16-3: Tip delighter.

The Tip calculator on the Delighters and Shortcuts panel also figures out how to split the ticket and calculates the per-person charge per check. That trick may not make you a math whiz, but it will impress the waiter.

Waitstaff frequently work for subminimum wage. Do give them a decent tip. They earn it.

Your Daily Schedule

"What's a datebook, Grandpa?"

Well, never mind. You don't have to worry about having or using a datebook or even knowing what one is, because you have a phone. The phone has the

Calendar app. It's well suited to keep track of your schedule and your appointments, and it even reminds you before an event and tells you how to get there:

⊭ The Fire phone's Calendar app is coordinated with your online accounts. If you use the Google calendar, the Yahoo! calendar, or even a corporate calendar, as long as those accounts are associated with your phone, their scheduled appointments appear in the Calendar app.

⊭ See Chapter 2 for information on adding accounts to the phone.

Browsing dates and appointments

Figure 16-4 shows the Calendar app's three views: List, Day, and Month. Tap the Today icon to instantly zoom to the current day. The Shortcuts and Delighters panel shows your next, immediate event.

Figure 16-4: The Calendar app.

Place the phone into the horizontal orientation to see Week view, shown in Figure 16-5. I check this view at the start of the week to remind me of what's coming up.

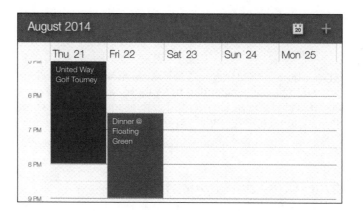

Figure 16-5: Week view.

- Events are color-coded based on the source as well as on individual calendar categories.

- Swipe the screen left and right to scroll the various calendar views: Day, Week, and Month.

- The current day is highlighted in Month view and Week view. A horizontal bar marks the current time in Day view.

Reviewing appointments

To see more detail about an event, touch it. When you're using Month view, touch the event's date to see Week view. Then choose the event again to see its details, similar to the event shown in Figure 16-6.

The details you see depends on how much information was recorded when the event was created. Some events have only a minimum of information; others may have details, such as a location for the event. When the event's location is listed, you can touch that location, and the Maps app pops up to show you where the event is being held:

- Birthdays and a few other events on the calendar may be pulled from the phone's address book or from certain social networking apps. That probably explains why some events are listed twice: They're pulled in from two sources.

- To quickly view upcoming events, choose the Calendar app from the Home screen's Carousel. It lists all your upcoming appointments.

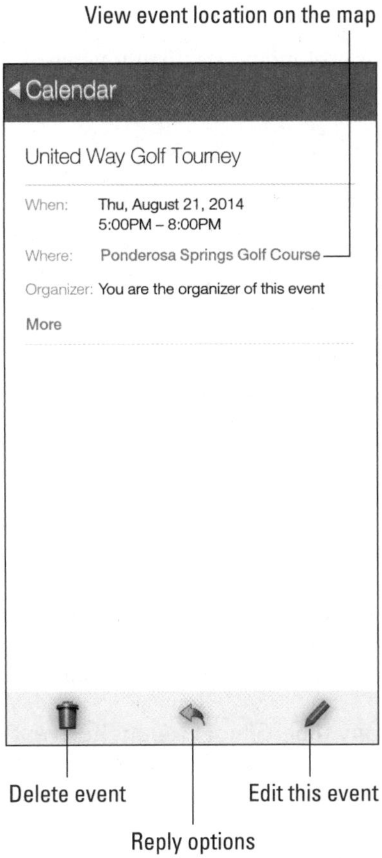

View event location on the map

◀ Calendar

United Way Golf Tourney

When: Thu, August 21, 2014
            5:00PM – 8:00PM

Where: Ponderosa Springs Golf Course

Organizer: **You are the organizer of this event**

More

Delete event   Edit this event

Reply options

Figure 16-6: Event details.

Creating an event

The key to making the calendar work is to add events: appointments, things to do, meetings, or full-day events such as birthdays or teeth cleaning. To create an event, follow these steps in the Calendar app:

1. **Select the day for the event.**

   It's best to use Day view, where you can touch the starting time for the new event.

2. **Touch the New icon.**

   The New Event screen appears. Your job now is to fill in the blanks to create the event.

3. **Set information for the event.**

   The basic information you can set includes the following:

   - Event title

   - Event date, starting time, and ending time

   - Whether the event repeats

   - A reminder for the event

   - The account or calendar or event category

   The more information you supply, the more detailed the event, and the more you can do with it on your phone.

4. **Touch the Done or Save button to create the event.**

   The Done button has a check mark by it, and it's located in the upper-right corner of the New Event screen.

The new event appears on the calendar, reminding you that you need to do something on such-and-such a day.

When an event's day and time arrives, an event reminder notification appears on the lock screen. You can also peruse event reminders by pulling down the Notification panel. The event reminders persist until you dismiss them:

- ✔ You can change an event at any time: Simply touch the event to bring up more information, and then touch the Edit icon to make modifications (refer to Figure 16-6).

- ✔ My advice is to type location information for an event as though you're typing a search query for the Maps app. When the event is displayed, the location becomes a link; touch the link to see where on the map you need to go.

- ✔ When the event lasts all day, such as a birthday or your mother-in-law's visit that was supposed to last for an hour, touch the All Day box to add a check mark.

- ✔ When you have events that repeat twice a month (say, on the first and third Mondays), you need to create two separate events — one for the first Monday and another for the third. Then have each event repeat monthly.

- ✔ You can set additional reminders by touching the Add Reminder icon.

- ✔ To remove an event, touch the event to bring up more information and then touch the Delete icon. Touch the OK button to confirm. When deleting repeating events, you need to specify whether all events are being removed or only the one.

Let's Play a Game

For all its seriousness and technology, one of the best uses of the Fire phone is to play games. I'm not talking about silly arcade games (though I admit that they're fun). No, I'm talking about some serious portable gaming.

To whet your appetite, the Fire phone comes with a small taste of what the device can do in regard to gaming; look for preinstalled game apps on the Apps Grid. That will get you started.

Additional games are available at the Appstore, which is covered in Chapter 17:

> ✔ The best games are those custom-designed to use the Fire phone's Dynamic Perspective feature. The Monkey Buddy game features this effect. I confess that it's not very engaging, however.

> ✔ Some games offer Amazon coins as a bonus. See Chapter 17 for more information on Amazon coins.

Don't Tell Kindle

Your Fire phone isn't a Kindle phone, but you can read all the books and magazines available to the Kindle, thanks to the Kindle eBook reader app. It's preinstalled on your phone and available on the App Grid.

Using the Kindle app

The Kindle app's main interface is illustrated in Figure 16-7. It shows a scrolling list of your eBook library — plus, it gives you quick access to the Kindle Store to buy even more books. And everyone should buy more books.

Books in your Kindle library are saved in the Amazon cloud. You have access to them only when the phone has Internet access — that is, unless you choose to save a copy of the books on your phone. Two such books are shown as saved in Figure 16-7.

To keep a book on the phone, or the "device," long-press the book in the library and choose the Download command. The book is then saved, and made available for reading even when an Internet connection isn't available — like in an airplane.

Book is saved on device   Search   Shop

Navigation panel   Library   Shortcuts and Delighters

Figure 16-7: The Kindle app.

Getting some reading material

You can get two types of books for reading on your Fire phone: good and terrible. Regardless of their satisfaction level, the two types of books can be free or paid. Mostly older titles and classics are free; the rest are paid. Shopping for books works like this:

1. **Start the Kindle app.**

2. **Display the Navigation pane.**

3. **Choose Shop.**

   The Shop category has many subcategories, so if you see something more specific, choose it.

   One category worthy of checking is Monthly Deals. If you're an avid reader, you may appreciate some of the offers presented.

4. **Search for the book you want, or browse the categories.**

   As a suggestion, search for *free classics* to find something free to download.

5. **Touch to select a title.**

   The Price button tells you how much the title costs, such as Buy for $3.99. A free title has Free to Buy listed as its price; otherwise, you see the book's cost displayed.

If you're timid about paying for an eBook, choose the Download Sample button instead. A snippet from the book is downloaded, which you can peruse at your leisure at no charge.

6. **Touch the Buy button.**

   The purchase is made instantly.

   Purchases are made by using the payment method you've configured for 1-Click buying. See Chapter 17 for details.

7. **Touch the Read Now button to read your new book, or keep shopping.**

   As an author, I recommend that you keep shopping. Never stop buying books.

See the next section for tips on reading eBooks:

✔ You receive an email confirmation message describing your purchase. The email appears even when you "buy" a free eBook.

✔ Not every title is available as an eBook.

Reading on your phone

The whole point of getting an eBook is so that you can read the thing, flipping the digital pages just the same as you would in a real book, although I don't recommend that you lick your finger to turn the page. (See Chapter 23 for information on cleaning the phone's screen.)

After choosing a book from the Kindle app's library, you see it open on the touchscreen. (The book may have to download first, if it's not already stored on your phone.)

The first time you open a book, you see the first page. Otherwise, you see the page you were last reading.

Figure 16-8 illustrates the basic reading maneuvers: You can touch the left or right sides of the screen to flip a page left or right, respectively. You can also swipe the pages left or right.

You can drag the progress meter at the bottom of the screen to skim back and forth through the book.

Display the Navigation panel to view the eBook's table of contents. Tap a chapter heading to jump to that location in the book.

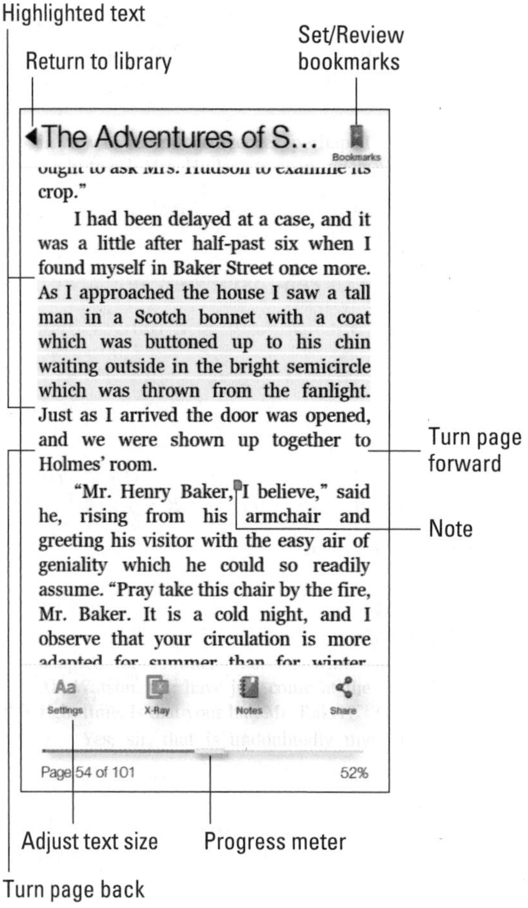

Highlighted text

Return to library

Set/Review
bookmarks

◄The Adventures of S... 🔖
                        Bookmarks

ought to ask Mrs. Hudson to examine its
crop."

I had been delayed at a case, and it
was a little after half-past six when I
found myself in Baker Street once more.
As I approached the house I saw a tall
man in a Scotch bonnet with a coat
which was buttoned up to his chin
waiting outside in the bright semicircle
which was thrown from the fanlight.
Just as I arrived the door was opened,
and we were shown up together to
Holmes' room.

"Mr. Henry Baker, I believe," said
he, rising from his armchair and
greeting his visitor with the easy air of
geniality which he could so readily
assume. "Pray take this chair by the fire,
Mr. Baker. It is a cold night, and I
observe that your circulation is more
adapted for summer than for winter

Aa   📖   📔   <
Settings X-Ray   Notes   Share

Page 54 of 101   52%

Turn page
forward

Note

Adjust text size   Progress meter

Turn page back

Figure 16-8: Reading with Kindle.

Long-pressing text selects the text on the screen, similar to selecting any text
on the Fire phone, as discussed in Chapter 4. You can choose to highlight the
text, share it, copy it, or use it to search the web. Figure 16-9 illustrates your
options.

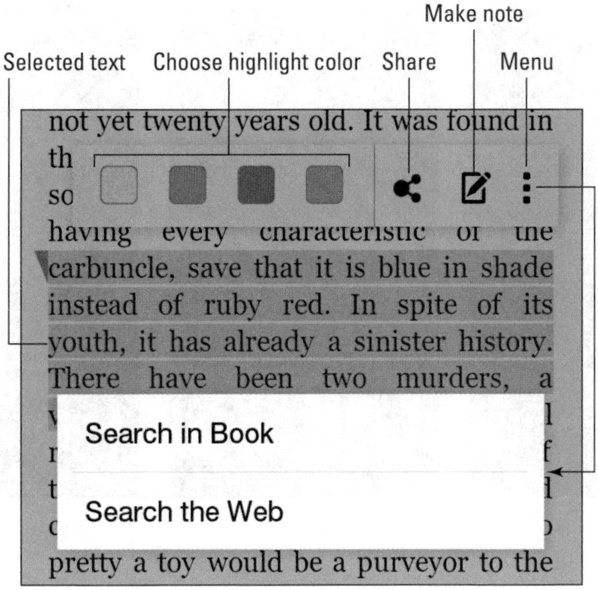

Make note

Selected text   Choose highlight color   Share   Menu

not yet twenty years old. It was found in
th
so

having every characteristic of the
carbuncle, save that it is blue in shade
instead of ruby red. In spite of its
youth, it has already a sinister history.
There have been two murders, a

Search in Book

Search the Web

pretty a toy would be a purveyor to the

Figure 16-9: Selecting text in an eBook.

The Video Player

It's not possible to watch "real" TV on your phone, but a few apps come close. One that comes supplied with the Fire phone is Instant Video. It allows you to rent or buy movies or TV shows. The Instant Video app is shown in Figure 16-10.

Browse for video by perusing the categories, or use the Search icon to look up specific titles. When you find a title that piques your interest, you can view more information, similar to what's shown in Figure 16-11. The options for viewing include buying, renting, and even watching at no cost.

To buy or rent a movie, tap either the Buy or Rent button. The button changes; you have to tap it a second time to make the purchase. The charge is made according to whatever payment source you've specified for your Amazon account's mobile 1-Click setting. See Chapter 17 for details on 1-Click settings.

You can watch the video at any time. If you leave the Instant Video app, you can check your library again and resume watching at any time.

Watching video on your phone uses a ton of data. I highly recommend that you establish a Wi-Fi connection for watching the film. If you watch over the mobile data connection, you will incur surcharges.

| Navigation | Main | Shortcuts and Delighters |

Figure 16-10: Now playing on your Fire phone.

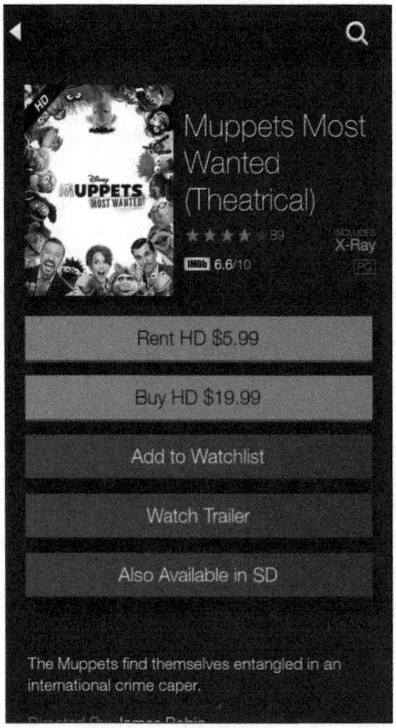

Figure 16-11: Viewing options for a video.

✔ As this book goes to press, the YouTube app is not available for the Fire phone. Similar apps are available, and some that appear to be YouTube, but they're not.

✔ As an alternative to YouTube, consider the Vimeo app.

✔ You can use Firefly to gather information about playing videos and potentially buy or rent what you see. Press the Camera/Firefly button, tap the TV icon (shown in the margin), and let the phone listen to the audio. Upon success, you see options for renting or purchasing the film or TV show.

✔ You can view videos on the phone on the big screen, by which I mean an HDMI monitor or TV. To do so, you need to obtain a Miracast adapter. It's a hardware doohickey that you attach to the HDMI monitor or TV. Obtain the corresponding app for the Miracast adapter, and then you can share an app's output, watching a video or even playing a game on a humongous screen.

Let's Go Shopping

In This Chapter

▶ Shopping at Amazon

▶ Using the Firefly feature

▶ Configuring your payment options

▶ Browsing at the Appstore

▶ Getting a new app

▶ Using a computer to install apps

*W*ho doesn't love to shop? Especially when you're spending someone else's money, shopping can be a wonderful thing. More care and diligence are involved when handing over your own money, but shopping is still an enjoyable pastime, hobby, or business, depending on who's paying whom.

Digital shopping also has its pleasures. Because it's tied into the largest online retailer, obviously the Amazon Fire phone will have shopping as a priority. That includes shopping for real stuff as well as for new apps for your phone. Leading the way is the Firefly app and its corresponding button on the phone. In a way, shopping is one of the reasons for the phone's existence.

Shop with Your Phone

Why go to the store? Let the store come to you by using your Amazon Fire phone to take care of your shopping needs, both vital and trivial:

   ✔ Refer to Chapter 15 for information on purchasing music by using the Music app and the online Amazon Music Store.

   ✔ Chapter 16 offers specifics on buying eBooks as well as information on buying and renting video.

Using the Shop Amazon app

Don't bother using the Silk browser app to visit Amazon on the Internet. Instead, use the Shop Amazon app, found on the App Grid. It's your key to digital shopping paradise, or as close as your credit card allows you to reach that nirvana.

The Shop Amazon app's main screen is shown in Figure 17-1. The Shortcuts and Delighters tab is greatly influenced by your shopping history. As you can see from the figure, *sto imparando l'Italiano.*

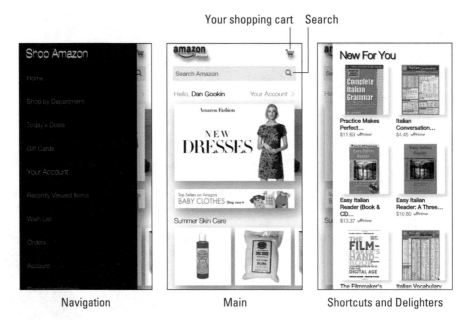

Your shopping cart   Search

Navigation   Main   Shortcuts and Delighters

Figure 17-1: The Shop Amazon app.

Browse the categories presented in the Shop Amazon app, use the Navigation panel to locate items, or tap the Search icon.

Before you set out shopping, confirm your payment method. See the later section "Setting your payment method."

You find an item you desire, tap the Add to Cart button to place it in your shopping cart, and keep browsing. You can also tap the Buy Now with 1-Click button to both purchase the item and have it shipped to your address.

If you elect to collect items, tap the Shopping Cart icon to review your purchases. Proceed through the checkout process, choosing your shipping address and method of payment. Tap the Place Your Order button to buy the item(s).

Eventually, you receive an email confirmation of the purchase. You can also choose the Orders item from the Navigation panel to peruse items you've recently ordered:

✓ Your shopping cart reflects items chosen by using the Shop Amazon app, as well as items you may have chosen earlier by using a computer's web browser or from another source.

✓ Unlike buying music or other items (refer to Chapters 15 and 16), you can cancel an Amazon store purchase after it's made. I recommend doing so on a computer, although the Shop Amazon app is up to the task: Choose Orders from the Navigation panel to browse recent purchases. Touch the Cancel Item button to undo the purchase.

Shopping with Firefly

There is a zone where shopping in the digital realm meets living in the real world. That zone is served by the Firefly app. You can start the app from the App Grid or just press and hold the Camera/Firefly button to summon Firefly.

Just like using the phone as a camera, you use Firefly by starting the app and then pointing the phone at an object. It can be a photo of a product or the product itself, and Firefly works best when the item has text on it, as shown in Figure 17-2.

Figure 17-2 shows Firefly in action, scanning a product label for additional information. To scan for music, tap the Music icon; to listen to movies, TV shows, and other video, tap the Video icon.

When a match is found, it appears at the bottom of the screen. Tap that card to see additional information, shown on the right in Figure 17-2. To buy the item, choose a shopping command, such as those shown in the figure:

✓ When Firefly cannot recognize what you're scanning, a message appears. Try again from another angle, or:

✓ It really helps if you can scan a label or other text. A barcode is perfect.

✓ Also see Chapter 24 for a tip on how to use Firefly to read in phone numbers.

Setting your payment method

When purchasing items by using the Shop Amazon app, you can select a preset payment type — or input a new type — directly in the app. Additionally, you can purchase items by using 1-Click. That means you click on the Buy button and the item is instantly purchased. The Music, Kindle (eBook), and Video stores all use this technique.

Listen for music   Scan for video

Scanning   Found information

Figure 17-2: Firefly, doing its thing.

To confirm your 1-Click payment method, follow these steps:

1. **Open the Settings app.**

2. **Choose My Accounts.**

3. **Tap the item Manage Your Amazon Payment Method.**

   The Payment Options screen appears.

4. **Choose 1-Click Payment.**

5. **Sign in to your Amazon account.**

   Your email address (the one you used to sign up for the Amazon account) is already specified. Type the password and tap the Sign-in button.

   You see your billing method shown on the 1-Click Payment screen, similar to what's shown in Figure 17-3, although your credit card should appear there instead of mine.

   Spread your fingers on the screen to zoom in.

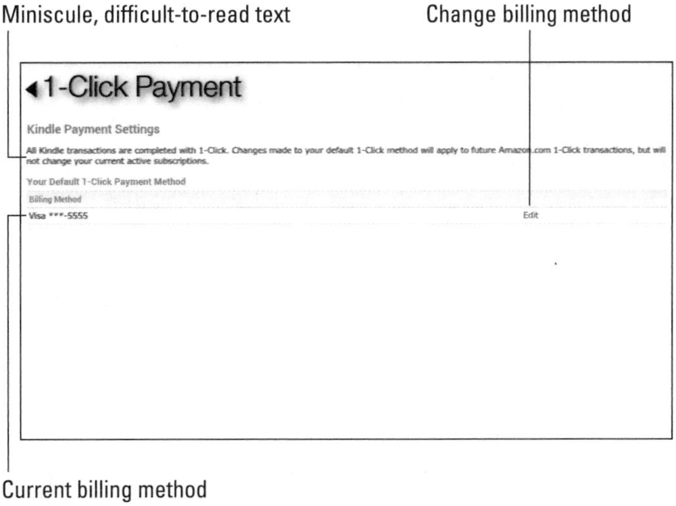

Miniscule, difficult-to-read text   Change billing method

◀ 1-Click Payment

Kindle Payment Settings

All Kindle transactions are completed with 1-Click. Changes made to your default 1-Click method will apply to future Amazon.com 1-Click transactions, but will not change your current active subscriptions.

Your Default 1-Click Payment Method

Billing Method

Visa ***-5555   Edit

Current billing method

Figure 17-3: Checking the 1-Click payment method.

6. **Tap the Edit button if you desire to change your billing options.**

   You can select another credit card that you have on file with Amazon. You can also enter information for a new credit card.

7. **Tap the Continue button after you've set a new option.**

8. **Choose a billing address.**

   Review the information to confirm.

You should also check the 1-Click Settings item in the Shop Amazon app: Open that app and choose Account from the Navigation panel. Tap the 1-Click Settings item to review your options. You can switch the master control by moving Mobile 1-Click Ordering to the Off position to disable 1-Click purchases in the Shop Amazon app.

Amazon Coins

Another way to shop for goodies is to collect Amazon Coins. This digital currency works a lot like a gift card: You can purchase the coins directly for one cent each, or you can earn coins by purchasing specific apps or playing games. Coins can be redeemed at the Appstore. Choose the Amazon Coins item from the Navigation panel in the Appstore app to see more details.

Apps from the Appstore

For shopping in the digital realm, specifically for your phone, you use the Amazon Appstore — specifically, the Appstore app.

The *Appstore* is a repository of over 200,000 apps. They expand the abilities of what your phone can do. The apps run the gamut from productivity apps, references, tools, and games to anything else you can imagine. The good news is that many of them are free. Even the paid apps often have "Lite" or trial versions you can try before you buy. It all happens at the Appstore:

✓ This section talks about getting apps for your phone. For information on getting music, see Chapter 15. Chapter 16 covers buying eBooks as well as buying or renting movies and TV shows.

✓ *App* is short for application. It's a program, or software, that you can add to your phone to make it do new, wondrous, or useful things.

✓ All apps you obtain from the Appstore reside on the App Grid. See Chapter 22 for more information about managing apps and using the App Grid.

✓ I highly recommend that you connect your phone to a Wi-Fi network if you plan to obtain apps from the Appstore. Wi-Fi not only gives you speed but also helps you avoid data surcharges. See Chapter 18 for details on connecting your phone to a Wi-Fi network.

Visiting the Appstore

To get more apps, open the Appstore app, found on the App Grid. After opening the app, you see the main screen, similar to the one shown in Figure 17-4. Swipe the screen up and down to view various categories and highlighted apps. You can use the Navigation panel to help you get somewhere quickly, and check out the Shortcuts and Delighters panel for app suggestions.

When you have an idea of what you want, such as an app's name or even what it does, searching works fastest: Touch the Search icon at the top of the Appstore screen (refer to Figure 17-1). Type all or part of the app's name or perhaps a description.

To see more information about an item, touch it. Touching an app doesn't buy it but instead displays a more detailed description, screen shots, comments, and additional details, as shown in Figure 17-5.

Return to the main Appstore screen by touching the Triangle icon in the upper-right corner of the screen, illustrated in Figure 17-5. Or you can choose Appstore Home from the Navigation panel.

Search for apps

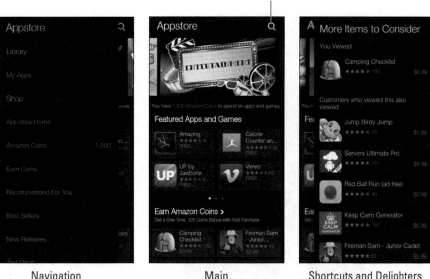

Navigation   Main   Shortcuts and Delighters

Figure 17-4: The Appstore app.

✔ You can be assured that all apps that appear in the Appstore can be used with your phone. There's no way to download or buy something that's incompatible.

✔ Pay attention to an app's ratings. Ratings are added by people who use the apps — people like you and me. Having more stars is better. You can see additional information, including individual user reviews, by swiping down the app's description.

✔ The Appstore is not the same thing as the Google Play Store, and it's definitely not the Apple App Store. Just because you can find an app for an Android phone or an iPhone doesn't mean that the same app is available for the Fire phone. More apps are written every day, and Amazon is approving new apps as fast as it can.

Obtaining a new app

After you locate an app you want, the next step is to download it from the Appstore into your phone. The app is installed automatically, building up your collection of apps and expanding what the phone can do.

Good news: Most apps are free. Better news: Even the apps you pay for don't cost dearly. In fact, it seems odd to sit and stew over whether paying 99 cents for a game is "worth it."

Return to Appstore

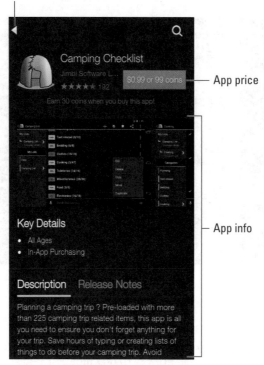

App price

App info

Figure 17-5: Info on a specific app.

I recommend that you download a free app first, to familiarize yourself with the process. Then try your hand at downloading a paid app.

Free or not, the process of obtaining an app works pretty much the same. Follow these steps:

1. **Open the Appstore app.**

2. **Find the app you want and open its description.**

   The app's description screen looks similar to the one shown in Figure 17-5.

   The difference between a free app and a paid app is found on the button used to obtain the app. For a free app, the button says *Free*. For a paid app, the button shows the price or the number of Amazon coins required for purchase.

3. **Touch the FREE button to get a free app; for a paid app, touch the button with the price on it.**

   The button changes after you tap it.

   For a free app, the button says *Get App*.

For a paid app that you can purchase with Amazon coins, you see a screen where you can choose to use the coins or pay with real money by using your 1-Click settings.

4. **Tap the Confirm or Get App button.**

   The app is downloaded and then installed. You're free to do other things on your phone while the app is downloaded and installed.

5. **Touch the Open button to run the app.**

   Or, if you were doing something else while the app was downloading and installing, check the Notification panel. You see an entry for the app with the words *Successfully Installed* shown beneath. Choose that notification to open and run the app.

At this point, what happens next depends on the app you've downloaded. For example, you may have to agree to a license agreement. If so, touch the I Agree button. Additional setup may involve setting your location, signing in to an account, or creating a profile, for example.

After you complete the initial app setup, or if no setup is necessary, you can start using the app:

- Apps you download are added to the App Grid, made available like any other app on your phone.

- You receive an email confirmation for any app you obtain, free or paid.

- See Chapter 22 for information on uninstalling apps, should the app not meet with your expectations.

What about viruses?

Relax. You can rest assured that all apps available at the Appstore are legitimate. Each has been tested. The security risk for getting a virus or obtaining an app that doesn't do what it claims to do is extremely low, if it exists at all. Unlike other app stores for other smartphones, Amazon is diligent about which apps are available.

Even given such assurances, I highly recommend that you remain vigilant about those apps you obtain. Avoid the temptation to get an app that does something questionable. Don't try to install apps via a text message or email or pay heed to your friend's pal who knows a neat trick but just needs to see your phone for a few minutes. Don't do it!

Computer viruses would have no effect on the Fire phone. There's no need to worry about a curious email attachment, but I recommend that you remain vigilant. Websites may alert you to a virus or compromised file on your phone. Ignore these messages because they're likely bogus. Instead, close the browser tab and move on.

Installing apps from a computer

You don't need to use the Appstore on your phone to install apps. Using a computer, you can visit Amazon on the web, drop by the Appstore, and obtain apps to install remotely on your Fire phone. Here's how it works:

1. **Use your computer's web browser to visit the Amazon Appstore on the Internet.**

   Visit Amazon at www.amazon.com and click on the link that takes you to the Appstore. It may say *Android Appstore,* and you may have to click on a suggested app link to get there. (Hopefully, Amazon updates its web page to make the Appstore more accessible.)

2. **If necessary, log in to your account on the Amazon web page.**

3. **Browse for something.**

   You can hunt down apps, books, music — the whole gamut. It works just like browsing the Play Store on your phone.

4. **Click the Get App button to obtain a free app; click the Spend Amazon Coins or Buy button for a paid app.**

   The app is made available for your Fire phone, but you have to synchronize the phone to obtain it.

5. **Pull down the Notification panel.**

   The panel also contains quick actions at the top.

6. **Tap the Sync Quick Action.**

   After tapping that Quick Action, and enjoying the animation, look in the notifications for a Download Manager. It's the process that's fetching your software from Amazon's Appstore servers and copying the app(s) into your phone.

7. **Display the App Grid.**

   Press the Home button twice.

8. **Slide the master control atop the screen to Cloud.**

   You see your apps present.

9. **Tap the app.**

   It doesn't open. Instead, it's copied from cloud storage to your device. From this point on, you'll find the app on your device, on the App Grid.

After the app has been fully installed, you can run it just like any other app. The only difference is that you used a computer to obtain it.

Part V
Nitty Gritties

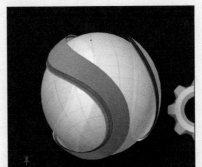

In this part . . .

- Figure out wireless networking and devices
- Connect, share, and store information
- Explore the world with your Fire phone
- Customize and configure your phone
- Thrill over managing your apps
- Maintain and troubleshoot your phone

Fireless Wireless

In This Chapter

▶ Understanding wireless networking
▶ Connecting to a Wi-Fi network
▶ Setting up a mobile hotspot
▶ Configuring Bluetooth
▶ Connecting to a Bluetooth headset
▶ Printing from your phone

*T*he whole mobile paradigm implies an utter lack of wires. Indeed, cell phones in the 1970s were unpopular due to the burdensome amount of cable that was required to operate the device remotely. Things are better today. Though that's bad news for the companies that make those table-size spools of wire, it's good news for you because your Amazon Fire phone can be as completely wireless as you desire.

🔒 **Imperial Wambooli**
Connected

Wireless Networking

Your Fire phone handles many forms of wireless networking. These capabilities are made possible thanks to a host of wireless networking radios neatly crammed into the device. The two that first come to mind are the radios that provide the phone with that vital Internet connection. These are the cellular modem and the Wi-Fi radio.

🔒 **Underground Wambooli**

LuckyDog-guest

🔒 **FunnyEagle**

Understanding the mobile data network

You pay your cellular provider a handsome fee every month. The fee comes in two chunks. One chunk (the less expensive of the two) is for the telephone service. The other chunk is the data service, which is how your phone accesses the Internet. This system is the *mobile data network*.

Several types of mobile data networks are available. When your phone uses one, an icon appears on the phone's status bar, cluing you in to which network the phone is accessing. Here's the gamut:

- ✔ **4G LTE:** The fourth generation of wide-area data networks is comparable in speed to standard Wi-Fi Internet access. It's fast. It also allows for both data and voice transmission at the same time.

- ✔ **3G:** The third generation of wide-area data networks is several times faster than the previous generation of data networks.

- ✔ **1X:** Several types of the original, slower mobile data signals are still available. They all fall under the 1X banner. It's as slow as pouring molasses on a cold day.

Your phone always uses the best network available. So, when a 4G LTE network is within reach, that network is used for Internet communications. Otherwise, the 3G network is chosen, and then 1X as a form of last-ditch desperation:

- ✔ Use the peek gesture to view the status bar. Or you can pull down the notification drawer to view the Mobile Data Network icon.

- ✔ The Mobile Data Network notification icon appears next to the Signal Strength icon. The Signal Strength icon refers to the phone service, not the mobile data connection.

- ✔ When a data network isn't available, no icon appears on the status bar. In fact, it's entirely possible for the phone to have no data signal but still be able to make phone calls.

- ✔ See Chapter 24 for information on how to monitor mobile data usage and avoid surcharges.

- ✔ Your phone uses the Wi-Fi signal whenever it's available, prioritizing it over the mobile data connection. Data transferred via a Wi-Fi network doesn't count against your cellular data usage. Therefore, I recommend connecting to and using a Wi-Fi network wherever possible. That's because:

- ✔ Accessing the mobile data network isn't free. Your phone most likely has some form of subscription plan for a certain quantity of data. When you exceed that quantity, the costs can become frighteningly prohibitive.

Using the Wi-Fi connection

The mobile data connection is nice and is available pretty much all over, but using it costs you money. A better option, and one you should seek out when it's available, is *Wi-Fi,* or the same wireless networking standard used by computers for communicating with each other and the Internet.

Making Wi-Fi work on your Fire phone requires two steps. First, you must activate Wi-Fi by turning on the phone's wireless radio. The second step is connecting to a specific wireless network.

Wi-Fi stands for *wireless fidelity*. It's brought to you by the numbers 802.11 and the letters A, B, N, and G and combinations of those letters, inclusive.

Activating Wi-Fi

Follow these steps to activate the Wi-Fi radio on your Fire phone:

1. **Open the Settings app.**

   At the Home screen, press the Home button to display the App Grid. If necessary, swipe the screen from bottom to top until you locate the Settings app icon. Tap that icon.

2. **Choose Wi-Fi & Networks to expand that item (if necessary).**

3. **Choose Connect to Wi-Fi.**

4. **Ensure that the Wi-Fi master control icon is on.**

   If not, slide the master control from Off to On to activate the phone's Wi-Fi radio.

If you've already configured your phone to connect to an available wireless network, it's connected automatically. Otherwise, you have to connect to an available network, which is covered in the next section.

To turn off Wi-Fi, repeat the steps in this section, but in Step 4 slide the Master Control icon from On to Off. Turning off Wi-Fi disconnects your phone from any wireless networks:

- ✔ You can quickly activate (or deactivate) the phone's Wi-Fi settings by choosing the Wi-Fi Quick Action. See Chapter 3 for more information on Quick Actions.

- ✔ Using Wi-Fi to connect to the Internet doesn't incur data usage charges.

- ✔ The Wi-Fi radio places an extra drain on the battery, but it's truly negligible. If you want to save a modicum of juice, especially if you're out and about and don't plan to be near a Wi-Fi access point for any length of time, turn off the Wi-Fi radio.

Connecting to a Wi-Fi network

After activating the Wi-Fi radio on your Fire phone, you can connect to an available wireless network. Heed these steps:

1. **Open the Settings app.**

2. **Choose the Connect to Wi-Fi item, found under Wi-Fi & Networks.**

   Tap the Wi-Fi & Networks area to expand it, if necessary.

You see a list of Wi-Fi networks. In Figure 18-1, the Imperial Wambooli network is connected. That's my office network.

3. **Choose a wireless network from the list.**

When no wireless networks are shown, you're sort of out of luck regarding Wi-Fi access from your current location.

4. **If prompted, type the network password.**

Put a check mark in the box by the Hide Password option if you fear that some shoulder surfer will bogart the password.

5. **Touch the OK button to connect.**

You should be immediately connected to the network. If not, try the password again.

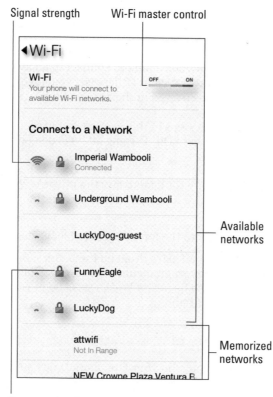

Figure 18-1: Hunting down a wireless network.

When the phone is connected, you see the Wi-Fi icon appear on the status bar. (Use the peek gesture to view the status bar.) The icon, shown in the margin, indicates that the phone's Wi-Fi is on, connected, and communicating with a Wi-Fi network:

- You can quickly access the Connect to Wi-Fi item from the Carousel, if you've used it previously. Just swipe the Carousel until you see the Settings icon. Look for the Connect to Wi-Fi hero widget below the app icon.

- Not every wireless network has a password. They should! I don't avoid connecting to any public network that lacks a password, but I don't use that network for shopping, banking, or any other secure online activity.

- Some public networks are open to anyone, but you have to use the web browser app to get on the web and find a login page that lets you access the network. Simply browse to any page on the Internet, and the login page shows up.

- The phone automatically remembers any Wi-Fi network it's connected to as well as its network password. An example is the `attwifi` network, shown in Figure 18-1.

- To disconnect from a Wi-Fi network, simply turn off Wi-Fi. See the preceding section.

- Compared with the mobile data network, a Wi-Fi network's broadcast signal has a limited range. My advice is to use Wi-Fi when you plan to remain in one location for a while. If you wander too far away, your phone loses the signal and is disconnected.

Finding no-name Wi-Fi networks

Some wireless networks don't broadcast their names, which adds security but also mystery. You can access such a network only when you know its name, or SSID.

To access a Wi-Fi network that doesn't broadcast its SSID, obey these steps:

1. **Visit the Connect to Wi-Fi screen in the Settings app.**

   Refer to Steps 1 and 2 from the preceding section.

2. **Tap the Add Network button.**

   The button is found at the bottom of the list of available Wi-Fi networks. You may have to swipe the screen from bottom to top to find the button.

3. **Type the Network SSID.**

   You can obtain the SSID from the guy with the green hair who just sold you coffee, or from whoever is in charge of the wireless network at your location.

4. **Choose the Security type (if available) and, optionally, type a password.**

   Again, this information is provided by the person with the SSID.

5. **Tap the OK button to connect.**

The average housefly lives only two weeks. I know this trivial tidbit isn't related to Wi-Fi networking, but I like to end a section with a paragraph of text.

The Wi-Fi Hotspot

Your Fire phone accesses the Internet anywhere the mobile data signal is available. Other devices have to wait, either for an available Wi-Fi signal or some type of wired connection. Pity their plight, but there is something you can do about it: You can share the mobile data connection as a Wi-Fi hotspot.

When you create a mobile hotspot, you're using the Fire phone's mobile data connection to create a Wi-Fi network. Other Wi-Fi devices — computers, laptops, tablets, and so on — can then use that Wi-Fi network to access the Internet. The process is referred to as *creating a Wi-Fi hotspot,* though no heat is involved.

To create a mobile hotspot, heed these steps:

1. **Plug the phone into a power source.**

   The Mobile Hotspot feature uses a lot of power.

2. **Open the Settings app.**

3. **Tap the Wi-Fi & Networks item to open that category.**

4. **Choose Set Up a Wi-Fi Hotspot.**

5. **Slide the master control by Wi-Fi Hotspot to the On position.**

   The hotspot is on, but you may want to confirm some of the settings.

   If the hotspot doesn't come on or the item is disabled, that feature is unavailable under your data subscription plan, or it simply isn't allowed.

6. **Choose the Configure Hotspot item to give the hotspot a name, or *SSID,* and then review, change, or assign a password.**

   Touch the fields on the Configure Hotspot screen to assign a name (SSID), password, and other options. Touch the Save button to set your changes.

To turn off the mobile hotspot, slide the master control to the Off position, as described in Step 5:

- ✔ The range for the mobile hotspot is about 30 feet. Items such as walls and dinosaurs can interfere with the signal, rendering it much shorter.

- ✔ Data consumption over the mobile data network increases rapidly when the mobile hotspot is in use. Up to five people can access the Internet through the phone's Wi-Fi hotspot, which increases many-fold the amount of data consumed.

- ✔ Don't forget to turn off the mobile hotspot when you're done using it.

Beautiful Bluetooth

Another wireless communications standard available to your Fire phone is Bluetooth. Yes, it's a curious name.

Unlike Wi-Fi, Bluetooth is used to wirelessly connect two devices, such as your Fire phone and some peripheral device, such as a headset, keyboard, speakers, or a printer. That connection is handy to have — plus, it fits in well with this chapter's wireless theme.

Understanding Bluetooth

To use Bluetooth to wirelessly connect a gizmo to your phone, you need to understand a few Bluetoothy peculiarities.

First, you need a Bluetooth peripheral, such as one of those wireless ear things you see attached to some phone users' ears. The variety of Bluetooth peripherals goes beyond ear thingies, although that's typically what people think of when Bluetooth is mentioned.

Second, you need to make the device (or your phone) discoverable. That is, you turn on the Bluetooth radio and tell it to say "Hello?"

Finally, you connect the two Bluetooth gizmos. This process is known as *pairing*.

After a device is paired with your phone, you can use it just as though it were connected by wire, but it's not:

- ✔ You can connect a number of Bluetooth devices to your phone and use them all at the same time. Each device must be paired individually.

- ✔ When you're done using a Bluetooth peripheral, you simply turn it off. Because the Bluetooth gizmo is paired with your phone, it's automatically reconnected the next time you turn it on.

✔ Bluetooth devices are marked with the Bluetooth logo, shown in the margin. It's your assurance that the gizmo can work with other Bluetooth devices.

✔ Bluetooth was developed as a wireless version of the old RS-232 standard, the serial port on early personal computers. Essentially, Bluetooth is wireless RS-232, and the variety of devices you can connect to and the things you can do with Bluetooth are similar to what you could do with the old serial port standard.

Activating Bluetooth

You must turn on the phone's Bluetooth radio before you can use one of those Borg-earpiece implants and join the ranks of the walking connected. To turn on Bluetooth, follow these directions:

1. **Open the Settings app.**

2. **Choose Wi-Fi and Networks.**

3. **Choose Pair Bluetooth Devices.**

4. **Slide the master control to the On position.**

   The Bluetooth radio is on.

To turn off Bluetooth, repeat the steps in this section, but slide the master control to the Off position:

✔ You can turn on Bluetooth also by choosing the Bluetooth Quick Action from the notifications drawer. See Chapter 3.

✔ Activating Bluetooth can quickly drain the phone's battery. Be mindful to use Bluetooth only when necessary, and remember to turn it off when you're done.

Pairing with a Bluetooth device

To make the Bluetooth connection between your phone and another gizmo, such as a Bluetooth headset, follow these steps:

1. **Ensure that Bluetooth is on.**

   Refer to the preceding section.

2. **Turn on the Bluetooth gizmo or ensure that its Bluetooth radio is on.**

   Some Bluetooth devices have separate power and Bluetooth switches.

3. **Open the Settings app.**

4. Choose Wi-Fi and Networks and then Pair Bluetooth Devices.

You see a list of available and paired devices, similar to Figure 18-2. Don't fret if the device you want doesn't yet appear in the list.

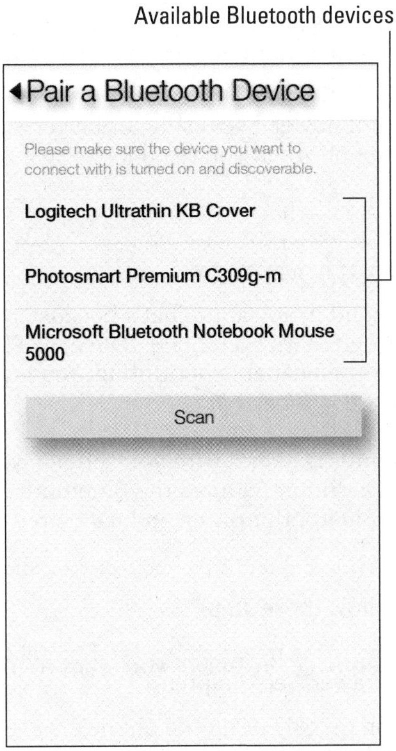

Available Bluetooth devices

◄ Pair a Bluetooth Device

Please make sure the device you want to connect with is turned on and discoverable.

Logitech Ultrathin KB Cover

Photosmart Premium C309g-m

Microsoft Bluetooth Notebook Mouse 5000

Scan

Figure 18-2: Finding Bluetooth gizmos.

5. If the other device has an option to become visible, select it.

For example, some Bluetooth gizmos have a tiny button to press that makes the device visible to other Bluetooth gizmos.

6. Choose the device.

The phone and Bluetooth device attempt to pair. You may be required to type the device's passcode or otherwise acknowledge the connection.

After pairing, you can begin using the device. For a headset, the device should be active right away: Tap the headset's button to answer an incoming call, for example. Many other peripherals are accessed by choosing the Bluetooth icon from a Share menu or screen. See the next section:

- Bluetooth peripherals are connected as long as they're on. To break the connection, you can either turn off the gizmo or disable the Bluetooth radio on your phone. Because the devices are paired, when you turn on Bluetooth and reactivate the device, the connection is instantly reestablished.

- When a Bluetooth headset is paired, a Bluetooth icon appears on the in-call screen. Use that icon to switch between a Bluetooth headset and the phone's microphone and speaker.

- Bluetooth can use a lot of power. Especially for battery-powered devices, don't forget to turn them off when you're no longer using them with your phone.

Printing to a Bluetooth printer

You won't find a Print command in any app. That's because printing isn't really something people associate with a mobile device, like the Fire phone. Even so, your phone is more than capable of printing: You just need to know the secret word, and that word is *Bluetooth.*

As long as the Bluetooth printer is paired with your phone, you can print documents on the printer. Such a printer features the Bluetooth logo, shown in the margin. As long as it's a Bluetooth printer, and it's paired with the phone, you can print.

To make printing happen, follow these steps:

1. **View the document, web page, or image you want to print.**

2. **Touch the Share icon.**

   If the Share icon isn't visible in the app, look for a Share command on a menu.

3. **Choose Bluetooth.**

   If the Bluetooth option isn't available, you can't print from the app.

4. **Choose your Bluetooth printer from the list of Bluetooth peripherals.**

5. **If a prompt appears on the printer, confirm that your phone is printing a document.**

   The document is uploaded (sent from the phone to the printer), and then it prints.

You can view the upload status by checking the phone's notifications. Check for the Bluetooth Share: Sent Files notification.

Printing from your phone to a Bluetooth printer works, but it's not a perfect solution. For printing lots of material, consider emailing the information to yourself or sharing it on a cloud drive. You can then use a computer to handle the printing task.

Unpairing a Bluetooth peripheral

You don't need to worry about unpairing Bluetooth peripherals: Turn off a device you don't want to use. Simple.

When you truly need to unpair a device, for example to use a peripheral with another phone, follow these steps:

1. **Open the Settings app.**

2. **Choose Wi-Fi & Networks.**

3. **Choose Pair Bluetooth Devices.**

4. **Tap the Edit (pencil) icon next to the peripheral you want to unpair.**

5. **Choose Forget This Device.**

    The device is unpaired.

You can always pair with the peripheral again, if you need to. Unlike breakups in the human world, Bluetooth peripherals are very forgiving.

More wireless with NFC

The Fire phone comes equipped with an NFC wireless radio, where *NFC* stands for Near Field Communications. This radio can be used with the proper app to read NFC devices. For example, you could get a wallet-type of app and use your phone to pay for a meal or a new pair of welding goggles if the merchant features an NFC payment system.

The phone's NFC radio must be activated before you can use this feature: In the Settings app, choose Wi-Fi & Networks, and then Enable NFC. Slide the master control to the On position.

Alas, you cannot use NFC on the Fire phone to directly send information to another smartphone. This feature, commonly known as Android Beam, might be available in the future.

Share and Store

*B*eing a mobile device and living a wild, free, untethered existence is most likely what a Fire phone enjoys the most. Such a life can, however, be lonely. Therefore, from time to time, your phone desires to connect with other devices, to share the things it has. Happily, a lot of that sharing takes place wirelessly. When necessary, a wire can be used to share information, moving it hither and thither and possibly even yon.

The Cloud Connection

The best way to share pictures, music, media, and files between your phone and a host of other devices is to use cloud storage. Though the term *cloud* is nebulous, the reality of this connection is that it makes swapping and sharing quite easy.

Understanding cloud storage

The amazing thing about the term *cloud* is that it's completely nontechnical. It's not jargon that the nerds would have made up. They would have concocted a cryptic acronym or called it *FROOF* or something and then dreamt up an acronym to match. No, the high-tech marketing team loves the term *cloud storage*, but what do they know? Half of them were hawking shoes last month.

Cloud storage is just fancy talk for storing files on the Internet.

Cloud storage also refers to information on the Internet, such as an address book, calendar appointments — even music and books. When that stuff is stored "in the cloud," it's available to a variety of devices:

- Because all devices that share the cloud storage are instantly synchronized, you don't need to worry about specific file transfers. All files saved to cloud storage are available to all devices that can access that storage.

- Many cloud storage options exist, such as Dropbox, Google Drive, Microsoft OneDrive, and more. An app for OneDrive is available. Hopefully, in the future, apps for the other services will be available as well.

- See Chapter 17 for information on obtaining apps for your phone.

- The opposite of cloud storage is local storage, or information that exists on only one device. That generally can't be shared unless you specifically copy, or *export,* the information. That's a pain, which is why cloud storage is so popular.

Setting up the Amazon cloud

Seeing that the Fire phone is from Amazon, what Amazon would just love for you to do is set up and configure the Amazon Cloud for use with your device. This is an optional procedure, but it does make certain features more useful.

Because you have an Amazon account, you have access to storage on the Amazon website. If you've been taking pictures with your phone, they're already stored in the cloud.

You can access your Amazon cloud storage by visiting www.amazon.com on a computer. Under the Your Account menu, choose the command Your Cloud Drive. You see a screen similar to Figure 19-1, which is an online folder and file manager. (You may need to first log in to your Amazon account.)

You can also obtain an Amazon cloud storage desktop program for your computer. Visit the following website and download the software:

https://www.amazon.com/clouddrive

To access Amazon cloud storage on your Fire phone, open the Docs app. The Docs app shows documents stored only in the `Documents` folder in your cloud storage: Display the Navigation panel, and slide the master control to Cloud to view the online documents.

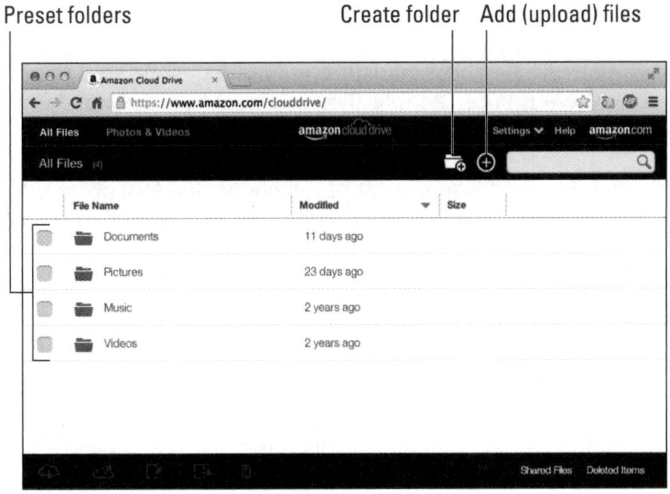

Preset folders   Create folder Add (upload) files

Figure 19-1: Amazon cloud storage.

Using cloud storage

All files saved to cloud storage are synchronized instantly with all devices that access the storage. Change a file on a computer and it's updated on your phone. The files are also available directly on the Internet from a web page. Even so, I recommend that you use a specific cloud storage app on your phone to access the files.

To make the file transfer from the computer to the phone, save a file in the cloud storage folder. For example, save a document from your PC on Amazon cloud storage in the Documents folder. That file is instantly available on the Fire phone: Open the Docs app.

Between Phone and Computer

The wireless way to swap files between your phone and a computer is to use cloud storage. The wired way is to plug the phone directly into a computer by using a USB cable. Coincidentally, a USB cable comes with the phone. Despite this coincidence, more is involved with the phone-and-computer connection than merely plugging in the cable.

Connecting the phone to a computer

The physical phone-computer connection involves using a USB cable. Specifically, it's a USB cable with an A adapter on one end and a Micro USB adapter on the other.

Which adapter is which?

It doesn't matter! They both plug into only one device, so if the plug doesn't fit, try the other end of the cable. The connectors are shaped differently and cannot be attached incorrectly.

The battery is charged when the phone is connected to a powered USB port. If possible, plug the USB cable into the computer itself or into a powered USB hub.

Configuring the USB connection

Your Fire phone presents itself to a computer in one of two ways:

- ✔ As a file storage device, such as a thumb drive or memory card
- ✔ As a digital camera, which is well-suited for transferring pictures and movies

The file storage device option is usually the best choice, although you can switch between these settings by following these steps on the Fire phone:

1. **Open the Settings app.**
2. **Choose Battery & Storage to expand that area.**
3. **Choose the item Change USB Connection Type.**
4. **Choose either File Transfer or Photo Transfer.**

   The File Transfer option is the preset option.

When connected under the File Transfer option, the computer treats the phone as any external storage device. When Photo Transfer is chosen, the computer recognizes the phone as a digital camera, and it may start a photo importing app, which is handy if you just want to transfer pictures and movies to your computer.

Connecting to a PC

The PC connection is pretty straightforward for your Fire phone. The key is to look for the AutoPlay dialog box for Windows 8 and for earlier, more popular versions of Windows. The Windows 7 AutoPlay dialog box is shown in Figure 19-2.

Choose the option Open Device to View Files, shown in Figure 19-2. A folder window opens, showing the Fire phone's internal storage. Open that item to browse folders on your phone — if that's what you want to do.

Figure 19-2: The AutoPlay dialog box.

Another option to choose is Sync Digital Media Files to This Device, which opens the Windows Media Player program. You can use this program to transfer pictures, movies, and music between the PC and your phone.

See the later section "Transferring files between the phone and a computer" for details.

Though you can copy Windows Media Audio (WMA) music files to the Fire phone, the Music app won't play them. See Chapter 15 for information on copying music from your computer to the Amazon cloud.

Connecting to a Mac

You need special software to manage files on your Fire phone by using a Macintosh. That's because the Mac prefers to recognize other phones, those that might rhyme with the words *pie phone*. Weird, huh?

To work with files on a Fire phone when you have a Macintosh, you need to obtain special software: the Android File Transfer program. Yes, the Fire phone pretends that it's not an Android phone, but secretly, deep down inside, it is.

On your Mac, download that program from this website:

```
www.android.com/filetransfer
```

Install the software. Run it. From that point on, when you connect your Android Fire phone to the Macintosh, a special window appears, similar to the one shown in Figure 19-3. It lists the phone's folders and files. Use that window for file management, as covered later in this chapter.

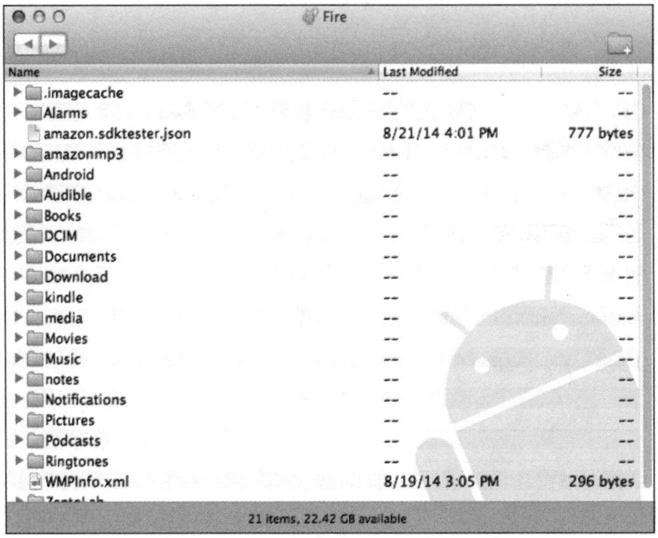

Figure 19-3: The ~~Android~~ Fire Phone File Transfer program.

See the next section for information on file transfers using the blankity-blank File Transfer program.

Transferring files between the phone and a computer

I can think of plenty of files you would want to copy from a computer to your Fire phone: pictures, videos, and audio files. You can also copy vCards exported from your email program, which helps to build the phone's address book. Likewise, you may want to copy files from the phone to the computer. Either way, it works the same. Follow these steps:

1. **Connect the phone and the computer by using the USB cable.**

   Specific directions are offered earlier in this chapter.

2. **On a PC, if the AutoPlay dialog box appears, choose the Open Folder to View Files option.**

   When the AutoPlay dialog box doesn't appear, you can view files manually: Open the Computer window, and then open the phone's icon, found at the bottom of that window. Open the storage icon to view files.

   The phone's folder window looks like any other folder in Windows. The difference is that the files and folders in that window are on your Fire phone, not on the computer.

   On a Macintosh, the Android File Transfer program should start (refer to Figure 19-3).

3. **Open the source and destination folder windows.**

   Open the folder that contains the files you want to copy. The folder can be found on the computer or on the phone. Then open the folder on the computer or phone where you want the file copied. Have both folder windows, computer and phone, visible on the screen, similar to what's shown in Figure 19-4.

Specific folders on the phone

Drag files to here
to copy to the 'root'

Files on your computer

Files on the phone

Figure 19-4: Copying files to your phone.

4. **Drag the file icon from one folder window to the other.**

   Dragging the file copies it, either from phone to computer or from computer to phone.

   If you want to be specific, drag the file to the phone's folder or to the root folder, as shown in Figure 19-4. On the PC, drag it to the My Documents, My Pictures, or My Videos folder, as appropriate. You can also drag directly to the desktop and decide later where to store the file.

   The same file-dragging technique can be used for transferring files from a Macintosh. You need to drag the icon(s) to the Android File Transfer window, which works just like any folder window in Finder.

5. **Close the folder windows and disconnect the USB cable when you're done.**

Although this manual technique works, a better way is to transfer files via cloud storage, as described earlier in this chapter:

✔ Not every file you copy over is digestible by the phone. To view or open the file, you must have the proper app.

✔ Copying over PDF or eBook documents directly may work, but there's a good chance it won't work. Unless an app can open that document, you're out of luck.

✔ Files you've downloaded on the phone are stored in the `Download` folder.

✔ Pictures and videos on the phone are stored in the `DCIM/Camera` folder.

✔ Music on the phone is stored in the `Music` folder, organized by artist.

Disconnecting the phone from the computer

The process of disconnecting your phone from the computer is cinchy: When you've finished transferring files, music, or other media between a computer and the phone, close all open programs and folders on your computer — specifically, those you've used to work with the phone's storage. Then you can disconnect the USB cable. That's it:

✔ It's a Bad Idea to unplug the phone while you're transferring information or while a folder window is open on your computer. Doing so can damage the phone's storage, rendering unreadable some of the information that's kept there. To be safe, close the programs and folder windows you've opened before disconnecting.

✔ Unlike other external storage on the Macintosh, there's no need to eject the phone's storage when you're done accessing it. Simply disconnect the phone. The Mac doesn't get angry when you do so.

Phone Storage

Somewhere deep in your phone's bosom lies a storage device. It's like the hard drive in a computer: The thing can't be removed, but that's not the point. The point is that the storage is used for your apps, music, videos, pictures, and a host of other information. This section describes what you can do to manage that storage.

Reviewing storage stats

To see how much storage space is available on your phone, open the Settings app and choose the Battery & Storage category. Tap the command View Available Storage. The Storage screen details information about storage space, similar to what's shown in Figure 19-5.

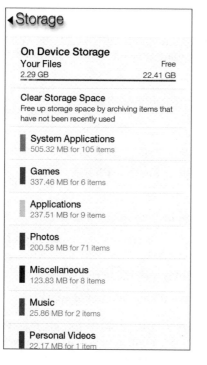

Figure 19-5: Phone storage information.

Touch a category on the Storage screen to view details on how the storage is used or to launch an associated app. For example, touching Applications (refer to Figure 19-5) displays a list of apps, on both the cloud and the phone itself (device). Choosing Photos lets you view pictures:

✔ The Fire phone makes excellent use of cloud storage, so most of the media you access is stored there (on the Internet) as opposed to on the phone itself. That's good news because videos, music, and pictures consume the most storage space on a phone.

✏ Don't bemoan the knowledge that the Free value is far less than the phone's storage capacity. For example, in Figure 19-5, a 32GB phone shows only 24.7GB free. (That's 2.29GB used plus 22.41GB available.) The missing space is considered overhead, as are several gigabytes taken by the government for tax purposes.

Clearing storage space

The Fire phone clears up storage space by taking items you've downloaded from the cloud to the device and removing them from the device. The items can still be accessed — and downloaded again — but the duplicate copy is removed.

To clear out any download duplicates, follow these steps:

1. **Open the Settings app.**

2. **Choose the Battery & Storage category to expand that area.**

3. **Select the command Free Space on Your Phone.**

   You see a list of downloaded items.

4. **Place a check mark by the items you desire to purge.**

   Some items already feature check marks, which means that the phone is completely okay with your removing those items.

5. **Tap the Delete icon at the bottom of the screen.**

   The items are removed, freeing up a modicum of space.

One reason to download something to the phone is for when you travel. A copy of a web page, music, photo, or movie is handy to have when you're away from the Internet on an international flight. See Chapter 20 for information on traveling with your Fire phone.

Taking the Fire with You

You're in a land far, far away. The sun shines warmly upon your face. A gentle breeze wafts over crashing waves. You wiggle your toes in the soft, grainy sand. And the number-one thought on your mind is, "Can my phone get a signal?"

The vernacular term is *bars,* as in the signal bars you see when the phone is actively communicating with a cellular network. That network pretty much covers the globe these days. That means from Cancun to the Gobi Desert, you probably can use your phone. How that happens and how to make it happen less expensively are the topics of this chapter.

Where the Phone Roams

The word *roam* takes on an entirely new meaning when applied to a cell phone. It means that your phone receives a cell signal whenever you're outside your cell phone carrier's operating area. In that case, your phone is *roaming.*

Roaming sounds handy, but there's a catch: It almost always involves a surcharge for using another cellular service — an *unpleasant* surcharge.

Relax: Your Fire phone alerts you whenever it's roaming. The Roaming icon appears on the status bar whenever you're outside your cellular provider's signal area. The big *R* is your clue that the phone is finding a signal outside its home turf.

To avoid incurring roaming charges, move to a location where your primary cellular provider has service. That may be difficult, which is why the phone still works when it's roaming.

You can disable the phone's ability to roam or confirm that that ability has already been disabled, by following these steps:

1. **Open the Settings app.**

2. **Choose Wi-Fi & Networks.**

3. **Choose Turn Off Cellular Data Access.**

4. **Slide the master control from Data Roaming to the Off position.**

   Data roaming is just the first step. That disables the mobile data network, another source of surcharges. To disable phone roaming, continue with Step 5.

5. **Choose the Advanced item.**

6. **Slide the master control by the option Automatic Operator Selection to the Off position.**

   This action disables mobile roaming, but this feature might be disabled by your cellular provider.

Your phone can still access the Internet over the Wi-Fi connection when it roams. Setting up a Wi-Fi connection doesn't make you incur extra charges, unless you have to pay to get on the Wi-Fi network. See Chapter 19 for more information about Wi-Fi.

The lock screen may also announce that the phone is roaming. You might see the name of the other cellular network displayed. The text *Emergency Calls Only* might also appear.

Airplane Mode

The rules about flying on an airplane with a cell phone are changing. Where it was once outright forbidden to even look at a cell phone while the plane was aloft, governments around the world have left it up to each airline to determine in-flight usage.

Generally speaking, follow the crew's direction when it comes to using your cell phone. They'll let you know when and how you can use the phone: specifically, whether it needs to be turned off for take-off and landing and, once in the air, whether you can use it to make phone calls or enable any wireless features, such as Wi-Fi and GPS.

Traditionally, cell phones are placed into what's commonly called *Airplane mode* during a flight. In that mode, it's okay to use the phone and access many of its features, except for cellular network access. So you can listen to music, play games, or use the in-flight Wi-Fi if your bankroll can afford it.

To activate Airplane mode on your Fire phone, pull down the Notifications panel and tap the Airplane Mode Quick Action. When the icon is highlighted (orange), Airplane mode is active.

To exit Airplane mode, repeat the steps in this section, but in Step 3 remove the check mark.

Fire phone air-travel tips

I don't consider myself a frequent flyer, but I travel several times a year. I do it often enough that I wish the airports had separate lines for security: one for seasoned travelers, one for families, and one, of course, for frickin' idiots. That last category would have to be disguised by placing a Bonus Coupons sign or a Free Snacks banner over the metal detector. That would weed 'em out.

Here are some of my cell phone and airline travel tips:

- **Charge your phone before you leave.** This tip probably goes without saying, but you'll be happier with a full cell phone charge to start your journey.

- **Take a cell phone charger with you.** Many airports feature USB chargers, so you might need just a USB–to–micro-USB cable. Still, why risk it? Bring the entire charger with you.

- **At the security checkpoint, place your phone in a bin or put it into your backpack or carry-on luggage.** Your pockets need to be empty when you go through the metal detector. This is important. I know.

- **If the flight crew asks you to *turn off* your cell phone for take-off and landing, obey the command.** That's *turn off,* as in power off the phone or shut it down. It doesn't mean that you place the phone in Airplane mode. Turn it off.

- **Use the phone's Calendar app to keep track of flights.** The combination of airline and flight number can serve as the event title. For the event time, I insert take-off and landing schedules. For the location, I add the origin and destination airport codes. Referencing the phone from your airplane seat or in a busy terminal is much handier than fussing with travel papers. See Chapter 16 for more information on the Calendar app.

- **Some airlines feature apps you can use while traveling.** Rather than hang on to a boarding pass printed by your computer, for example, you simply show your phone to the scanner. See Chapter 17 for information on looking for such apps.

✔ When the phone is in Airplane mode, a special icon appears in the status area, similar to the one shown in the margin. You might also see the text *No Service* on the phone's lock screen.

✔ Bluetooth networking is disabled in Airplane mode, as is NFC communications. See Chapter 18 for more information.

You Can Take It with You

What's the point of sitting in an airplane cabin for four or more hours with a Fire phone and nothing to do? No, I'm not trying to urge you to use the overpriced in-flight Wi-Fi service. Instead, prepare for your tip beforehand by saving some Internet-only items for offline enjoyment.

For example, save a few web pages in the Silk browser — sites you normally visit but may not have time to read. To save a web site for later viewing, follow these steps:

1. **Open the Silk browser app and visit the site you want to save.**

   If it's a new site, open the article you want to read.

2. **Tap the Menu icon, to the right of the address bar.**

   A menu appears.

3. **Choose the Save Page command.**

   The page is downloaded to the device.

Repeat these steps for several pages. You never know how bored you'll be.

Later, when you're stuck on the flight and bored from watching the crew dispense beverages, open the Silk browser app and display the Navigation panel. Choose the Saved Pages command to view the Saved Pages screen. Tap the page you saved to read it offline.

Just as you can save web pages for viewing in an aluminum tube at 36,000 feet, consider downloading some of your music or a few books from cloud storage.

In the Music app, long-press an album or song and choose the Download command. Ditto for the Books (Kindle) app: Long-press a book and choose the Download command. The downloaded item stays on your phone. It's available whether or not you have Internet access:

✔ Save several web pages for offline viewing.

✔ Saving a web page for later viewing is great, but remember that none of the links on the page works, nor does any streaming video. On the positive side, the text is still readable and the images show up just fine.

✔ To remove a saved web page, display the Saved Pages screen and tap the Edit icon. Select one or more pages, and then tap the Delete icon at the bottom of the screen.

✔ Also see Chapter 19 for information on freeing phone storage by removing items downloaded from the cloud.

International Calling

You can use your Fire phone to dial up folks who live in other countries. You can also take your cell phone overseas and use it in another country. Completing either task isn't as difficult as properly posing for a passport photo, but it can become frustrating and potentially expensive when you don't know your way around.

Dialing an international number

A phone is a bell that anyone in the world can ring. To prove it, all you need is the phone number of anyone in the world. Dial that number and, as long as you both speak the same language, you're talking!

To make an international call with a Fire phone, you merely need to know the foreign phone number. That number includes the international country-code prefix, followed by the local phone number.

Before dialing the international country-code prefix, you must first dial a plus sign (+) when using the Phone app. The + symbol is the _country exit code,_ which must be dialed to flee the national phone system and access the international phone system. For example, to dial Finland on your phone, you dial +358 and then the number in Finland. The +358 is the exit code (+) plus the international code for Finland (358).

To produce the + code in an international phone number, press and hold down the 0 key on the Phone app's dialpad. Then type the country prefix and the phone number. Touch the Dial Phone icon to complete the call:

✔ Dialing internationally involves surcharges, unless your cell phone plan provides for international dialing.

✔ In most cases, dialing an international number involves a time zone difference. Before you dial, be aware of what time it is in the country or location you're calling. The Clock app's World Clock feature can handle that job for you: Summon a clock for the location you're calling and add it to the Word Clock screen in the Clock app.

✔ The + character isn't a number separator. When you see an international number listed as 011+20+xxxxxxx, do not insert the + character in the number. Instead, dial +20 and then the rest of the international phone number.

✔ International calls fail for a number of reasons. One of the most common is that the recipient's Phone Company or service blocks incoming international calls.

✔ Another reason that international calls fail is the zero reason: You need to omit a leading zero in the phone number that follows the country code. So, if the country code is 254 for Kenya and the phone number starts with 012, you dial +254 for Kenya and then 12 and the rest of the number.

✔ Know which type of phone you're calling internationally — cell phone or landline. The reason is that an international call to a cell phone might involve a surcharge that doesn't apply to a landline.

Sending an international text

Just as you can make an international phone call with the Fire phone, you can also send a text message. And just like placing an international call, you may also find a per-message surcharge for both sending and receiving international texts.

To send an international text, type the complete phone number, including the plus sign (+) and international access code. If you have a contact with an international number, you can use the contact's name, just as you would when sending any text:

✔ See Chapter 8 for texting info.

✔ Contact your cellular provider to confirm the text message rates. Generally, you'll find two rates: one for sending and another for receiving text messages.

✔ If texting charges vex you, remember that email has no associated per-message charge.

Taking your phone abroad

The easiest way to use a cell phone abroad is to rent or buy one in the country where you plan to stay. I'm serious: Often, international roaming charges are so high that it's cheaper to simply buy a temporary cell phone wherever you go, especially if you plan to stay there for a while.

When you opt to use your Fire phone rather than buy a local phone, things should run smoothly — if a compatible cellular service is in your location. Not every foreign country uses the same cellular network. Things must match before the phone can work. Plus, you may have to deal with foreign carrier roaming charges.

The key to determining whether your phone is usable in a foreign country is to turn it on. The name of that country's compatible cellular service should show up at the top of the phone, where the name of your carrier appears on the main screen. So where your phone once said *AT&T Wireless,* it may say *Wambooli Telcom* when you're overseas:

- ✔ You receive calls on your cell phone internationally as long as the phone can access the network. Your friends need only dial your cell phone number as they normally do; the phone system automatically forwards your calls to wherever you are in the world.

- ✔ The person calling you pays nothing extra when you're off romping the globe with your Fire phone. Nope — *you* pay extra for the call.

- ✔ While you're abroad, you need to dial internationally. When calling home (for example, the United States), you need to use a 10-digit number (phone number plus area code). You may also be required to type the country exit code when you dial.

- ✔ When in doubt, contact your cellular provider for tips and other information specific to whatever country you're visiting.

- ✔ Be sure to inquire about texting and cellular data (Internet) rates while you're abroad.

- ✔ Using your phone over a Wi-Fi network abroad incurs no extra fees (unless data roaming is on, as discussed earlier in this chapter). In fact, you can use the Skype app on your phone over a Wi-Fi network to call the United States or any international number at inexpensive rates. See Chapter 12.

Customize and Configure

Customizing your Fire phone doesn't involve sprucing up the phone's case, so put away that Bedazzler. The kind of customization this chapter refers to involves fine-tuning the way the phone's interface (as well as other aspects) is presented. Not everything you see — or hear or touch — on the Fire phone is fixed. You have the liberty to make adjustments, providing that you know where to look.

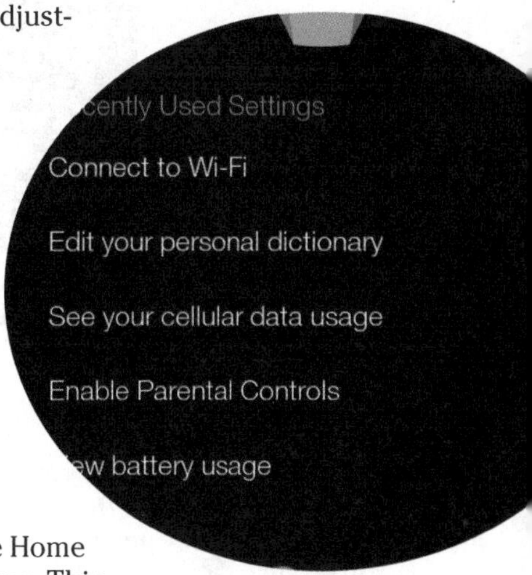

Carousel Pruning

App icons appear on the Home screen's Carousel as you use the apps. More recent apps appear on the left, and you can swipe the screen right-to-left to view apps you used a while back. App icons eventually drop off the list. Though you can't control how the apps are presented, you can add and remove app icons from the Carousel as a way to customize the Home screen:

cently Used Settings

Connect to Wi-Fi

Edit your personal dictionary

See your cellular data usage

Enable Parental Controls

ew battery usage

▶ Unlike with other phones, you cannot change the Home screen background, or *wallpaper,* on the Fire phone. This feature might be added at a future date.

▶ You can change the image that appears on the lock screen. See the later section "Changing the lock screen scene."

▶ The widgets that appear below apps on the Carousel depend on what you've done with the app. You cannot manually add or remove app widgets.

Sticking an app on the Carousel

To keep an app affixed to the Carousel, long-press its icon. Choose Pin to Front from the menu.

Pinned icons appear on the far left end of the Carousel, always showing up first when you view the Home screen, as shown in Figure 21-1. They appear in the order you pin them, most recently pinned first.

Pin

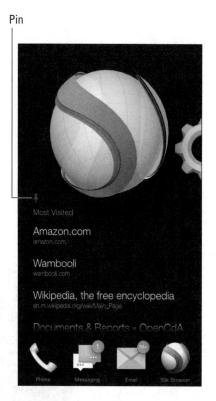

Figure 21-1: A pinned Carousel icon.

When you start other apps, they appear to the right of the pinned apps on the Carousel. Also, when you visit the Home screen, you see the first unpinned app; pinned apps appear to the left of that app:

- If you want an app to appear on the far left end of the Carousel, or "up front," long-press its icon and choose the command Move to Front.

- To unpin an app, long-press its icon and choose the command Unpin from Carousel. The app vanishes, although you can still find it (and start it) from the App Grid.

Removing an app from the Carousel

An app appears on the Carousel whenever you open that app. If you don't want that app on the Carousel, long-press its icon and choose the command Remove from Carousel. The app is gone.

Removing an app from the Carousel doesn't prevent it from appearing again the next time you start that app. It simply removes it from the Carousel until the next time you start the app.

To remove a pinned app, first unpin it as described in the preceding section. Then remove the app.

Lock Screen Modifications

The lock screen provides ample opportunities for customization, from the vain to the critical. The vain includes changing the lock screen background, or *scene,* and controlling whether notifications appear. The critical involves setting a screen lock more secure than the standard swipe lock.

Changing the lock screen scene

The image you see when you first unlock the phone is the *lock screen scene.* The Fire phone is preset to show a 3D image on the lock screen, one that takes advantage of the phone's Dynamic Perspective feature. Many such images ship with the phone, and a new image rotates in every day.

You can direct the phone to display one particular image if you like, or stir in your own images for the lock screen. To do so, follow these steps:

1. **Open the Settings app.**

2. **Choose Lock Screen to expand that area.**

3. **Tap the command Select a Lock Screen Scene.**

    You see a scrolling list of available lock screen images on the Scene screen.

To add your own image, tap the Your Photo icon. Browse the phone's photo album for a suitable image. Tap the Done icon on the next screen to set that image.

With your own image set, the phone disables the Rotation feature. If you want your image thrown in with the others, tap the Rotate Scene icon and choose Every Day or Every Week to set the rotation interval. Choosing Never means that the same image is shown on the lock screen all the time.

- You can choose only one of your photos at a time as the lock screen scene. To replace the current photo, tap its icon on the Scene screen.

- If you're fond of one of the preset images, choose Never as the rotation option, and then tap the image you want to use. Touch the Done icon to set that image as the lock screen scene.

- Images you capture by using the camera's Lenticular mode do not show up in 3D on the lock screen.

- Refer to Chapter 14 for information on taking a 3D photo with your Fire phone's camera.

Adding or removing lock screen notifications

When new email arrives, a calendar appointment looms, you miss a call, or any of a number of events happen, a notification icon appears on the lock screen. It's echoed in the Notifications panel, so if you miss the wee li'l icons, you're not sore out of luck. But you can also prevent the icons from showing up in the first place.

To show or hide the lock screen notifications, obey these steps:

1. **Open the Settings app and choose Lock Screen.**

2. **Choose the command Turn On Notifications On the Lock Screen.**

3. **Slide the master control by Notifications to the On position.**

Whether or not you see the notification depends upon whether you're paying attention. Beyond that, they appear in the top part of the lock screen based on what events are taking place on the phone.

You cannot deal with a notification on the lock screen until you've unlocked the phone. Then check the Notifications panel or start a specific app to deal with the notification.

Setting a secure screen lock

Be honest: The swipe screen lock isn't difficult to work. If you have vital information stored in your phone, and you most likely do, you need to apply a more secure screen lock. You have two choices, both of which are recommended by security experts: PIN and Password.

To set a PIN or Password lock for your Fire phone, obey these directions:

1. **Open the Settings app and tap the Lock Screen item.**

   Lock screen options appear.

2. **Choose the command Set a Password or PIN.**

3. **Enter a PIN or Password if one has already been set.**

   The Lock Method screen shows up. Three options are available:

   - *None,* or the standard swipe screen lock
   - *PIN,* where you must type a personal identification number (PIN) to get access
   - *Password,* where you must type a password, which can include letters, numbers, and symbols

4. **If you don't need a secure password, say out loud, "I'm one crazy human being," and choose the None option. Otherwise, proceed** with Step 5.

   Choosing the None option is also how to disable the PIN or password locks.

5. **Choose PIN or Password to set the appropriate lock.**

   You're required to type the PIN or Password twice to confirm that you know it.

After confirming the PIN or password, lock the phone to try it out.

The PIN or password you set appears after you unlock the screen by using the standard swipe-from-bottom-to-top action on the lock screen. Type the PIN or password and you're granted immediate access to the phone:

- ✔ You don't need to work the PIN or Password locks when you answer an incoming call. You're prompted, however, to unlock the phone if you want to use its features while you're on a call.

- ✔ To remove the PIN or Password screen lock, repeat these steps and choose None in Step 4.

- ✔ The password must be at least 4 characters long.

- ✔ The best passwords contain a mix of upper- and lowercase letters, numbers, and at least one symbol.

- ✔ Don't forget the PIN or password. As a bit of advice, I recommend that you write them down somewhere inauspicious, like maybe as a random work in the margin in this book.

- ✔ See Chapter 2 for details on unlocking your phone.

Various Phone Adjustments

If you need some time to kill, take a leisurely walk through the Settings app. Behold all the interesting and useful controls. Play with each one! Or you can just read this section, which highlights some of the more interesting and useful settings.

Changing display settings

The Display item in the Settings app deals with touchscreen settings. This section lists some popular settings worthy of your attention.

To access the Display settings items, open the Settings app and choose Display. To see all options in one spot, as shown in Figure 21-2, choose the first item, Adjust Screen Brightness. Otherwise, follow the steps as mentioned for each of the following items.

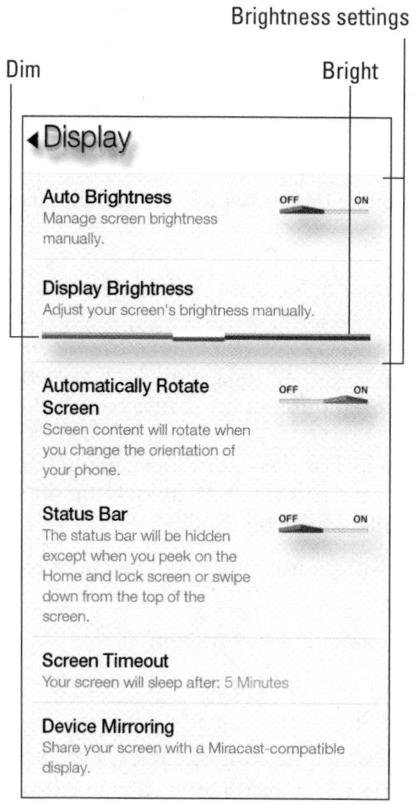

Brightness settings

Dim   Bright

◄Display

Auto Brightness OFF ON
Manage screen brightness
manually.

Display Brightness
Adjust your screen's brightness manually.

Automatically Rotate OFF ON
Screen
Screen content will rotate when
you change the orientation of
your phone.

Status Bar OFF ON
The status bar will be hidden
except when you peek on the
Home and lock screen or swipe
down from the top of the
screen.

Screen Timeout
Your screen will sleep after: 5 Minutes

Device Mirroring
Share your screen with a Miracast-compatible
display.

Figure 21-2: Adjusting display settings.

Screen brightness: In the Display area, choose the item Adjust Screen Brightness. Use the slider to set how bright the screen appears. If you prefer that the phone use its light sensor to set the brightness, slide the Auto Brightness master control to On.

The screen brightness settings are also accessible from the Quick Actions on the Notification panel.

A dimmer screen uses less battery power and therefore makes the phone's battery last longer.

Screen rotation: The Fire phone adjusts the screen's orientation depending on how you hold the phone: vertically or horizontally. If you want to fix rotation to one way or the other, orient the phone and then set the master control by Automatically Rotate Screen to Off.

Sleep timeout: The Screen Timeout value determines when the phone automatically locks, turning off the touchscreen display. The standard value is 1 minute: After 50 seconds of inactivity, the screen dims, and then 10 seconds later, the screen "sleeps" and the phone is locked.

Tap the Screen Timeout item on the Display screen (refer to Figure 21-2) to select a new timeout value. Choosing a value of Never means that the screen locks only when you press the Power/Lock button.

Show the Status Bar: Normally, the Fire phone shows the status bar only when you pull down the Notification panel or you use the Tilt gesture. To show the status bar all the time, set the master control by Status Bar to the On position.

Controlling the sound

The Sounds & Notifications area in the Settings app helps you control the various sound, noise, and silence features of the Fire phone. This section lists a few key controls for setting sounds.

Sound level adjustment: In the Settings app, in the Sounds & Notifications area, choose the Change Volume Levels item. You see a screen similar to the one shown in Figure 21-3. Use the sliders to adjust the volume levels for each individual sound-generating item.

The descriptions below each heading describe which events generate that type of sound (refer to Figure 21-3). For example, the video game volume is set by using the Media slider. When you're on the phone, the In-Call setting is used.

You can set the volume for whatever activity you're doing by using the Volume button on the side of the phone.

Notification sounds: Beneath the Sounds & Notifications heading in the Settings app, choose Manage Notifications. You see the App Notifications screen, which lists all apps on the phone that generate notifications. You can change the sound used for individual apps by choosing them from the list.

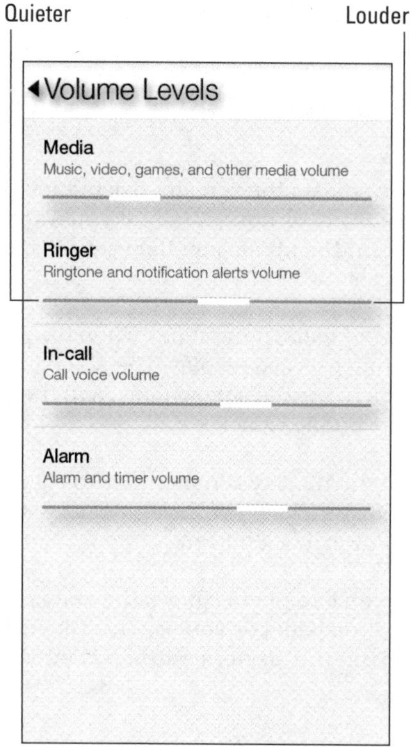

Quieter   Louder

◀Volume Levels

Media
Music, video, games, and other media volume

Ringer
Ringtone and notification alerts volume

In-call
Call voice volume

Alarm
Alarm and timer volume

Figure 21-3: Setting sound levels.

For example, if you want a unique sound to play whenever new email appears, choose the Email app. On the Email screen, tap Sound. Choose a ringtone from the list. That sound plays, and if you tap the Done icon, it's set as the Email app's notification sound.

If you don't want an app to play a sound when a notification is generated, choose the No Sound ringtone.

Vibration mode: In the Settings app's Sounds & Notifications area, tap the Change Your Ringtone command. Slide the master control by Vibrate to the On position. The phone now vibrates in addition to playing sound.

I find that Vibration mode comes in handy when I'm at locations where I may not hear my phone's ringtone. The phone vibrating in my pocket works well to grab my attention.

Turning on vibration puts a wee extra drain on the battery. See Chapter 23 for more information on power management for your phone.

Modifying keyboard settings

The onscreen keyboard is packed with a lot of power. Most of that power is accessed via special controls on the Keyboard screen, as shown in Figure 21-4.

◄Keyboard

Auto-correct   OFF   ON
Words spelled incorrectly will
be corrected automatically as
you type.

Auto-capitalize   OFF   ON
Words at the beginning of
sentences will be capitalized
automatically.

Advanced Keyboard   OFF   ON
Secondary keys will be
accessible by pressing and
holding.

Check Spelling   OFF   ON
Words spelled incorrectly will
be underlined.

Trace Typing   OFF   ON
You can enter words by tracing
from key to key.

Keyboard Language
English (United States)

Personal Dictionary

Figure 21-4: The Keyboard screen.

To get to the Keyboard screen, open the Settings app and choose Keyboard. Tap the item Manage Advanced Keyboard Features.

One feature that comes in handy, which is disabled by default on the Fire phone, is the Advanced Keyboard setting: Slide that item's master control to the On position, as shown in Figure 21-4.

When the Advanced Keyboard setting is active, the onscreen keyboard changes to show wee character previews above the primary keys. You can access those secondary characters by long-pressing the keys, as illustrated in Figure 21-5.

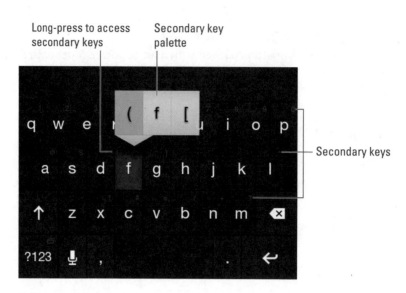

Figure 21-5: Secondary keys are active.

Some people enjoy having quick access to the secondary keys, but it seems to drive a majority of people nuts. If you have a heavy hand (or finger), keep this feature turned off. Otherwise, you may find quick access to the secondary keys a blessing.

App Central

*W*ith over 200,000 apps available at the Appstore, you would think that the object of owning a Fire phone would be to collect them all. And that's true. Actually, it's true with a limitation: Collect all the apps you need, those that do the job you intended when you obtained your Fire phone.

Beyond finding, installing, and using apps, a necessary task involves managing those apps and keeping them neat and tidy. It's neither heavy-duty nor frequent, but it's something you may find yourself doing on occasion. This chapter offers information to help keep your apps under control.

Manage Your Apps

Some Fire phone users go to school for years to learn how to practice good app management. On the other hand, you need only read this section. Not only that, you need to refer to this information only when you believe app management is necessary. Hopefully, that need doesn't arise too often.

Reviewing your apps

The central location for all the apps you have installed or are available to your phone is the App Grid. It's the same place you go to when you want to start an app. It's that convenient.

Display the App Grid from the Home screen by swiping the screen from bottom to top. You can also press the Home button twice to view apps on the App Grid, shown in Figure 22-1.

Master control

Home row

App Grid index

Figure 22-1: The App Grid.

The App Grid may be several screens tall. An index appears on the right side of the App Grid, indicating how many screens are present and which screen you're viewing, as shown in Figure 22-1.

The master switch at the top of the App Grid lets you view apps installed on your phone as well as apps not installed but available on cloud storage. The cloud storage represents apps you may have obtained previously, but removed. If you tap one of those app icons, the app is again downloaded to your phone.

Updating an app

App developers frequently offer *updates,* or newer versions of their software. The updates happen all the time, and they address issues, bugs, or offer new features. The good news is that after you pay for an app, you don't have to pay again for its update. Better news is that Fire phone apps are updated automatically. You never need to do a thing.

To review recent app updates, follow these steps:

1. **Open the Appstore app.**

2. **Summon the Navigation panel.**

3. **Choose App Updates.**

You see a screen similar to Figure 22-2, although the screen may be blank if no apps have been updated.

Update details

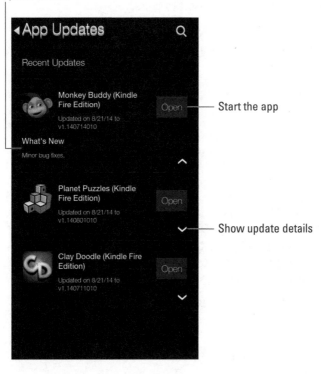

Start the app

Show update details

Figure 22-2: Reviewing app updates.

The App Updates screen lists those apps that have been recently updated and the date when the updates occurred; plus, you can tap the chevron to view update details, as shown in the figure.

App updates are automatic on the Fire phone.

Uninstalling apps

On the Fire phone, you don't uninstall apps as much as you put them away. Essentially, you exile the unwanted app to cloud storage, where it sadly sits and awaits the day when you want it again. That's okay, and it's an excellent system because it means you never pay twice for the same app.

To uninstall an app or, more correctly, to remove an app from the phone and banish it to the cloud, follow these steps:

1. **Display the App Grid.**

   All installed apps appear on the App Grid.

2. **Long-press the app you want to remove.**

   The phone vibrates a bit, and then a menu appears below the app icon.

   If the menu doesn't appear, the app cannot be removed from the phone.

3. **Choose the command Remove from Device.**

   The app icon disappears.

The app is removed from the phone, but it remains available from the cloud: Slide the master control to Cloud and you'll see the app listed. (Refer to Figure 22-1 for the location of the master control.)

- Purging apps you no longer use does free up some space on the phone. Generally speaking, however, apps aren't the lead culprits when your phone gets low on space. See Chapter 19 for more information on increasing storage space on your phone.

- You can always reinstall apps you've removed, even apps you've paid for. Simply slide the master control to Cloud and tap the app icon. You aren't charged twice for reinstalling a paid app.

- You can't remove apps that are preinstalled on the phone by either the phone's manufacturer or your cellular service provider. These apps are necessary for the phone's operation. If you don't plan on using them, consider sticking them into a folder or collection. See the later section "Building an app collection."

Shutting down an app run amok

It happens. Sometimes an app goes crazy and just won't stop. Though Amazon tries to keep unstable apps out of the Appstore, not all technology is perfect. If you need to smite an errant app, follow these steps:

1. **Open the Settings app.**

2. **Choose Applications & Parental Controls.**

3. **Choose Manage Applications.**

   You see a list of running apps. If not, tap the Filter By command and choose Running Services.

4. **Swipe the screen to look for the app that's vexing you.**

   For example, a game is stuck and it's repeating some heinous sound.

5. **Tap the app to open its Manage screen.**

   A sample Manage screen is shown in Figure 22-3.

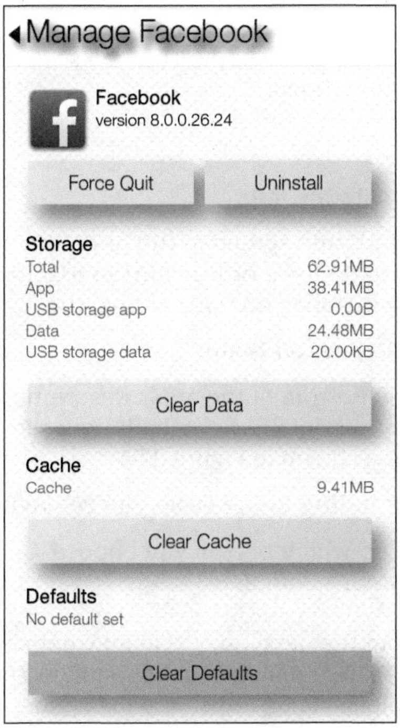

◀Manage Facebook

f   Facebook
    version 8.0.0.26.24

| Force Quit | Uninstall |

Storage
Total	62.91MB
App	38.41MB
USB storage app	0.00B
Data	24.48MB
USB storage data	20.00KB

Clear Data

Cache
| Cache | 9.41MB |

Clear Cache

Defaults
No default set

Clear Defaults

Figure 22-3: The Manage screen.

6. Tap the Force Quit button.

You see a warning prompt.

7. Tap the OK button to stop the app.

Be careful with these steps! Only stop an app that you truly cannot stop in any other way. Many apps feature a Quit command or Exit command. Try that first. Also see the next section.

The problem with randomly quitting an app is that data may get lost or damaged. At worst, the phone may become unstable. The only way to fix that situation is to restart the device.

Reporting app problems to the developer

Yet another advantage of having a Fire phone is that when you have trouble with an app, you can easily get in touch with the app developer to help resolve issues. Though reporting a problem doesn't guarantee a response from the developer — or a fix, for that matter — it's good to know that the line of communication is open.

To report app problems to the app developer (the folks who wrote and produced the app), obey these directions:

1. Open the Appstore app.

2. Browse or search to locate the app.

You need to view the app's Info screen in the Appstore. It's the same screen where you tapped the Free or Buy button to initially obtain the app. Because the app is installed on your phone, the button says Open.

3. Choose the command Report an Issue.

You have to swipe to the bottom of the app's description screen and paste the reviews and other details. Eventually, you see the reporting screen, similar to the one shown in Figure 22-4.

4. Tap the button corresponding to the issue you're having.

The next steps depend on which button you choose. Continue working through the process until it's complete.

You may not hear a reply from the developer. You may not see the issue resolved in your lifetime. I still recommend that you follow the steps in this section when you have problems using apps on your phone.

It's at this point that the kind people at Amazon would like for me to remind you that they have in place a vetting process for all apps found at the Appstore. If you find a bad or questionable app, they really want to hear from you.

Figure 22-4: The Issue Report menu.

Organizing Your Apps

You might be under the assumption that your Fire phone's apps organize themselves. To a degree, that's true: As new apps are installed, they're placed on the App Grid. Their order, however, isn't fixed. You can rearrange apps to your heart's content. You can also organize apps into folders, called app *collections*. It's a voluntary activity, but one you may pursue in the future.

Also see Chapter 21 for information on working with apps on the Home screen Carousel.

Rearranging apps on the App Grid

It may appear as though apps on the App Grid are solidly attached to the screen. They're not. You can pick up and move the apps at any time.

The secret to moving an app on the App Grid is to long-press the app. After a moment, the phone vibrates. Keeping your finger down, you can then drag the app icon to another location on the App Grid. The icons all jiggle around to make room for the one icon you've moved. Figure 22-5 illustrates the process.

You can also drag an icon to another App Grid screen: Long-press to lift the icon, and then drag your finger down to another screen. If no other screen exists, dragging down the icon creates that screen:

✓ The App Grid can't have any blank spots. When you move an icon, all other icons rearrange themselves to fill in any blanks.

Icon to move   Long-press   Drag to new location   Icons rearrange to make room

Figure 22-5: Moving an icon on the App Grid.

⚓ Though you can create a new App Grid screen by dragging an icon to it, you can't create a blank screen. When the last icon is removed from an App Grid screen, that screen is removed.

Placing an app on the Home row

The top row of apps on the App Grid also appear at the bottom of the Home screen. That makes this location a great place for your most-often-used apps. The location is officially known as the *Home row*. Refer to Figure 22-1 for its location.

The Fire phone comes preconfigured with four apps on the Home row: Phone, Messages, Email, and the Silk browser. You're free to replace these apps with others you use more frequently. To do so, simply drag another app icon to the Home row as described in the preceding section:

⚓ I highly recommend retaining the Phone app on the Home row.

⚓ Important apps can also be pinned to the Carousel. See Chapter 21.

Pinning media

Beyond apps, the App Grid can be home to media you view on the Fire phone. You can place media icons into the grid, which gives you quick access to music, books, photos, and videos.

To pin media to the App Grid, you first need to open and enjoy the media, such as listening to an album by using the Music app. When the album appears on the Carousel, long-press its icon. Choose the command Pin to Home Grid, as shown in Figure 22-6.

Long-press the Media icon   Media on the App Grid

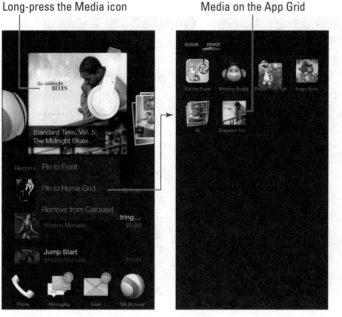

Carousel   App Grid

Figure 22-6: Pinning media to the App Grid.

Now, why they call the command Pin to Home Grid and not Pin to App Grid is anyone's guess. Perhaps someone didn't get a memo? Regardless, you'll find the media located on the App Grid (look near the bottom), as shown in Figure 22-6.

- Media pinned to the App Grid can be moved just like any other icon. See the earlier section "Rearranging apps on the App Grid."

- To remove media from the App Grid, long-press its icon and choose the command Unpin from Home Grid.

- Removing media from the App Grid doesn't uninstall or remove the media from your phone.

Building an app collection

On any other device, an app collection would be called a *folder.* It's a single icon that contains multiple icons. Creating an app collection allows you to organize similar apps into a single spot, and it also helps keep the App Grid from becoming too long and tawdry.

Figure 22-7 illustrates what an app collection looks like. Tap the icon to view its contents, also shown in Figure 22-7. To start an app held in a collection, open the collection and then tap the icon.

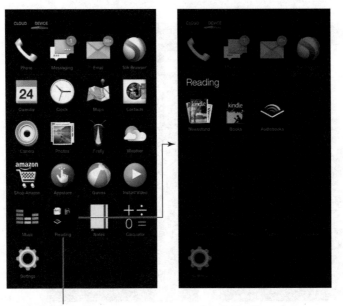

App Collection icon   App Collection contents

Figure 22-7: An app collection.

To create an app collection, on the App Grid drag one icon over another. Upon failure, the two icons swap positions. Upon success, you see the Name App Collection prompt. Type a short, descriptive name for the collection. Tap the OK button to create the collection.

Add icons to the collection by dragging them over the collection icon.

To remove an icon from a collection, open the collection and long-press the icon. Choose the command Remove from Collection. When you remove the last icon from a collection, the collection itself is discarded:

- ✓ Keep the collection name short and descriptive. The name appears below the collection icon on the App Grid, so if it's too long you don't see the whole thing.

- ✓ It's best to create an app collection of similar icons — for example, a collection of games, social networking apps, and shopping apps.

Maintenance, Troubleshooting, and Help

on't blame yourself; no one likes to do maintenance. Okay, well, I like maintaining my stuff. I even change the belt on my vacuum cleaner every six months. Did you know that the vacuum cleaner manual tells you to do so? Probably not. I read that in *Vacuum Cleaner Maintenance For Dummies*. This book is *Amazon Fire Phone For Dummies*, which is why it contains topics on maintenance, troubleshooting, and help for the Fire phones, not for vacuum cleaners.

Battery Care and Feeding

Perhaps the most important item you can monitor and maintain on your phone is its battery. The battery supplies the necessary electrical juice by which the phone operates. Without battery power, your phone is about as useful as a tin-can-and-a-string for communications. Keep an eye on the battery.

Monitoring the battery

The battery's current state is reflected by a status icon on the status bar, lurking at the top of the screen. Use the Peek gesture to see the status bar, although it's also visible when you pull down the Notification panel.

Various icons are used to display the battery status. Figure 23-1 displays the variety. As the battery drains, the battery icon appears to drain as well. When the icon is red, the battery is very low. Charge at once!

 Battery is fully charged

 Battery is draining

 Battery is precariously low!

 Battery is charging

Figure 23-1: Battery status icons.

You might also see the icon for a dead or missing battery, but for some reason I can't get my phone to turn on and display it:

✔ See Chapter 3 for more information on the Peek gesture.

✔ Heed those low-battery warnings! The phone sounds a notification whenever the battery power gets low. The phone sounds another notification whenever the battery gets *very* low.

✔ When the battery is too low, the phone shuts itself off.

✔ The best way to deal with a low battery is to connect the phone to a power source: Either plug the phone into a wall socket or connect the phone to a computer by using a USB cable. The phone charges itself immediately; plus, you can use the phone while it's charging.

✔ The phone charges more efficiently when it's plugged into a wall socket rather than a computer.

✔ You don't have to fully charge the phone to use it. If you have 20 minutes to charge and the power level returns to only 70 percent, that's great. Well, it's not great, but it's far better than a 20 percent battery level.

✔ Battery percentage values are best-guess estimates. Just because you talked for two hours and the battery shows 50 percent doesn't mean that you're guaranteed two more hours of talking. Odds are good that you have much less than two hours. In fact, as the percentage value gets low, the battery appears to drain faster.

Determining what is drawing power

The Battery screen on your Fire phone lets you review which activities have been consuming power when the phone is operating from its battery. This informative screen is shown in Figure 23-2.

To view the Battery Usage screen on your phone, open the Settings app and choose Battery & Storage. Choose the item View Battery Usage.

Touch an item in the list to view its details. For some items, the Details screen contains an icon that you can touch to adjust the setting. For example, touch the Music item (shown in Figure 23-2) to view additional details and turn off the music. Or, if Wi-Fi shows up on the list, tap the Wi-Fi button to control the phone's Wi-Fi settings. Turning off Wi-Fi can extend battery life should the situation grow dire.

The number and variety of items listed on the Battery Use screen depend on what you've been doing with your phone between charges and how many different apps you've been using. Don't be surprised if an item (such as the Books app) doesn't show up in the list. Not every app consumes copious quantities of battery power.

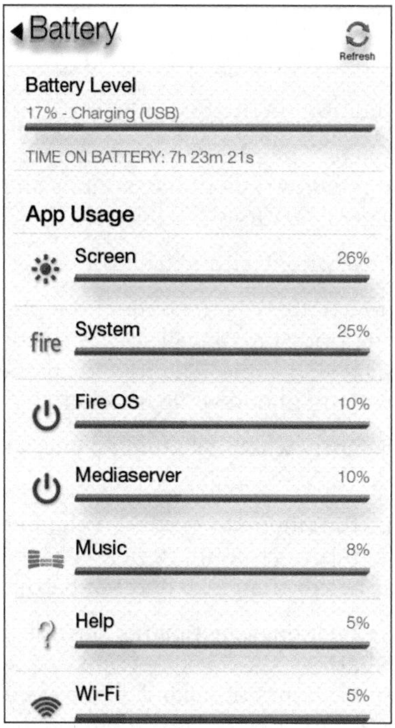

Figure 23-2: Battery usage info.

Saving battery life

Here's a smattering of things you can do to help prolong battery life for your Fire phone:

Dim the screen. The display is capable of drawing down quite a lot of battery power. Although a dim screen can be more difficult to see, especially outdoors, it definitely saves on battery life. Adjust the screen brightness from the Settings app, or choose the Brightness Quick Action from the Navigation panel.

Disable vibration options. The phone's vibration is caused by a teensy motor. Although you don't see much battery savings by disabling the vibration options, it's better than no savings. To turn off vibration, follow these steps:

1. **Open the Settings app.**

2. **Choose Sound & Notifications.**

3. **Choose Change Your Ringtone.**

4. **Slide the master control by Vibrate to the Off position.**

Additionally, consider lowering the volume while the battery is low: Just press the Volume button to lower the volume almost all the way.

Deactivate Bluetooth. When you're not using Bluetooth, turn it off: Display the Notification panel and tap the Bluetooth icon. See Chapter 18 for information on Bluetooth.

Turn off Wi-Fi. The phone's Wi-Fi radio places only a modest drain on the battery, but it's still a drain. You can quickly disable Wi-Fi by pulling down the Notification panel and tapping the Wi-Fi icon.

Regular Phone Maintenance

Unlike draining the lawn mower's oil once a year (you do that, right?), regular maintenance of a phone doesn't require a drip pan or a permit from the EPA. In fact, the Fire phone requires only two basic regular maintenance tasks: cleaning and backing up.

Keeping it clean

You probably already keep your phone clean. I must use my sleeve to wipe the touchscreen at least a dozen times a day. Of course, better than your sleeve is something called a *microfiber cloth*. This item can be found at any computer- or office-supply store:

✔ Never use ammonia or alcohol to clean the touchscreen. These substances damage the phone. Use only a cleaning solution specifically designed for touchscreens.

✔ If the screen continually gets dirty, consider adding a *screen protector*. This specially designed cover prevents the screen from getting scratched or dirty while still allowing you to interact with the touchscreen. Ensure that the screen protector you obtain is intended for use with your specific phone.

✔ You can also find customized cell phone cases, belt clips, and protectors, which can help keep the phone looking spiffy. Be aware that these items are mostly for decorative or fashion purposes and don't prevent serious damage should you drop the phone.

Backing up your phone

A *backup* is a safety copy of the information on your phone. It includes any contact information, music, photos, videos, and apps you've recorded, downloaded, or installed, plus any settings you've made to customize your phone. Copying this information to another source is one way to keep the information safe, in case anything happens to the phone.

Because the Fire phone heavily relies upon the cloud, you don't really need to back up a thing. Any new information you create or input on the phone is instantly stored on the Internet. Information about apps, music, and books is coordinated with the Amazon cloud. Other information, such as contacts and calendar events, is associated with individual accounts you've added to the phone.

To confirm that automatic backups are taking place, open the Settings app. In the Device area, choose the item Disable Auto Backups. Ensure that the master control by Device Backup is set to the On position.

If you desire to copy specific information from the phone to a computer, you can use cloud storage or perform a manual file copy between the phone and a computer. See Chapter 19 for information on both of these backup methods.

Updating the system

Every so often, a new version of your phone's operating system becomes available. When that update occurs, a notification appears on the phone, indicating that a system upgrade is available. Follow the directions for that update, which should install in only a few minutes.

You can manually check for updates, although doing so is kind of futile. Follow these steps:

1. **Open the Settings app and choose Device.**

2. **In the Device area, choose Install System Updates.**

   If an update is available, you'll see so on the System Updates screen. Otherwise:

3. **Tap the Check Now button.**

   Odds are good that the phone tells you, "No updates found."

I recommend connecting the phone to a power source during an update. The reason is that you don't want the phone to run out of juice in the middle of the process.

Help and Troubleshooting

Getting help isn't as bad as it was in the old days. Back then, you could try two sources for technological help: the atrocious manual that came with your electronic device or a phone call to the guy who wrote the atrocious manual. It was unpleasant. Today, the situation is better. You have many resources for solving issues with your gizmos, including your Fire phone.

Finding help

The Fire phone offers you plenty of opportunities for obtaining help. They start by opening the Help app found on the App Grid. You'll also find the Quick Start app, which has the word *Fire* as its icon.

Your first and best opportunity for help comes from the Mayday feature: Open the Help app, and on the Mayday screen, tap the Connect button. Mayday puts you in direct contact with a real, live human being. You can see the person on the screen after you start the feature, similar to what's shown in Figure 23-3.

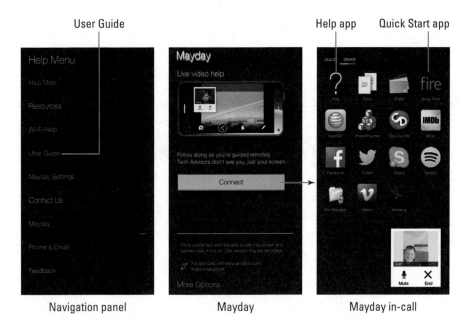

Figure 23-3: Getting help via Mayday.

Ask the Mayday assistant your question, and they'll provide an answer. They can even control your phone to show you how things work, but you must first grant them permission to do so. Also, know that although you can see the assistant (refer to Figure 23-3, on the far right), they cannot see you. So feel free to ask for help while you're improperly clothed.

For additional Help options, for example, when you believe that the Mayday assistant *can*, in fact, see you, consider browsing the Fire phone documentation: Open the Help app and swipe in the Navigation panel. Choose User Guide to view the documentation:

- ✓ When you're done with a Mayday call, you see a prompt offering feedback to Amazon. Be sure to respond accordingly about whether your issue was resolved.

- ✓ Use the Search command while viewing the documentation to help you quickly find and resolve certain issues.

Getting cellular support

Beyond Mayday, you may need help from your cellular provider. They can provide assistance when you're having problems with the cellular network as well as with the mobile data network (Internet).

As this book goes to press, the Fire phone is offered only on the AT&T network in the United States. Even so, I've listed all the major carriers in Table 23-1. Use the information presented in the table to get cellular assistance, should you need it.

Table 23-1		U.S. Cellular Providers	
Provider	*From Cell*	*Tollfree*	*Website*
AT&T	611	800-331-0500	www.att.com/esupport
Sprint Nextel	*2	800-211-4727	mysprint.sprint.com
T-Mobile	611	800-866-2453	www.t-mobile.com/Contact.aspx
Verizon	611	800-922-0204	http://support.vzw.com/clc

Your cellular provider's Help phone number is already present in the phone. To locate it, open the Settings app. In the Phone category, choose the item Contact Your Carrier. The next screen details contact information.

Fixing random and annoying problems

Aren't all problems annoying? A welcome problem doesn't exist, unless the problem is welcome because it diverts attention from another, preexisting problem. And random problems? If problems were predictable, they would serve in office. Or maybe they already do?

Here are some typical problems and my suggestions for a solution:

You have general trouble. For just about any problem or minor quirk, consider restarting the phone: Turn off the phone, and then turn it on again. This procedure will most likely fix a majority of the annoying and quirky problems you encounter when using your Fire phone.

To restart the Fire phone, press and hold the Power/Lock button. From the menu that appears, tap the Restart button. The phone instantly restarts. Hopefully, that fixes whatever has gone awry.

When restarting doesn't work, consider turning off the phone, waiting about 15 seconds, and then turning it on again.

The data connection needs to be checked. Sometimes the data connection drops but the phone connection stays active. Check the status bar. If you see bars, you have a phone signal. When you don't see the 4G, 3G, 1X, or Wi-Fi icon, the phone has no data signal (Internet access).

Occasionally, the data signal suddenly drops for a minute or two. Wait, and it comes back around. If it doesn't, the cellular data network might be down, or you may simply be in an area with lousy service. Consider changing your location.

For wireless connections, you have to ensure that Wi-Fi is set up properly and working. Setup usually involves pestering the person who configured the Wi-Fi signal or made it available, such as the cheerful person in the green apron who serves you coffee.

Some older Wi-Fi routers cannot handle the increased load of multiple wireless devices. In some cases, turning off the phone's Wi-Fi and then turning it on again may restore the connection: Pull down the Notification panel and tap the Wi-Fi icon. Wait a moment. Then tap the Wi-Fi icon again to see if that restores the connection.

The phone's software must be reset (a drastic measure). When all else fails, you can do the extreme thing and reset all software on the phone, essentially returning it to the state it was in when it popped out of the box. Obviously, you should not perform this step lightly. In fact, consider finding support (see the earlier section "Finding help") before you start:

1. **Open the Settings app.**

2. **Choose Device to expand that area.**

3. **Choose Factory Reset Your Fire.**

   Nothing scary happens yet.

4. **Place a check mark in the box by Back Up Device Before Reset.**

   That sounds like a good idea.

5. **Tap the Reset button.**

   Still nothing scary.

6. **Touch the OK button to proceed with the erase-and-reset.**

   Scary: All the information you've set or stored on the phone is purged.

Again, *do not* follow these steps unless you're certain that they will fix the problem or you're under orders to do so from someone in tech support.

You can, however, follow these directions should you decide to sell, give away, or return your phone. In that case, erasing all your personal information makes a lot of sense.

Fire Phone Q&A

I love Q&A! That's because not only is it an effective way to express certain problems and solutions but some of the questions might also cover topics I've been wanting to write about.

"The touchscreen doesn't work!"

The touchscreen, such as the one used on a Fire phone, requires a human finger for proper interaction. The phone interprets complicated electromagnetic physics between the human finger and the phone to determine where the touchscreen is being touched.

You can use the touchscreen while wearing special touchscreen gloves. Yes, they actually make such things. But wearing regular gloves? Nope.

The touchscreen might also fail when the battery power is low or when the phone has been physically damaged.

"The screen is too dark!"

Your phone features a teensy light sensor on the front. The sensor is used to adjust the screen's brightness based on the amount of ambient light at your location. If the sensor is covered, the screen can get very, very dark.

Ensure that you aren't unintentionally blocking the light sensor. Avoid buying a case or screen protector that obscures the sensor.

The Automatic Brightness setting might also be vexing you. See Chapter 21 for information on setting screen brightness.

"Dynamic Perspective isn't working!"

The Dynamic Perspective feature, where objects appear to be 3D on the screen, is pretty nifty, but it doesn't work all the time. For example, if the phone's sensors don't see a human face, the feature doesn't work.

Ensure that the four sensors, one in each corner on the front of the phone, aren't being obscured. Also, the feature may not work if your face is covered.

When the battery gets low, Dynamic Perspective is disabled to save power. See the section "Saving battery life," earlier in this chapter, for information on what to do when the battery gets low.

"The battery doesn't charge!"

Start from the source: Is the wall socket providing power? Is the cord plugged in? The cable may be damaged, so try another cable.

When charging from a USB port on a computer, ensure that the computer is turned on. Computers provide no USB power when they're turned off. A powered USB hub works best for charging the phone. Use a USB connection directly on the computer to be sure.

"The phone gets so hot that it turns itself off!"

Yikes! An overheating phone can be a nasty problem. Judge how hot the phone is by seeing whether you can hold it in your hand: When the phone is too hot to hold, it's too hot. If you're using the phone to keep your coffee warm, the phone is too hot.

Turn off the phone. Let it cool.

If the overheating problem continues, have the phone looked at for potential repair. The battery might need to be replaced.

"The phone won't do Landscape mode!"

Just because an app doesn't enter Landscape mode doesn't mean that it *can* enter Landscape mode. Not every app takes advantage of the phone's capability to orient itself in Landscape mode. For example, the Home screen doesn't "do Landscape."

One app that definitely does Landscape mode is the web browser, which is described in Chapter 10.

Confirm that the Automatic Screen Rotation feature is enabled before you blame the phone. See Chapter 21 for information on adjusting this setting.

Part VI
The Part of Tens

Enjoy a Part of Tens list online at www.dummies.com/extras/amazonfirephone.

In this part . . .

- ✓ Glean ten tips, tricks, and shortcuts
- ✓ Remember ten important things

Ten Tips, Tricks, and Shortcuts

In This Chapter

▶ Using the Flashlight app
▶ Controlling kids' phone access
▶ Jotting down notes
▶ Organizing loyalty cards
▶ Controlling the phone with your voice
▶ Setting default apps
▶ Avoiding data surcharges
▶ Controlling the personal dictionary
▶ Using Firefly to read information
▶ Finding a lost phone

A *tip* is a handy suggestion, something spoken from experience or insight, and something you may not have thought of yourself. A *trick* is something that's good to know, something impressive or unexpected. And a *shortcut* is the path you take through the graveyard because it's a lot faster — not minding that the groundskeeper may, in fact, be a zombie.

Although I'd like to think that everything I mention in this book is a tip, trick, or shortcut for using your Android phone, I can offer even more information. This chapter provides ten tips, tricks, and shortcuts to help you get the most from your phone.

Log Manager
47.85MB

android.downloads:3202
44.65MB

Mayday
16.52MB

Shine Some Light on the Subject

It's dark. You can't find the front-door keyhole. Or maybe you're touring a sewage treatment plant and the only light switch is on the far side of the Toxic Sludge room.

If you're a dork, you'll just power-on your phone and use the touchscreen as a makeshift flashlight. You're not a dork, however, because you have a Fire phone. It features a built-in flashlight.

To turn on the flashlight, which is really the rear camera's flash or LED, pull down the Notification panel. Tap the Flashlight icon. The LED comes on. *Fiat lux!*

To turn off the flashlight, tap the Flashlight icon again.

Having the flashlight on consumes battery life at an alarming pace. Ensure that you turn off the flashlight as soon as you no longer need it.

Parental Controls

What kind of fool would let a child use a sophisticated piece of electronics like a Fire phone? Well, I would. Kids of any age can operate the phone, providing you give them a few key words of advice and perhaps employ some of the phone's parental-control features.

The Fire phone's parental controls can be employed to block specific apps, restrict access to content, as well as control what a wee one can do with the phone. For discussion purposes, *wee one* refers to any human under the age of 26.

To enable the parental controls, follow these steps:

1. **Open the Settings app.**

2. **Choose Applications & Parental Controls.**

3. **Choose Enable Parental Controls.**

   The Parental Controls screen appears. It's rather sparse when the controls are off, so:

4. **Slide the master control to the On position.**

5. **Use the onscreen keyboard to set a parental password.**

   The password is unique, different from any other password, so make up something you won't forget and your kid won't guess.

6. **Tap the Submit button.**

   The Parental Controls screen springs to life, offering a slew of options and settings to make your rug rat's phone life a little less permissive.

With the parental controls enabled, two types of restrictions are applied to the content and apps on your phone: Block Content and Password Protection.

Block Content: A list of apps appear with the Blocked button to the left. When an app is blocked, the phone operator cannot use that app. If they attempt to do so, they see a pop-up warning appear, similar to the one shown in Figure 24-1.

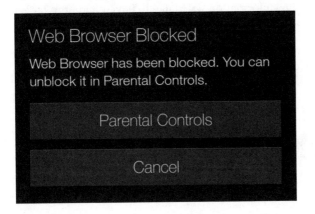

Web Browser Blocked

Web Browser has been blocked. You can unblock it in Parental Controls.

Parental Controls

Cancel

Figure 24-1: An app's content is blocked.

The phone operator must return to the Parental Controls screen and tap the Blocked button, changing it to read *Unblocked,* for the operator to use the app.

Choose the item Block Content Types to apply even more blocking restrictions to various media and app types.

Password Protection: Several phone features are listed, with a master control to the right of each feature. All master controls are preset to the On position, meaning that the phone operator must type the Parental Controls password to reset the master control for that feature and then use the feature.

For example, the Password Protect Purchases feature restricts access to online shopping. To shop, the operator would have to type the Parental Controls password, slide the master control for password-protected purchases to the Off position, and then try again to buy something:

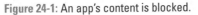

 ✔ To disable the parental controls, slide the main master control to the Off position. You have to type the password and tap the Submit button to complete the process.

 ✔ The parental controls lack a feature that ensures your offspring will immediately return a call or text. That's probably one of the most frustrating things about being the parent of a child with an instant communications device like a smartphone.

Take Some Notes

The Fire phone comes with a simple note-taking app called Notes. This fact may seem trivial, but you'd be surprised by how many smartphones don't come with such an app. It's truly a good thing to have, not only for jotting down notes but also for keeping information you'd like to have handy but have nowhere else to put. For me, that's my dress shirt size. (Authors don't get out much.)

Open the Notes app from the App Grid. You see an overview of the notes you've already created, similar to what's shown in Figure 24-2.

Figure 24-2: The Notes app.

Tap a note card to open it, view its contents, or make changes.

Tap the New Note icon to start a new, blank note.

While you're editing a note, tap the Camera icon to add a photo; tap the Microphone icon to take an audio note. Both media, the photo and the audio clip, are embedded into the note.

To remove a note, long-press its card and choose the Delete command from the pop-up menu. Tap the OK button to confirm.

Whip Out Your Wallet

Relax: The Wallet app isn't about copying your credit card information. That would probably be a dumb idea, although in the future the smartphone may replace the wallet. I'll be an old fogey on that topic and say, "No!" But until then, you can use the Wallet app to keep track of all your customer loyalty and gift cards.

To use the Wallet app, touch its icon on the App Grid. You see a list of any cards you've already added to the Wallet. To use a card, choose it from the list. The card's barcode appears on the phone's touchscreen. Present that code to the scanner at checkout to use your card.

If you haven't yet added any cards, follow these steps:

1. **Tap the Add icon.**
2. **Choose the card type, such as Rewards or Loyalty Card.**
3. **Fill in the card's information.**

   Type the store name, account number, PIN, and other information copied from the card.

   To quickly enter the card number, tap the Scan Barcode button. Use the phone's camera (Firefly, actually) to scan the barcode and input the number.

4. **Use the phone's camera to snap a picture of the card's front, back, or both.**

   Tap the Front of Card button to take a picture of the card's front; tap the Back of Card button to take a picture of the card's backside.

5. **Tap the Save icon to save the card.**
6. **Repeat the steps to enter another card.**

Some store scanners cannot read the image from a touchscreen. Things are getting better than they were in the past, but you may still have problems.

Turn on the phone's NFC to take advantage of NFC card readers at checkout. See Chapter 18 for more information about NFC.

Voice Commands

It's possible to control the Fire phone using only your voice. That's not entirely true, because to activate the Voice Commands feature, you have to press and hold the Home button. If you can get past that effort, then you can command the phone without touching it.

When you press and hold the Home button, you see the Voice Commands screen, similar to what's shown in Figure 24-3.

Figure 24-3: The phone is listening.

At this point, you can direct the phone to carry out specific tasks, but you must know what to see. Here are some common commands and phrases:

> *Make a call*
>
> *Call Barack Obama's cell phone*
>
> *Send a text message*
>
> *Send an email*

Search the web for Hungarian restaurants

Shop for adult diapers

After you bark an order, the phone may ask for more information. Respond as prompted. For example, say "Yes" or "No" or utter the name of a contact.

Say "Cancel" when you want the voice interaction to stop.

Choose Default Apps

As you use your phone, you may see the Complete Action Using prompt. It asks you to pick an app to complete an action. Then you tap Just Once or Always.

When you choose Just Once, you see the prompt again. When you choose Always, that same app is used to complete the action; the prompt never shows up again. That is, unless you completely undo that choice.

My advice is to choose Just Once until you're sick of seeing the Complete Action Using prompt. At that point, after choosing the same app over and over, choose Always.

The fear, of course, is that you'll make a mistake. But you can't make a mistake, because the Always decision is reversible. Here's how to undo that setting:

1. **Open the Settings app.**

2. **Choose Applications & Parental Controls.**

3. **Choose Manage Applications.**

   The Manage Applications screen appears.

4. **Tap Filter By, and on the next screen choose All.**

   At this point, all installed applications — including a few secret ones that you won't recognize and definitely shouldn't touch — appear in the list.

5. **Locate the app you assigned to the Always choice.**

   Here is where the steps may become difficult. You need to remember which app you chose, such as the Photos app.

6. **Tap the app's entry to display its detailed information screen.**

7. **Touch the Clear Defaults button.**

   The phone immediately forgets to always use that app.

You can't screw up by following these steps. The worst that happens is that the Complete Action Using prompt appears again. The next time you see it, however, make a better choice.

Avoid Data Overages

A vital concern for anyone using a cell phone is whether you're about to burst through your miserly monthly mobile data quota. Surcharges can pinch the wallet, but your Fire phone has a handy tool to help you avoid data overages. It's the Data Usage screen, shown in Figure 24-4.

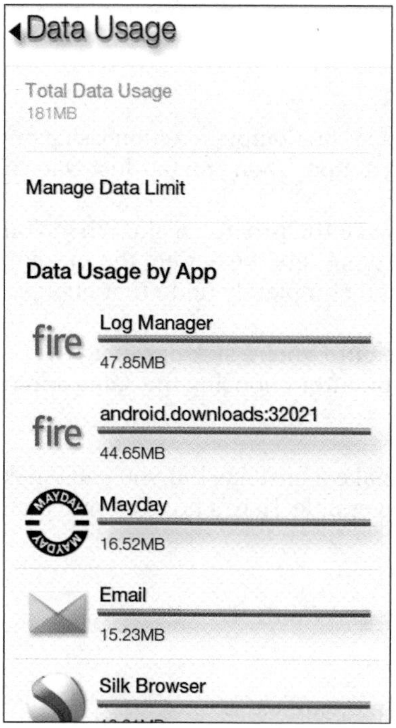

◄Data Usage

Total Data Usage
181MB

Manage Data Limit

Data Usage by App

fire   Log Manager
        47.85MB

fire   android.downloads:32021
        44.65MB

MAYDAY Mayday
        16.52MB

        Email
        15.23MB

        Silk Browser

Figure 24-4: The useful Data Usage screen.

To access the Data Usage screen, follow these steps:

1. **Open the Settings app.**

2. **Choose Wi-Fi & Networks.**

3. **Choose See Your Cellular Data Usage.**

The main screen details data usage for the current cycle. Beneath that is a list of apps that access the mobile data network along with the quantity of data downloaded by each.

The best thing you can do on the Data Usage screen is to set warnings and limits for your data usage: Choose the command Manage Data Limit. You see the Manage Data Limit screen, shown in Figure 24-5.

◀Manage Data Limit

Data Usage Cycle
Aug 14 – Sep 13

Data Limit   OFF   ON
Your device will turn off data
access when the limit is
reached.

Data Limit
5.0 GB

Data Limit Warning   OFF   ON
You will receive an alert when
you reach the specified data
limit.

Data Limit Warning
4.0 GB

Figure 24-5: Managing data consumption.

Slide the master control by Data Limit to the On position to apply a data limit. Choose Data Limit to set a limit, such as 4.0GB for a plan that limits your monthly mobile data usage to 4.0GB. When your data usage hits that amount, mobile data is disabled. That should save you some surcharges.

In addition to limiting mobile data, or along with it, you can set the Data Limit Warning (refer to Figure 24-5). When your usage hits the amount specified, a warning appears on the touchscreen, alerting you that your data usage has passed the limit. This is a great setting to apply to family members when you have a shared data plan.

Accessing the Internet by using Wi-Fi doesn't affect mobile data usage. Even if you establish and reach a Data Limit setting, your phone can still access the Internet over a Wi-Fi network.

Manage the Dictionary

The Fire phone sports a dictionary. It's not an English language dictionary, although you can obtain such an app at the Appstore. No, the dictionary I'm referring to is the one to which unknown spelling words are added.

When you type on the onscreen keyboard and a word isn't recognized, you can choose to add that word to the Fire phone dictionary. Chapter 4 explains how it works. To review additions or otherwise examine the phone's dictionary, follow these steps:

1. **Open the Settings app.**

2. **Choose Keyboard.**

3. **Choose Edit Your Personal Dictionary.**

   You see a list of words added to the dictionary, similar to Figure 24-6.

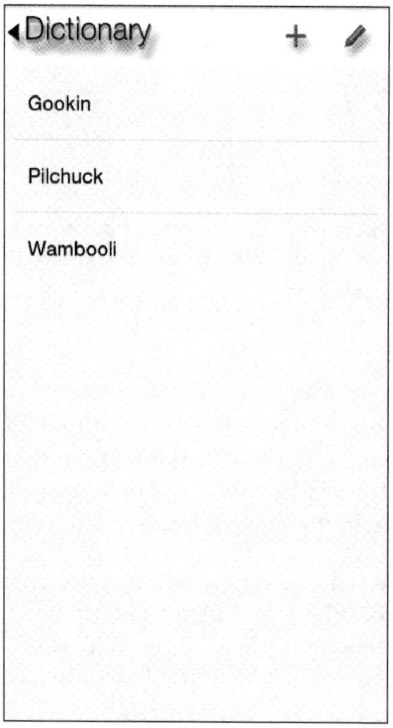

Figure 24-6: Words in the personal dictionary.

To add a new word, tap the Add icon. Type the word you want the Fire phone spell checker to recognize, such as your last name, street name, or whatever other unusual name you type frequently.

To edit a word, long-press it. Use the onscreen keyboard and your powers of onscreen editing (both honed in Chapter 4) to fix the word. Tap the OK button to save your changes.

Tap the Edit icon to purge words from the dictionary: Tap to place a check mark by a word, and then tap the Delete icon at the bottom of the screen.

Words placed in the dictionary are no longer flagged as incorrectly spelled when you type them on your phone.

Use Firefly to Dial a Number

When you're out and about, or just staring at someone's business card, don't bother typing in the number you see. Instead, long-press the Camera/Firefly button on the side of the phone. The Firefly app starts.

Point the phone at the phone number. In half a jiffy, the phone number is scanned and recognized. Tap the phone number's entry on the screen to dial that number:

- ⤶ Similarly to phone numbers, Firefly also recognizes email addresses and websites. You can choose those items from the onscreen list as well.

- ⤶ Firefly can best find phone numbers, email addresses, and websites that have been printed. Handwritten information can also be scanned, although the handwriting must be very, very good for Firefly to read it.

Find Your Lost Phone

Someday, you may lose your beloved Fire phone. It might be for a few panic-filled seconds, or it might be for forever. The hardware solution is to weld a heavy object to the phone, such as a chimney, yet that strategy kind of defeats the entire mobile/wireless paradigm. The software solution is to use the phone's Find Your Phone feature.

To enable the Find Your Phone feature, or to confirm its settings, obey these steps:

1. **Open the Settings app.**

2. **Choose Location Services.**

3. **Choose Enable Find Your Phone.**

   The Location screen appears.

4. **Ensure that the master control by Find Your Phone is in the On position.**

   This setting isn't available unless you activate Location Services, which is found on the same Location screen.

After the feature is on, you can generally forget about it.

When that terrible day comes and you need to locate your lost phone, follow these steps:

1. **Visit the web page at** `amazon.com/mycd`.

   If prompted, log in to your Amazon account. Eventually, you see the Manage Your Content and Devices web page.

2. **Click the Your Devices tab.**

3. **Choose your Fire phone from the list of devices.**

   The phone may have already been selected; if not, click on it.

4. **Choose an action from the Device Actions menu.**

   What you do next depends on how lost the phone is.

For example, if you can't find the phone around the house, choose the Remote Alarm command. The phone's ringer sounds for two minutes, which helps you locate it in the couch cushions.

If the phone is really lost, choose the Find Your Phone command. A map appears on the screen, detailing the phone's last known location.

When you believe the phone to be stolen or deliberately messed with, choose the Remote Lock command. You'll be able to apply a PIN lock to the phone that renders the device useless.

As a drastic step, choose the Remote Factory Reset command. This command removes all your personal data from the phone. After using this command, however, you can no longer track the device.

For the Find Your Phone feature to work, your Fire phone must be turned on and connected to the Internet, either over the mobile data network or a Wi-Fi network. The phone must also have at least a 30 percent charge on the battery.

Ten Things to Remember

*I*f only it were easy to narrow to ten items the list of all the things I want you to remember when using your Fire phone. Even though you'll find in this chapter ten good things not to forget, don't think for a moment that there are *only* ten. In fact, as I remember more, I'll put them on my website, at www.wambooli.com. Check it for updates about your phone and perhaps for even more things to remember.

The Back Gesture

The Fire phone uses its accelerometer to pick up subtle movements called *gestures*. The common gestures are Auto Scroll, Peek, Swivel, and Tilt. These are all described in Chapter 3.

Another gesture, one that's just as useful (and quite popular), is Back. Alas, the Back gesture doesn't involve moving the phone. Instead, you move your finger, dragging it from the bottom of the screen to the top. That's the Back gesture, and it comes in very handy when you use the phone. Because it's not a phone motion, however, people tend to forget it:

- Use the Back gesture to return to the previous screen, like backing up.

- Use the Back gesture to dismiss the onscreen keyboard or any onscreen notice.

- For an alternative, you can tap the screen title in the upper-left corner of an app, although not every app uses this technique. The Back gesture is, however, universal.

Quickly Switch Apps

Apps on your phone don't quit. Sure, some of them have a Quit command or Sign Out command, but most apps lurk inside the phone's memory while you do other things. The phone's operating system may eventually kill off a stale app. Before that happens, you can deftly and quickly switch between all running apps.

The key to making the switch is to use the Quick Switch command: Quickly press the Home button twice. The list of running apps appears on the screen. Swipe it left or right to browse running apps. Tap an app to switch to it.

Hands-Free Mode

The Fire phone doesn't really have a hands-free mode as much as it has several features that lend themselves well toward hands-free operation. Chief among these are the gestures, covered in Chapter 3 — specifically the Auto Scroll gesture, which lets you automatically scan long documents.

Beyond the gestures, the phone offers voice commands: Press and hold the Home button to enter Voice Command mode. Speak a command at the phone. You can literally ask the phone a question and it responds, although a limited set of commands are available.

The Voice Command screen offers suggestions on what you can say. For additional commands, refer to Chapter 24.

Lock the Phone on a Call

Whether you dialed out or someone dialed in, after you start talking, you should lock your phone. Press the Power/Lock button. By doing so, you disable the touchscreen and ensure that the call isn't unintentionally disconnected.

Of course, the call can still be disconnected by a dropped signal or by the other party getting all huffy and hanging up on you. But by locking the phone, you prevent a stray finger or your pocket from disconnecting (or muting) the phone.

I especially recommend locking the phone when you're using the earphones on a call.

Use Landscape Orientation

The natural orientation of the Fire phone is vertical — its *portrait* orientation. Even so, that doesn't mean you have to use an app in portrait orientation.

Turning the phone to its side makes many apps, such as the Silk browser app and the Maps app, appear wider. It's often a better way to see things, such as more available items on certain menus, and to give you larger key caps on which to type if you're using the onscreen keyboard:

✔ Not every app supports landscape orientation.

✔ You can lock the orientation so that the touchscreen doesn't flip and flop. See Chapter 21 for information on making that adjustment.

Get the Most from the Onscreen Keyboard

Don't forget to take advantage of the onscreen keyboard's Predictive Text feature; use the suggestions that appear above the onscreen keyboard while you type. Choose a word to greatly expedite the ordeal of typing on a cell phone. Plus, the Predictive Text feature may instantly display the next logical word for you.

When predictive text fails you, keep in mind that you can use trace typing instead of the old hunt-and-peck. Dragging your finger over the keyboard and then choosing a word suggestion works quickly — when you remember to do it.

See Chapter 4 for information on activating these phone features.

Things That Consume Lots of Battery Juice

Three items on your phone suck down battery power faster than a 4-year-old fleeing the confines of your car to see whether Grandpa has candy:

- Navigation
- Bluetooth
- The display

Navigation is certainly handy, but because the phone's touchscreen is on the entire time and dictating text to you, the battery drains rapidly. If possible, try to plug the phone into the car's power socket when you're navigating. If you can't, keep an eye on the battery meter.

Bluetooth requires extra power for its wireless radio. When you need that level of connectivity, great! Otherwise, turn off your Bluetooth gizmo as soon as necessary to save power.

Finally, the touchscreen display draws a lot of power. You can try using the Auto Brightness setting, but it can get too dark to see or, more frequently, take too long to adjust to a high- or low-light setting. So if you avoid the Auto Brightness setting, remember how that bright display can drain the battery.

See Chapter 23 for more information on managing the phone's battery.

Check for Roaming

Roaming can be expensive. The last non-smartphone (dumbphone?) I owned racked up $180 in roaming charges the month before I switched to a better cellular plan. Even though you might have a good cell phone plan, keep an eye on the phone's status bar to ensure that you don't see the Roaming status icon when you're making a call.

Well, yes, it's okay to make a call when your phone is roaming. My advice is to remember to *check* for the icon, not to avoid it. If possible, try to make your phone calls when you're back in your cellular service's coverage area. If you can't, make the phone call but keep in mind that you will be charged roaming fees. They ain't cheap.

Snap a Pic of That Contact

Here's something I always forget: Whenever you're near one of your contacts, take the person's picture. Sure, some people are bashful, but most folks are flattered. The idea is to build up your phone's address book so that all contacts have photos. Receiving a call is then much more interesting when you see the caller's picture, especially a silly or an embarrassing one.

When taking the picture, be sure to show it to the person before you assign it to the contact. Let the person decide whether it's good enough. Or, if you just want to be rude, assign a crummy-looking picture. Heck, you don't even have to do that: Just assign a random picture of anything. A plant. A rock. Your dog. But seriously, the next time you meet up with a contact, keep in mind that the phone can take that person's picture.

See Chapter 14 for more information on using the phone's camera.

The Search Command

Amazon wanted to ensure that the Search command was available all over the Fire phone — and it succeeded. Just about every app — even the technical ones, like Settings — features a Search command. The command is most frequently represented by the Search icon, shown in the margin.

Touch the Search icon to look for information such as locations, people, text — you name it. It's handy. It's everywhere. Use it.

Index

About the Author

Dan Gookin has been writing about technology for over 25 years. He combines his love of writing with his gizmo fascination to create books that are informative, entertaining, and not boring. Having written over 140 titles with 12 million copies in print translated into over 30 languages, Dan can attest that his method of crafting computer tomes seems to work.

Perhaps his most famous title is the original *DOS For Dummies,* published in 1991. It became the world's fastest-selling computer book, at one time moving more copies per week than the *New York Times* number-one bestseller (though, as a reference, it could not be listed on the *Times'* Best Sellers list). That book spawned the entire line of *For Dummies* books, which remains a publishing phenomenon to this day.

Dan's most popular titles include *PCs For Dummies, Word For Dummies, Laptops For Dummies*, and *Android Phones For Dummies*. He also maintains the vast and helpful website www.wambooli.com.

Dan holds a degree in Communications/Visual Arts from the University of California, San Diego. He lives in the Pacific Northwest, where he enjoys spending time with his sons playing video games indoors while they enjoy the gentle woods of Idaho.

Publisher's Acknowledgments

Acquisitions Editor: Katie Mohr

Senior Project Editor: Mark Enochs

Copy Editor: Rebecca Whitney

Editorial Assistant: Claire Johnson

Sr. Editorial Assistant: Cherie Case

Project Coordinator: Sheree Montgomery

Cover Image: Amazon Fire Phone Courtesy of Amazon.com, Inc.; Background © iStock.com/NagyDodo

Apple & Mac

iPad For Dummies,
6th Edition
978-1-118-72306-7

iPhone For Dummies,
7th Edition
978-1-118-69083-3

Macs All-in-One
For Dummies, 4th Edition
978-1-118-82210-4

OS X Mavericks
For Dummies
978-1-118-69188-5

Blogging & Social Media

Facebook For Dummies,
5th Edition
978-1-118-63312-0

Social Media Engagement
For Dummies
978-1-118-53019-1

WordPress For Dummies,
6th Edition
978-1-118-79161-5

Business

Stock Investing
For Dummies, 4th Edition
978-1-118-37678-2

Investing For Dummies,
6th Edition
978-0-470-90545-6

Personal Finance
For Dummies, 7th Edition
978-1-118-11785-9

QuickBooks 2014
For Dummies
978-1-118-72005-9

Small Business Marketing
Kit For Dummies,
3rd Edition
978-1-118-31183-7

Careers

Job Interviews
For Dummies, 4th Edition
978-1-118-11290-8

Job Searching with Social
Media For Dummies,
2nd Edition
978-1-118-67856-5

Personal Branding
For Dummies
978-1-118-11792-7

Resumes For Dummies,
6th Edition
978-0-470-87361-8

Starting an Etsy Business
For Dummies, 2nd Edition
978-1-118-59024-9

Diet & Nutrition

Belly Fat Diet For Dummies
978-1-118-34585-6

Mediterranean Diet
For Dummies
978-1-118-71525-3

Nutrition For Dummies,
5th Edition
978-0-470-93231-5

Digital Photography

Digital SLR Photography
All-in-One For Dummies,
2nd Edition
978-1-118-59082-9

Digital SLR Video &
Filmmaking For Dummies
978-1-118-36598-4

Photoshop Elements 12
For Dummies
978-1-118-72714-0

Gardening

Herb Gardening
For Dummies, 2nd Edition
978-0-470-61778-6

Gardening with Free-Range
Chickens For Dummies
978-1-118-54754-0

Health

Boosting Your Immunity
For Dummies
978-1-118-40200-9

Diabetes For Dummies,
4th Edition
978-1-118-29447-5

Living Paleo For Dummies
978-1-118-29405-5

Big Data

Big Data For Dummies
978-1-118-50422-2

Data Visualization
For Dummies
978-1-118-50289-1

Hadoop For Dummies
978-1-118-60755-8

Language & Foreign Language

500 Spanish Verbs
For Dummies
978-1-118-02382-2

English Grammar
For Dummies, 2nd Edition
978-0-470-54664-2

French All-in-One
For Dummies
978-1-118-22815-9

German Essentials
For Dummies
978-1-118-18422-6

Italian For Dummies,
2nd Edition
978-1-118-00465-4

Available in print and e-book formats.

Math & Science

Algebra I For Dummies,
2nd Edition
978-0-470-55964-2

Anatomy and Physiology
For Dummies, 2nd Edition
978-0-470-92326-9

Astronomy For Dummies,
3rd Edition
978-1-118-37697-3

Biology For Dummies,
2nd Edition
978-0-470-59875-7

Chemistry For Dummies,
2nd Edition
978-1-118-00730-3

1001 Algebra II Practice
Problems For Dummies
978-1-118-44662-1

Microsoft Office

Excel 2013 For Dummies
978-1-118-51012-4

Office 2013 All-in-One
For Dummies
978-1-118-51636-2

PowerPoint 2013
For Dummies
978-1-118-50253-2

Word 2013 For Dummies
978-1-118-49123-2

Music

Blues Harmonica
For Dummies
978-1-118-25269-7

Guitar For Dummies,
3rd Edition
978-1-118-11554-1

iPod & iTunes
For Dummies, 10th Edition
978-1-118-50864-0

Programming

Beginning Programming
with C For Dummies
978-1-118-73763-7

Excel VBA Programming
For Dummies, 3rd Edition
978-1-118-49037-2

Java For Dummies,
6th Edition
978-1-118-40780-6

Religion & Inspiration

The Bible For Dummies
978-0-7645-5296-0

Buddhism For Dummies,
2nd Edition
978-1-118-02379-2

Catholicism For Dummies,
2nd Edition
978-1-118-07778-8

Self-Help & Relationships

Beating Sugar Addiction
For Dummies
978-1-118-54645-1

Meditation For Dummies,
3rd Edition
978-1-118-29144-3

Seniors

Laptops For Seniors
For Dummies, 3rd Edition
978-1-118-71105-7

Computers For Seniors
For Dummies, 3rd Edition
978-1-118-11553-4

iPad For Seniors
For Dummies, 6th Edition
978-1-118-72826-0

Social Security
For Dummies
978-1-118-20573-0

Smartphones & Tablets

Android Phones
For Dummies, 2nd Edition
978-1-118-72030-1

Nexus Tablets
For Dummies
978-1-118-77243-0

Samsung Galaxy S 4
For Dummies
978-1-118-64222-1

Samsung Galaxy Tabs
For Dummies
978-1-118-77294-2

Test Prep

ACT For Dummies,
5th Edition
978-1-118-01259-8

ASVAB For Dummies,
3rd Edition
978-0-470-63760-9

GRE For Dummies,
7th Edition
978-0-470-88921-3

Officer Candidate Tests
For Dummies
978-0-470-59876-4

Physician's Assistant Exam
For Dummies
978-1-118-11556-5

Series 7 Exam For Dummies
978-0-470-09932-2

Windows 8

Windows 8.1 All-in-One
For Dummies
978-1-118-82087-2

Windows 8.1 For Dummies
978-1-118-82121-3

Windows 8.1 For Dummies,
Book + DVD Bundle
978-1-118-82107-7

𝒆 **Available in print and e-book formats.**

Available wherever books are sold. **For more information or to order direct visit www.dummies.com**